7 16/ 3330.
10/9/4

Items should be returned on or before the last date
shown below. Items not already requested by other
borrowers may be renewed in person, in writing or by
telephone. To renew, please quote the number on the
barcode label. To renew online a PIN is required.
This can be requested at your local library.
Renew online @ **www.dublincitypubliclibraries.ie**
Fines charged for overdue items will include postage
incurred in recovery. Damage to or loss of items will
be charged to the borrower.

Leabharlanna Poiblí Chathair Bhaile Átha Cliath
Dublin City Public Libraries

Dublin City
Baile Átha Cliath

Date Due	Date Due	Date Due
18. OCT 11.		

John Scally works as a teacher in Dublin and was formerly a journalist and broadcaster. He is author of more than 20 books, including *100 GAA Greats*.

100 IRISH RUGBY GREATS

JOHN SCALLY

MAINSTREAM
PUBLISHING

EDINBURGH AND LONDON

First published in Great Britain in 2011 by
MAINSTREAM PUBLISHING COMPANY
(EDINBURGH) LTD
7 Albany Street
Edinburgh EH1 3UG

ISBN 9781845967734

A catalogue record for this book is available
from the British Library

Printed in Great Britain by
CPI Mackays, Chatham ME5 8TD
1 3 5 7 9 10 8 6 4 2

TO THE MEMORY OF THE ONE AND ONLY MOSS KEANE

CONTENTS

FOREWORD

I had the great privilege in my career to make wonderful friendships with incredible teammates including many featured in this book, such as Jim McCarthy and Paddy Reid, and some who have sadly passed on, like Karl Mullen, Tom Clifford and Des O'Brien. When Des died, Jim McCarthy and his wife Pat, Ronnie Kavanagh, Ronnie Dawson, Jimmy Nelson and myself went to Edinburgh for the funeral. He was a superb back-row player, a delightful man and great company. His funeral was a celebration of a wonderful life. He had left word that there was to be a party afterwards, and so we went back to his house and round the piano played and sang the old songs that he used to sing. It just highlighted the enduring friendships that rugby has created for me.

I had the good fortune to play on a Grand Slam-winning team for Ireland and then, 61 years later, to see an Irish team winning a second one. I have seen many great players wear the green jersey down the years who, by their prowess on the field over a long period, have claimed a permanent place in the memory of all who love the game. This book honours many of them.

I still enjoy meeting up with old comrades from the rugby fields and reminiscing about bygone days as the conversation ebbs and flows. I hope you will enjoy this celebration of great players and great characters.

It is a pleasure to write the foreword to a very interesting book. It will be a welcome addition to the history of rugby.

Jack Kyle, June 2011

INTRODUCTION

How do you select the 100 greats of Irish rugby? With great difficulty! Greatness, like beauty, is an extremely subjective concept. There are no criteria that will please everybody and there can be no selection that will gain universal approval. Invariably in a work like this, people latch on to who is *not* included. I am not claiming that the players are Ireland's greatest-ever players but arguing that for different reasons they merit the term 'great'. While this book features many of the greatest names in the rich history of Irish rugby, I did not want to simply 'round up the usual suspects'. I did go out of my way to include a few less obvious choices – at the expense of a few household names – to a large degree because of my desire to have as much diversity in the stories as possible. I offer this selection to stimulate debate rather than claiming to end it.

A number of options presented themselves in the writing of the book. One was to take a statistical approach and present the facts and figures of the chosen players' careers. Another was to recycle lengthy accounts of their most famous matches. I decided in the main to forego such approaches and go beneath the surface to present a more personal style of portrait, showing the characters of these sportsmen, the controversies they faced and sometimes created, their triumphs and their setbacks – through their own eyes or those of the men who played against them. I hope these portraits will in some way capture the unique magic and humour of Irish rugby.

I am very grateful to all the players who so generously gave interviews for this book, including some who have sadly passed on, such as Mick Doyle, Mick English, Karl Mullen, Con Murphy, Des O'Brien and, of course, the true legend Moss Keane. Two of the giants of world rugby who have unfortunately gone on to swap stories in the rugby sky, the incredibly entertaining and passionate Ray Gravell and the 'voice of rugby' Bill McLaren, were also very helpful to me.

My particular gratitude goes to Nigel Carr, David Irwin and Philip

INTRODUCTION

Rainey, who generously gave me their time in re-creating their most traumatic journey for me.

I must also acknowledge my special thanks to that most gentle and special of men, the legendary Jack Kyle, who greatly honoured me by writing the foreword for this book.

Not for the first time I must record my debt in particular to rugby's ultimate nice guy and the perfect 10, Ollie Campbell. It is always a great pleasure to link up with my first rugby hero, Tony Ward.

Mick Quinn and Ken Ging very graciously provided me with great stories.

Thanks for help with photos to Niall Barry, Nigel Carr, Dave Curran, Suzanne Costello, Carmel Dempsey, Eleanor Flew, Carol Hennessy, Scott LaValla, Eric Miller, Adam and Harry Minogue, John O'Shea and Teresa Scally.

While this book was being written, I was deeply saddened to hear the news that my aunt Mary Whelan had died at Christmas 2010. She was an exceptional woman who will be much missed, especially by those who loved her most – her 11 children.

Thanks to Susan Cahill and Patrick Geoghegan of Newstalk's *Talking History* programme for their support of some of my previous books.

Thanks also to all at Mainstream for backing this book.

John Scally, June 2011

1

OUR WILLIE IS BIGGER THAN YOUR CONDOM
WILLIE ANDERSON

Despite his 27 caps for Ireland, his then record of 78 caps for Ulster and his achievements as a coach, Willie Anderson will probably always be remembered as the player who precipitated an international diplomatic incident. He was on a tour of Argentina with the Penguins in 1980 when he took a shine to the Argentinean flag and decided to claim it as his own.

'Myself and another player were walking home to the hotel around midnight. I liked the look of the flag and its colours. Shortly after that, six guys came through the door with machine guns. They said, "Someone in here has an Argentinean flag."

'I immediately handed it back and said I was sorry. I was quickly told saying sorry was not good enough in this situation. As I was brought down to the jail, two Irish internationals, Dave Irwin and Frank Wilson, volunteered to come with me for moral support. For their consideration, they were both thrown in jail with me for three weeks!

'I was strip-searched and had 30 sets of fingerprints taken. I was in the interrogation chair for a whole day. Anyone who has seen the film *Midnight Express* will have an idea of the naked terror you can experience when you are in prison and there's a gun to your head. Things got worse before they got better. I was put into this tiny interrogation unit, which is the most frightening place in the world, before being taken to my cell. The cell was 6 ft by 4 ft and had nothing but a cement bed in the centre. The people who had been there before me had left their excrement behind. It was pretty revolting. The only blessing was that I wasn't put in the "open" cell with a crowd of prisoners, because I would have never survived.

'The next day, I was taken out in handcuffs, which is the ultimate in degradation. I was taken up the stairs and was stunned to discover that there were about 60 or 70 reporters and journalists waiting for me. For three or four days, I was not just front-page news in Argentina, I was the first three pages. To me, the press were not much better than terrorists.

WILLIE ANDERSON

As I had a British passport, they tried to whip up a nationalistic frenzy and portray me as an imperialist. They didn't print the truth. Some said I had urinated on the flag. Others said I had burned it. Yet more said I had done both. My lawyer got death threats.

'It was much more serious than anybody here realised at the time. I know for a fact that two or three army generals wanted to have me executed. Others wanted to make sure that I served at least ten years' hard labour. The whole episode cost my parents £10,000 in legal fees and so on, but you can't put a price on the mental anguish that they had to endure. I remember one letter I sent them home that I would hate to have to read again because I had struck rock bottom.

'The two lads and I were taken back to a cell where we came into contact with two South Koreans. They had tried to smuggle some Walkmans into the country. David Irwin taught me how to play chess and we had the World Chess Championships: South Korea v. Northern Ireland.

'One of the guards looked like a ringer for Sergeant Bilko. At one stage, he was marching us in the yard and Frank roared out, "Bilko."

'I said, "For Christ's sake, Frank, just keep your mouth shut." Thankfully, the guard didn't know who Bilko was.

'I think things could have been much worse had the warden not wanted to learn English. His colleagues would have been happy to throw away the keys to our cell. In that country, we were guilty until proved innocent.

'After three weeks, Frank and David were sent home. It was the loneliest day of my life. I had to wait for a further two months before my trial and release. I wouldn't wish what happened to me on my worst enemy. A great many rugby players contributed via the clubs to a fund to pay for the legal expenses. The people of Dungannon rallied around and raised a lot of money also. I owe them a lot. I wrote to my then girlfriend, now wife, Heather, every day. The following year, we got married.

'In rugby terms, I was to pay a heavy price for my indiscretion. I was perceived as a rebel and was quietly told later, by a prominent personality in Irish rugby, that my first cap was delayed because of the incident. In fact, I was 29 when I first played for Ireland. I met Denis Thatcher some years later and said to him that I could have told his wife the Argentineans were scrapping for a war.'

As a player, Anderson had many highs and lows; the highs included the 1985 Triple Crown and the night he captained a scrap Irish side to a famous victory over France at Auch in 1988 – Ireland's only victory over France on French territory in over 20 years. His appearances against France were memorable for his epic struggles with the French lock Jean Condom, leading to the banner that appeared in the crowd in Lansdowne Road at the Ireland–France match in 1985: 'Our Willie is bigger than your Condom'.

As Irish captain, he was also famous for a piece of sporting theatre before Ireland played the All Blacks in 1989 when he led the Irish team up to the noses of the New Zealanders in an effort to intimidate them. After the match, All Black Wayne Shelford was asked if he had been scared. He admitted that he had been absolutely petrified: 'I was terrified that Willie Anderson would kiss me!'

2

THE ITALIAN JOB
TREVOR BRENNAN

Tom Humphries, in one of his columns in the *Irish Times* dismissed rugby:

> Rugby people. Can't live with them. Can't shoot them. Mainly can't live with them. Can't afford to live with them. Haven't the bloodlines to live with them. Haven't the patience to love them. Haven't the language skills to live with them. Haven't the desire even. Rugby people have always been college scarves and jutting jaws and silly songs I don't know the words of. C-A-N-N-O-T live with them.

Tom obviously has spent very little time with former milkman Trevor Brennan, a player who brings immense passion and in-depth knowledge to the game. However, sometimes Trevor's passion gets the better of him, and in 2007 he retired prematurely after he was involved in a fracas with a fan in a Toulouse–Ulster game. Having won thirteen caps for Ireland, Brennan had moved to France, where he won two Heineken Cups with Toulouse.

Girvan Dempsey is loud in his praise of Brennan: 'Trevor is one of the great rugby characters. He is larger than life and has made a massive impact since he moved to play rugby in France. I was talking to some of the French players at the dinner after our Six Nations match in Paris in 2004 and they were all singing Trevor's praises. He's even opened a pub over there now.

'Trevor was responsible for my funniest moment in rugby. It was one of my first starts for Leinster and we were playing Treviso on a pre-season tour in Italy. After we flew into the airport and collected our bags, our manager at the time, Jim Glennon, came in to tell us there would be a delay because there was a difficulty with Dean Oswald's passport and that the problem was compounded by the fact that there was a language barrier. Trevor immediately piped up, "I'll sort it out for you. I know the lingo."

'We were all stunned because Trevor was not known for his linguistic skills. When we turned to him and asked him when he had learned to speak Italian, he coolly replied, "I worked in Luigi's chip shop one summer!"'

Ronan O'Gara is another fan of the man who won 13 caps for Ireland: 'Trevor Brennan also brought great freshness to the game and he was a real character in the Irish squad.'

Trevor features in one of Ronan's favourite stories. Munster faced Leinster in the inaugural Celtic League final in Lansdowne Road. Leinster's Eric Miller was sent off after only 20 minutes in the game, but Leinster won the final nonetheless. In the Leinster dressing-room afterwards, Eric was distraught. Sensing his pain, his teammates rallied and one by one went to console him. Finally, it was Trevor's turn to utter some comforting words. He grabbed a pale-faced Miller roughly by the shoulders and said, 'If we lost the game, you wouldn't be safe in Tora-f**king-Bora!'

Former Leinster manager and rugby raconteur Ken Ging tells two classic Brennan stories: 'One day, Sir Anthony O'Reilly was driving home in his brand-new Rolls-Royce. He was smiling because it was the most magnificent model. At a set of traffic lights, he pulls up beside a Mini with a black cloud of smoke trailing from the exhaust and black tape on the windows. Trevor Brennan gets out from the Mini and walks up to O'Reilly and signals to him to roll down the windows. The Lions legend duly does so and Trevor asks, "Do you have a telephone in there, Anto?"

'O'Reilly replies, "I have."

'"Do you have a TV and a DVD player?"

'"I do and before you ask I've also got a fully stocked cocktail bar."

'"Have you a bed?"

'"I haven't a bed."

'Trevor replies, "I've a bed in my car," and walks off.

'This really got to O'Reilly. The following day, he instructed his personal assistant to get a four-poster bed in his car. A few minutes later, the secretary returned and explained to O'Reilly that this would cost a fortune. O'Reilly snapped back angrily, "I don't care. Just get me that bed."

'Two weeks later, O'Reilly was driving home and feeling really proud of his state-of-the-art bed with beautiful satin sheets. Then he got dejected because he thought he would never see Trevor again to show him his new prize possession. He pulled up at Tesco to buy his groceries and to his great delight he spotted Trevor's Mini in the car park. He walked over and knocked at the window. Two minutes later, Trevor pulled down the window and said, "Ah, Anto, it's yourself."

'O'Reilly was nearly jumping for joy: "Trevor, Trevor, let me show you the great new bed I have installed in my car."

'Brennan shook his head and looked at him scornfully: "Do you mean to tell me you dragged me out of the shower just to show me a bed?!"

'The most famous Trevor tale goes back to the day he was walking down Dublin city centre when he saw a man dead on the street. He pulled out his mobile phone and rang the gardai. He told the guard the situation and the boy in blue replied, "OK, you're there in Exchequer Street. Spell Exchequer Street."

'Trevor started, "Exc, no Exh, no . . ." He paused and said, "Hang on a second. I'm just going to drag him round to Dame Street and I'll ring you back then."'

3

CAMPBELL'S KINGDOM
OLLIE CAMPBELL

Following the selectors' sensational decision to drop Tony Ward in Australia in 1979 in favour of Ollie Campbell, both players found themselves unwittingly embroiled in the long-running Ward–Campbell saga. Ollie jokes that he always carries two tickets for a cruise around the world in his pocket to give to the first person who talks to him without mentioning Tony Ward.

One of the few occasions when Campbell's kicking let him down was in his international debut against Australia in 1976.

'It was one of the biggest disappointments of my life. It was everything you want your first cap *not* to be. I was dropped from the side straight away, which was the only time in my career I was ever dropped off any team.'

It would be three years before Campbell regained his place in the Irish team on the Australian tour at the expense of Tony Ward. The following season, he set a new points record (46) for the Five Nations Championship.

Campbell's next close encounter with Ward was on the Lions tour in 1980. 'With the first Test looming and with both out-halfs (Gareth Davies and I) injured, a fit one was needed. Who was flown out? A.J.P. Ward. Not only did he play in the first Test but he scored 18 points, which was then a Lions individual points-scoring record in a Test match. Was there to be no escape from this guy?'

In 1981, Campbell was moved to the centre to allow for Ward's return as Irish out-half. How did he react to the change?

'I never minded the idea of playing in the same team as Tony – provided I was at out-half. Playing in the centre is a very different position and to be honest I was never really comfortable there. In 1981, we lost all four matches by a single score after leading in all four at half-time. It was Ireland's best-ever whitewash! I remember at the time Tom Kiernan repeatedly kept telling us that, whatever happens about the results, if there was to be a Lions tour that year, the country that would have the most representatives would be Ireland.

OLLIE CAMPBELL

I'm not sure if that was true but it certainly kept our morale and self-belief up.'

The following season, in 1982, things came together for the Irish side. A record score from Campbell, kicking all of Ireland's points (with 6 penalties and a drop goal) in their 21–12 victory over Scotland, allowed the Irish to clinch their first Triple Crown since 1949, ending a 33-year wait.

One of Campbell's enduring recollections of the game was of the fans: 'Probably my abiding memory of that whole season was the reaction of the crowd during the whole of the second half of that Scottish game, particularly in the East Stand because much of the half seemed to be played there. I think it was really the start of "Molly Malone" becoming the "anthem" of the Irish team. The atmosphere was just incredible. Most of the team had grown up with no international success. There was a huge sense of achievement and a bonding that has lasted since.

'When we won our first match, all we were trying to do was to bring a sequence of seven consecutive defeats to an end. Two weeks later, we won at Twickenham and suddenly we were in a Triple Crown situation. It was something as a team we had never thought about. But we knew we were on to something big when we saw the big crowds watching us in training. That was something we had never experienced before. It was a very exciting week as we had a general election at the time following the fall of Garret FitzGerald's first coalition government but nobody seemed to care about it. Everybody was more excited about the possibility of a Triple Crown – Ireland had never won one before at Lansdowne Road.

'The tension mounted but Tom Kiernan, the Irish coach, decided to have a closed practice session, on the Thursday before the game. Suddenly, the Triple Crown match became just another game and I have never felt so at ease and comfortable going into a game. It was a masterstroke as far as I was concerned. Two weeks previously, I had missed a penalty against England that would have sewn the game up. On the Sunday afterwards, I went to Anglesea Road with my five balls and kicked for two hours from the same spot I had missed the previous day. Ninety per cent of all the kicks I took in practice over the next two weeks were from this spot. After just three minutes of the Scotland game, when the first penalty arrived, I relaxed. Amazingly, it was from exactly the same spot. I felt I would have kicked it with my eyes closed but I didn't take the chance. We were on our way and, for me at least, never before had the value of practice been more clearly demonstrated.'

As well as his rugby talents, it seems one of Campbell's gifts is the ability to predict the future. 'A number of years ago, I was coaching Belvedere's Under-8s. We played Naas and lost narrowly. The lads were devastated. I told them not to worry because we would be playing them again before the end of the season and would beat them then. We won the return fixture and one of the boys came up to me and, with awe in his voice, said, "You can tell the future!"

'I commiserated with the Naas coach and he asked me what I thought of his team. I told him they were a good side and said, "The blond fellow is one to watch." He was Jamie Heaslip.'

4

TRIUMPH AND TRAGEDY
DONAL CANNIFFE

On a unique day in Irish rugby history, one player had a unique story.

The only biblical story that the four gospels have in common is the occasion when Jesus fed the multitude with a few loaves and fishes and managed to have twelve baskets of fragments left over. Munster's victory over the All Blacks in 1978 has spawned a similar miracle. Although the official attendance at the match was only 12,000, since then tens of thousands of people have said, often with the benefit of generous liquid refreshment, 'I was there the day Munster beat the All Blacks.'

The Clare hills provided a scenic background for the New Zealanders as they performed their traditional haka before the game. Somewhat against the run of play, Munster took the lead in the 11th minute – a delicate chip from Tony Ward was followed through and won by Jimmy Bowen, who made an incisive run, and, as he was caught from behind, he fed Christy Cantillon, who crossed the line beneath the posts. Ward kicked the conversion with ease. In the 17th minute, Ward dropped a goal.

The home side hung on to their 9–0 lead until half-time, but realised that a modern-day siege of Limerick awaited them in the second half when the men from Down Under would do all in their formidable power to protect their unbeaten record. Their fears were justified, as the All Blacks exerted enormous pressure, but the tourists did not know what hit them as they were stopped in their tracks with a series of crunching tackles by such players as Seamus Dennison, Greg Barrett and most notably Colm Tucker. The All Blacks coach Jack Gleeson subsequently described them as 'Kamikaze tacklers'.

As the seconds ticked by agonisingly slowly in the second half, the crowd became more and more frenzied, sensing that here lay history in the making. 'M-U-N-S-T-E-R! M-U-N-S-T-E-R!' rang out at a deafening level. Ward got the only score in the second half – a drop goal – and Munster held on. It was an extraordinary team performance.

The Munster team that day was: L. Moloney (Garryowen), M. Finn (UCC), S. Dennison (Garryowen), G. Barrett (Cork Constitution), J. Bowen (Cork Constitution), T. Ward (Garryowen), D. Canniffe (Lansdowne) (captain), G. McLoughlin (Shannon), P. Whelan (Garryowen), L. White (London Irish), M. Keane (Lansdowne), B. Foley (Shannon), C. Cantillon (Cork Constitution), D. Spring (Dublin University), C. Tucker (Shannon).

Donal Canniffe, a former Irish international, had been an inspirational captain to that Munster team. When his team gathered around at half-time leading 9–0, there was an eerie silence because the crowd could not cope with a shock of such massive proportions. To keep the team fired up, Canniffe uttered the immortal words: 'We're 40 minutes from immortality . . . believe it.'

Sadly, Donal's victory that day was overshadowed by personal sadness when his father, Dan Canniffe, collapsed and died in Cork while listening to the match. At the banquet in honour of the team's victory, a minute's silence was observed, and Pat Whelan, vice-captain, stood in for Donal.

The match was one of the biggest highlights of Whelan's career: 'In 1978, Munster rounded off a magnificent season by beating Leinster 12–3 in Lansdowne Road in December, to win their first Grand Slam since 1968, their first Championship outright since 1973 and to record their first win at Lansdowne Road since 1972. That game was played on a Sunday. The previous day, the All Blacks were playing against the Barbarians, and the Munster team watched the match in the hotel together. The All Blacks only won with a late drop goal and I still remember the roar that went up when they got that score because it meant that the All Blacks had won 17 out of 18, highlighting the uniqueness of Munster's achievement. It set us up for the performance the next day, and it was without question Munster's finest season. The magnitude of our achievement in defeating the All Blacks only sunk in years afterwards, but the personal tragedy for Donal Canniffe was immediately apparent to us all when we heard the news of his father's passing after the match.'

While Moss Keane was lucky enough to win 54 caps and be part of the Triple Crown-winning side in 1982, and go on a Lions tour, the famous Munster victory was the high point of his career: 'It's very hard to separate memories and say one match was more important than another. My first cap was a great feeling, so was my Lions Test appearance; Ginger's try in '82 was memorable, but the highlight was defeating the All Blacks. It was a great, great day, though my clearest memory of the day is the disappointment we all felt when we heard that the father of our scrum-half and captain, Donal Canniffe, died immediately after the match. Donal was a very fine player and it was a shame that he had such sadness on what should have been the happiest day of his life.'

5

THE GARDEN OF GET SOMEBODY
TOM CLIFFORD

No one encapsulated Munster's famed passion for the game of rugby better than Tom Clifford. He won the first of his 14 caps for Ireland against France in 1949 and was a key part of the Triple Crown victory in that season, and then toured with the Lions to New Zealand in 1950.

Jack Kyle has vivid memories of touring with Clifford on that tour: 'It was the last of the six-and-a-half-month tours. When you go along on a tour like that, it's years later before you really appreciate it. It's amazing how quickly people get used to the star treatment. Welsh coalminers who were reared on anything but the silver spoon quickly assume a new star persona. After a few weeks, we were all cribbing about the waitresses.

'One of the great finds of that 1950 Lions tour was Lewis Jones of Wales. He was only in his teens but he looked much older because he was losing his hair like lightning. With his big bandy legs, he was the first running full-back. That's the big difference between our time and now. Then, every player's first instinct was not to get tackled. Today their instinct is to make sure they get tackled with all this talk about recycling the ball. The first people to start this was the All Blacks. It's very effective but not very pretty to watch. It's not so much "win rugby" as no-loss rugby. I'm certain it's not the running game which William Webb Ellis envisaged.

'We were given two blazers and our jerseys and two pounds, ten shillings a week for expenses. If you adjusted that figure to allow for inflation, I can't see chaps playing international rugby accepting that today! From our point of view, the trip was a very enriching experience.

'We were gone for six months. Although we had journeyed to France to play an international, it was our first real experience of travel. We went out via the Panama Canal and home by the Suez Canal so it was really a round-the-world trip. We kept fit by running around the ship. Every afternoon, we had great discussions about rugby. I learned more about the game in those conversations than I ever had before or since.

'Our champion was Tom Clifford. Tom was famous on the tour for his singing. One of his favourite ditties was "When I was a wee wee tot, they put me on a wee wee pot, to see if I could wee or not".

'Apart from the normal luggage, Tom brought a massive trunk on to the ship. We were all puzzled about what he could have in it. As cabins were shared, players were instructed to only store essential items there but Tom insisted on bringing in his trunk, which immediately caused a lot of grumbles from his roommates, who were complaining about the clutter. They changed their tune the first night, though, when some of us said we were feeling peckish. Tom brought us into his cabin and opened his trunk, which was crammed with food his mother had cooked. So every night we dined royally in Tom's cabin. Someone said that we should all write a letter to Mrs Clifford because she fed us so well on that trip! Tom had a very healthy appetite. To break the monotony on the journey, we had all kinds of competitions. One night we had an eating competition. Tom won hands down because he got through the 30 courses that were on the menu!'

Tom Clifford's name lives on through 'Tom Clifford Park', a ground which has been variously described as 'The Killing Fields', 'The Garden of Get Somebody' and 'Jurassic Park'.

For Jim McCarthy, Clifford was not only one of the great props but also perhaps the greatest character in Irish rugby: 'He was the character among characters. I'll never forget his funeral. The church was teeming with rugby folk. The priest giving the homily had been a lifelong friend of Tom's and told us how he had invited the giant of Irish rugby to his ordination Mass. After the ceremony, he asked Tom what he thought of it. Tom replied, "You spoke too long. The next time, if you go on for longer than ten minutes, I'll set off an alarm clock in the church." The next Sunday, the priest saw Tom arriving at the church and noticed he had a bulge in his overcoat. When Tom caught his eye, he pulled out an alarm clock!

'Another typical Munster forward was Starry Crowley, a hooker. At one stage, we were playing in a ferocious match when he "made contact" with a player. He explained his motivation to me afterwards: "I was running across the pitch and I saw a head lying on the ground and I kicked not to maim but to kill."

'That kind of commitment is essential if you are to win matches. There's no doubt in my mind that, if you look back to the 1995 World

Cup, South Africa were the fourth-best team after the Wallabies, the All Blacks and France, but they were that bit hungrier, which allowed them to win the tournament. No one I knew played with more hunger than Tom Clifford.

'My clearest memory is of Tom playing for Munster against the Wallabies in 1948. Munster had a very simple way of dealing with touring sides. That was as soon as possible to bring them down to our level and then it was an even match! Tom was in the front row packing against Nick Shehadie, one of the stars of the Australian side, and said, "Come in here, son. You may as well die here as in f**kin' Sydney!"'

6

THE CLAW
PETER CLOHESSY

Peter Clohessy earned the nickname 'Judge Dredd' in the dressing-room because his word was law. The English language has yet to invent a word that adequately sums him up. 'Legend' and 'character' hint at his essence, but no more than that. He is one of a kind. It was Mae West who famously observed, 'A hard man is good to find.' In Irish rugby, we found one in Clohessy.

'The Claw' had the type of temperament and physicality to endear himself to the Limerick faithful, but there were the very occasional blips: 'One Tuesday evening, after a particularly galling loss to Shannon, I was heading onto the field to go training for Young Munster and there was this old lady – I'd say she was 85 if she was a day – and she called me over to the wire. I knew I was in for an earful straight away. She shouted at me, "What the hell was wrong with you on Saturday? You were hoisted so high in the scrum I was going to send you a parachute!"'

Clohessy had a sophisticated rugby intelligence, and there was a lot more to his game than 'hump it, bump it, whack it'. For those of a certain disposition, this approach might be a recipe for a good sex life, but it won't win you 54 caps and a Lions selection. Clohessy is said to be the only man in Limerick who can leave his car unlocked. His love of Limerick is immediately apparent when he is asked about the highlights of his career: 'I suppose my first highlight was winning the All-Ireland League with Young Munster in 1993. After that, the other highlights were my first cap for Ireland; beating France in Paris in 2000 and England in Twickenham in 1994.'

His Limerick bias is also evident when asked who he thinks the characters of rugby are: 'Mick Galwey, Philip Danaher, Keith Wood and Anthony Foley.'

Another great passion of his was Munster: 'The low points were losing two European Cup finals with Munster. To be so close twice and to lose on both occasions was very tough. We just seemed to always be the bridesmaids.'

The Claw did have some other setbacks. In 1997, he was selected for the Lions' tour to South Africa alongside an elite group of players: Martin Johnson, Neil Jenkins, Tim Stimpson, Nick Beal, John Bentley, Ieuan Evans, Tony Underwood, Allan Bateman, Scott Gibbs, Will Greenwood, Jeremy Guscott, Alan Tait, Paul Grayson, Gregor Townsend, Matt Dawson, Austin Healey, Rob Howley, Jason Leonard, Graham Rowntree, Tom Smith, David Young, Mark Regan, Barrie Williams, Keith Wood, Jeremy Davidson, Simon Shaw, Doddie Weir, Neil Back, Lawrence Dallaglio, Richard Hill, Eric Miller, Scott Quinnell, Tim Rodber and Rob Wainwright. However, although he made the trip to London to meet with the squad, he was forced to return home with injury.

Before the 2002 Heineken Cup semi-final, he faced a more serious injury when he was badly burned in a domestic accident. This prompted his wife to remark, 'I always knew you'd go out in a blaze of glory, but I didn't think you'd literally do it.' The small matter of multiple skin burns was not enough to deter Clohessy from playing in the game, and, in solidarity with the Claw, Munster fans wore T-shirts to the game saying, 'Bitten and burnt, but not beaten'.

There were happier times earlier that year when his son, Luke, accompanied him as he led the Irish team out against Wales in the Six Nations to celebrate his 50th cap. To add to the occasion, he was followed closely onto the Lansdowne Road turf by his great friend Mick Galwey, captaining his country for the first time on the famous sod. Clohessy played like a man possessed in Ireland's demolition job of the Welsh, even setting up a try for Geordan Murphy with a masterful reverse-pass. When he was substituted near the end, he received a massive standing ovation.

However, it was not always thus. Clohessy had unexpectedly found himself cast as the bête noire of Irish rugby in 1996. During a Five Nations match in Paris, he 'misplaced his boot' on Olivier Roumat's head during a ruck. Roumat himself was no angel. The 6 ft 6 in., 242-lb lock was once so incensed by the loud snoring of his roommate, Abdel Benazzi, on the eve of a Test that he ran over to his bed and punched the mighty Moroccan-born forward.

Clohessy's character was unfairly traduced after the affair, particularly as the amount of intimidation and provocation he was subjected to was largely ignored. He was quoted after one match against French opposition as saying: 'It's a bit much to have some

PETER CLOHESSY

French f**ker gouging you in the eyes without him grabbing you by the bollocks as well.'

It seems he didn't forget. In 2006, his rallying cry to his former teammates before Munster played in the Heineken Cup was: 'Sock it to these French bas***ds.'

7

VICTOR BRAVO
VICTOR COSTELLO

Along with the Welsh winger Nigel Walker, Victor Costello is part of an elite club of people who have competed in athletics in the Olympics and then gone on to play international rugby.

The most formative influence on Costello's career, which saw him win 39 caps, was his late father, Paddy. 'My first cap gave me great satisfaction. I will always remember ringing my dad from Atlanta to tell him I had been selected and him running down the corridor to tell my mum and then running back to tell me her reaction. It is a special family moment and is very personal to me. My father played once for Ireland in 1960 against France in Paris. I reminded him when I won my second cap that I had played twice as many times for Ireland as him!'

Victor also followed in his father's footsteps by excelling at athletics. 'My dad had been a national champion in the shot-put. I put a huge amount of pressure on myself to get to the Olympics. I grew up on athletics. My sister Suzanne also represented Ireland at athletics. I was good at it but I never was going to be a world champion. I didn't like the loneliness of life as a shot-putter. I didn't fancy spending all my time in a gym with just a German coach. I gave what I had to give to go to the Barcelona Olympics in 1992 and after that I didn't care.

'The year after I finished athletics, I was brought into the Irish squad. I went on the tour to Australia in 1994. In 1996, I went to Atlanta with the Irish squad for warm-weather training to get us ready for the Championship. It was ironic that it poured rain while we were there and it took us 36 hours to get home because we were caught in a snow storm and we had to return via Copenhagen and Manchester. At the end of the week, we played the USA on a rain-sodden pitch. I played reasonably well when winning my first cap, but I missed a tackle and they scored from it. My defence was questioned at the time. More than now, players got labelled back then. It is interesting that, in 1994, Keith Wood was the undisputed star of the Irish team on the tour to Australia. Yet, the following year, he was not the Irish hooker because people said he was "too loose a player".'

One of the controversies in Costello's career was about the manner of his departure from London Irish, which he acknowledges: 'I moved to London to advance my career. It was a case of the grass is always greener. It was universally believed at the time that there was a higher standard of rugby in England. I chose London Irish rather than a club like Saracens because I wanted a bit of "home". I didn't settle in and it wasn't a good move for me. My career was on a slippery slope and I called it early and came back to Ireland.'

There has been much speculation that he had an unhappy relationship with Clive Woodward during his sojourn in London, but Victor dismisses it: 'Everybody thinks I had a problem with him but I didn't. He was trying to do things with us that we weren't able to do. It was like when Brian Ashton was Irish coach. Brian couldn't communicate with the Irish team, and, when he did, it was way beyond what we were up to. Clive was a very hard worker and was very ambitious but didn't have the players. He recognised things weren't going to work out and went to Bath. There never was any bust-up or row between us. The money was good but I was on a downward curve and got back home quickly.

'That was the low point of my career. It was tough to get out and call it quits. To people back home, it probably looked as if I couldn't hack it outside my comfort zone. I was coming back to Ireland with my tail between my legs. When you do something like that, you feel that your peers have less esteem for you and you've got to start from scratch and do it all over again. At that time, in '97, my father had just died and unfortunately I was only climbing out of the bad patch when he passed away. I only had six caps when he died. Then again I mightn't have been able to win any more caps without his help up there. It would be very easy to say neither Clive Woodward nor Warren Gatland fancied me as a player but that would be too easy. I had to improve as a player.'

Eddie O'Sullivan's appointment as Irish coach was to resurrect Costello's international career. 'I approached Eddie in the summer of 2002 in our training camp in Poland because I was on the fringes of the squad but not actually in it, and I asked him what I had to do to get back into the squad. We sat through a couple of videos and he said, "Well, this is what you have to do to get in." I went out and did it, and he, true to his word, brought me back into the squad. I kind of pride myself on the fact that I listened to people I respect like Eddie

O'Sullivan or Declan Kidney, and when they asked me to do something I did my damnedest to get it done. That's why I was delighted to get back into the squad – at least I was back on the radar, despite those who were writing me off because of my age or for other reasons. After competing in the Olympics, I was really keen to play in the World Cup in 2003 because they are both the greatest stages of all, so when I got my chance to be selected for the team, I took it.'

8

THE GREMLIN
KEITH CROSSAN

On 20 February 1982, Ireland secured a 21–12 victory over Scotland thanks to six penalty goals and a dropped goal from Ollie Campbell. It was a historic victory – their first Triple Crown title in 33 years. The Irish team on that auspicious occasion was: Hugo MacNeill, Moss Finn, Michael Kiernan, Paul Dean, Keith Crossan, Ollie Campbell, Robbie McGrath, Phil Orr, Ciaran Fitzgerald (captain), Ginger McLoughlin, Donal Lenihan, Moss Keane, Fergus Slattery, Willie Duggan, John O'Driscoll. It was Keith Crossan's first cap. He replaced his injured Ulster colleague Trevor Ringland for that game and displaced Moss Finn for a permanent place on the team for the following seasons. With his try against Wales in Cardiff in 1985, he was rated as the best winger in the Championship.

As he broke into the Irish team, Crossan came face to face with the legend that was Moss Keane. It was a time when the Troubles in the North were at their height, and Moss told Crossan about a match he had played in Belfast. After the game, the lads stopped for a case of beer in an off-licence because the drink was so much cheaper up there and it would set them up nicely for the train journey home. That evening, though, there was a bomb scare which ruled out travelling by train, and after a long delay a bus arrived instead. The problem was that there was no room on the bus for Moss and some of the other players. Moss had already got through a couple of his beers and was not too happy with the prospect of having to wait even longer. He marched on to the bus and, according to folklore, said, 'Excuse me, this bus is going to crash.'

At first, nobody moved but then a little old man got up, timidly walked up to the towering figure of Moss and said, 'Excuse me, sir, but where did you say this bus was going to?'

Like the entire Irish team, Crossan had followed Moss's progress keenly when he went on his first tour to New Zealand with the Lions in 1977. Moss was the only player who the BBC had not interviewed in the first seven weeks, because they didn't think his strong Kerry brogue would work well with a British audience. Eventually, the Lions players said they would refuse to do any more interviews for the BBC until Nigel Starmer-Smith interviewed Moss. Nigel reluctantly agreed to this demand and, on live television, asked Keane, 'Well, Moss, you've been here now for two months and you've played in your first Lions Test, met the Maoris . . . What's been the best moment of the trip for you?'

In his thickest Kerry accent, Moss replied, 'When I heard that Kerry beat Cork in the Munster final.'

Moss explained to me that he had a mutual admiration society with Crossan: 'I loved playing with the Gremlin because he was such an exciting player and because he could score tries, with his speed and strength, when and where others couldn't. If you were picking the dream Irish team, you would have to seriously consider him for a position on the wing. He was that good and he should never be forgotten.'

Crossan was an integral part of Ireland's triumphs during their march to the Triple Crown in 1985. He enjoyed the camaraderie of his teammates: 'There was a great bond between the team. It was probably most evident at Cardiff Arms Park when we beat Wales 21–9. We hadn't won there for over 20 years but I will never forget that we linked arms before kick-off. It wasn't planned. It just happened naturally. It showed how united we were.'

The mood in the camp was helped by coach Mick Doyle and his wicked sense of humour. He was taking the squad for a Sunday-morning training session, and his prop-forward Jim McCoy – an RUC officer brought up in the Protestant tradition – was not moving as swiftly as Doyler would have liked. Doyler shouted at him, 'Hurry up, McCoy, or you'll be late for Mass!'

Crossan was, of course, central to Ireland's plans for the inaugural World Cup in 1987, although, for most players, it was a big disappointment. It was badly organised, and the hotels and training grounds were sub-standard. There was also an Irish fiasco when, before the opening game against Wales, the IRFU insisted that the national anthem ought not be played, and 'The Rose of Tralee' was chosen as a replacement.

Tony Ward was one of Crossan's many big admirers: 'Keith – or "The Gremlin" as he was affectionately known – was a great attacker but what was special about him was that he was such a competitor, as much at home in defence as attack. Like Trevor Ringland, he was fast without being blisteringly so. Keith was the type of player that, if you were going to war and digging deep into the trenches, you would want with you. He was the complete winger, good in timing the tackle and counterflagging an opponent on the other side as he put in a last-ditch try-saving tackle, which he did so often for Instonians, Ulster and Ireland. He had great hands and was a good kicker, competitive in defence but also fantastic in attack and scored many fine tries for Ireland.'

9

DALY CHORES
JACK DALY

Jack Kyle's clearest memory of the Triple Crown-winning side is of Jack Daly. 'It's not important to have a good captain when you have a good team because everybody knows exactly what they have to do. Karl Mullen was a great captain but that 1948–49 team had total commitment. We never contemplated losing at any stage. I think attitude is hugely important in rugby. You have to believe you will win before you win. At the time, we always faced playing the Welsh on their own patch with trepidation. In 1948, though, when we played them in Swansea, Jack sat in the dressing-room, punching his fist into his hand, saying, "I'm mad to get at them. I'm mad to get at them. I'm mad to get at them." His enthusiasm rubbed off on the rest of us.

'You have to remember that it was such a different set-up then from today. We came down from Belfast on the train in the morning and in the afternoon we went for a training session – using the term loosely – in Trinity College. Johnny O'Meara might throw me a few passes and that would be enough for me. We used an interesting word a lot at the time – "stale" – which I never hear now. Basically, we believed if we trained too hard, we would not perform on the Saturday. It was probably an excuse for us not to do any serious work!

'I always felt that, just as a girl who is born beautiful can only enhance her looks a little bit, you can only achieve a limited amount in rugby by coaching. It's really a question of natural ability. I only dropped a goal once for Ireland. It was from a very difficult angle. If I had thought about it, I could never have attempted it. It was just instinctive. A lot of times, we were working on a subconscious level. Another time, I combined with Jim McCarthy for Jim to score a great try. I got a letter afterwards telling me it was such a textbook score we must have practised it on the training ground. Looking back now, it's amazing how few set moves we had worked out came off. Jack Daly was more in the mode of Mick Doyle's give-it-a-lash philosophy. It certainly worked for him and he was a big part in our success.'

Another teammate on the Grand Slam-winning side was Des O'Brien,

38

who was a keen student of Daly's: 'Jack was an extraordinary character and one of rugby's great romantics. Before World War Two, he only played with the thirds for London Irish. As he departed for combat, he said, "When I come back, I'll be picked for Ireland." He was stationed in Italy during the war and had to carry heavy wireless equipment on his back. As a result, his upper-body strength was incredible. Before internationals, he did double somersaults to confirm his fitness. Having scored the winning try to give Ireland the Grand Slam in 1948, he was nearly killed by spectators at the final whistle. His jersey was stripped off his back and people were wearing pieces of it on their lapels for weeks afterwards. Jack was whisked off from the train station in Dublin the next day by a girl in a sports car whom he had never met but who was sporting a piece of his jersey on her blouse. He stayed with her for a week and lost his job when he went back to London!'

Jim McCarthy was another big fan of Daly's: 'Jack Daly from Cobh was a terrific player. He was a powerful man, and, after he scored the decisive try in Belfast that clinched the Triple Crown in 1948, he turned to Des O'Brien and said, "If Wales don't score now, I'll be canonised in Cobh tonight." In fact, at the end of the game, the fans tore his jersey off his back to keep as a souvenir because Ireland hadn't won the Triple Crown for 49 years. He also went on to play rugby league very successfully as Paddy Reid's teammate with the Huddersfield club.'

The past is a foreign country and, listening to Daly, it seems they really did do things differently there: 'We were really innocent. I suppose this was particularly shown when we went to Paris in 1948. We had our banquet in the Hotel Laetitia. It was a bit of an eye-opener! There were six different glasses, a different wine for every course, all vintage. I will never forget the wine waiter coming along to pour for some of the Irish lads and them telling him, "*Non, non merci, avez-vous un jus d'orange, s'il vous plaît?*" After that, we headed to the Folies Bergere, or, in the immortal words of Bill McKay, the Folies Bareskins! It came as a culture shock to be looking at women whose breasts were uncovered!'

10

MR D'ARCY
GORDON D'ARCY

Although he won a Grand Slam and a Heineken Cup in 2009, Gordon D'Arcy will always be remembered for his performances in 2004, which saw him becoming one of the elite Irish sports personalities chosen for a prestigious Texaco award and being voted the Northern Hemisphere player of the year. Few players have ever announced their arrival on the Six Nations stage with a louder blare of trumpets than D'Arcy did in 2004. One moment that will forever define his impact that season came in the last minute of the match against Scotland, which sealed Ireland's Triple Crown. Eddie O'Sullivan was making a bench clearance and D'Arcy was one of the players to be called ashore. After he had scored two tries and consistently tormented the Scottish defence with his powerful and intelligent running, the cheer for D'Arcy nearly raised the roof.

Before 2004, there had been a number of hints in newspaper articles that D'Arcy had a problem with his attitude. How accurate was that perception?

'When I first started playing rugby, I had a very blasé approach. I was enjoying playing rugby but I was carrying that casual attitude into my preparation and training, and it just gave off the wrong vibe, and it just took me a while to realise that more commitment was needed. When you have established yourself consistently as a top-class player, you don't have to be too worried about the vibe you give off, but when you are trying to break into a new team it is important because other people make judgements about you on the basis of that rather than what you can do on the pitch. It took me a while to adjust to that.

'What amazed me was that certain people in the media were looking for a story to latch on to and a story about Matt Williams finding me drunk got legs and started turning up everywhere. My attitude, though, was that one incident doesn't sum me up as a person. I was doing things my way. I was playing exciting rugby in my eyes, like running the ball from my own five-metre line – sometimes it came off, sometimes it didn't. As a 19-year-old, the consequences of your actions aren't all that relevant. People said I was a crazy, crazy kid. I wasn't. I was just a regular 19-year-old.'

D'Arcy was controversially omitted from the Irish World Cup squad in 2003, and he still remembers the disappointment he felt: 'That will go down as one of the low points of my life. I always said when I made the first World Cup in '99, I would like to play in four World Cups. If I play in 2011, it will be my third and not my fourth. It was between Paddy Wallace and myself for the one spot. It was a call that had to be made and you live and die by those calls. There have been calls that have gone my way since, like when Brian [O'Driscoll] was injured before the France game in 2004.

'I remember I was inconsolable when I heard I had missed out on the squad. I was talking to a schoolteacher friend of mine and I asked in a wailing tone, "What's going to happen to me now?" He calmly said, "Well, you're going to be able to play eight games at full-back for Leinster and you are always saying that you want to play at full-back." It helped me to start thinking positively again.'

The popular perception was that missing out on the World Cup was the catalyst D'Arcy needed to get his act together and finally fulfil his true potential. Not for the first time in his career, the real story was more complex.

'It was easy for people to write that missing out on the World Cup was the spur that made me perform in 2004 but that is not the case. When I wasn't getting picked for Ireland, I lost my enjoyment of playing rugby and I lost the things I enjoyed about the game, like beating a man one on one and putting in a good tackle. During the World Cup, I started to enjoy my rugby again, because at Leinster I was playing with my friends and a coach I got on brilliantly with, Gary Ella. He gave me literally a free role. I asked him before one game whether there was anything he wanted me to do and he said, "If you see it, do it."

'"Is there anything you don't want me to do?"

'"No, not really, mate."

'"OK."

'I was just smiling after a game and I was training well because I was so looking forward to playing again, and that was what re-energised me. I didn't consciously say I'm going to get my place on the Irish team or I'm going to train harder. I was just enjoying it more.'

His international redemption came almost by accident. 'There wasn't much cover in either Leinster or Ireland for the centre positions. In the run-up to a Leinster game, Gary Ella casually asked me one day, "Do you want to go 13?" It really was as casual as that. We were walking onto the pitch and we were having a little banter.

'I replied, "Well, do you want me to play 13?"

'"Well, what do you think?"

'"Yeah, OK. We'll see how it goes."

'It seemed to work for Leinster and Eddie O'Sullivan gave it a try against France.'

Brian O'Driscoll's injury allowed D'Arcy to take his place on the Irish team in the opening Six Nations fixture in Paris. Five years after winning his first cap against Romania in the '99 World Cup, D'Arcy was to finally stamp his distinctive mark on international rugby.

'There were a few moments before the France game that stand out for me. You train for the start of the week with a squad of 30. Then, on the Wednesday, a squad of 22 was announced. I was in the 22 and I went, "Wow. I'm going to be on the bench." I presumed they were going to go for a different combination in the centre, but I was pretty sure that I would win another cap at some stage in the match by coming on as a replacement.

'Then the team was called out. I heard, "D'Arcy 13." I was in a state of shock.

'After that, we went to training. Eddie [O'Sullivan] said to me, "Relax. Play your game and, when you get the ball, run hard."

'It was the best advice I ever got.

'The other thing I remember is going to the stadium before the match. I had heard a lot about it but never been in it. I remember, when we turned a corner on the team bus, there it stood in front of us and I actually couldn't see as far as the top of it because it was so huge. I walked out with Malcolm O'Kelly to throw the ball around. You nearly had to look straight up to see the sunlight.

'The Wales game for me personally was massive. It was my first start at home for Ireland and I felt really in the zone. The English game was special. All week, everybody was "locked and loaded" as Eddie liked to put it. The great thing was that the squad, players and staff were so well gelled together and our play on the field reflected that. Brian made a throwaway comment that he hoped Ireland might make the Twickenham crowd "choke on their prawn sandwiches". Of course, the English media whipped up a storm about it but we didn't let it faze us in the slightest.

'Before the game, we did a warm-up and you could feel the energy running through the side. "Rog" [Ronan O'Gara] was playing so well and was able to give Brian and myself the type of ball we needed and that made a huge difference. A big part of the game-plan for that match was for Rog to throw a wide, flat pass to Brian and myself. When we came in at half-time, the question was asked: "Is anybody tired?" The answer was an emphatic no from everyone. This is the world champions and we are going to win. They can't beat us. The try we scored from our own 22 is a favourite Ireland team try of mine.'

What was his own highlight from that magical season?

'My second try against Scotland was the last nail in the coffin and effectively sealed the Triple Crown, but it was my first try that day that was the most satisfying for me personally because it was a much better score.

'Eddie O'Sullivan was a great help to me making the transition to regular international rugby in 2004 in ways nobody ever saw. It was just the way he gave me a kick in the ass when I needed it, like the week up to the France game in 2004 when I did an interview for a newspaper article which I shouldn't have done. Eddie had a few words with me about it but I knew he was looking out for my best interests.

'In 2003, on the summer tour to Australia, he said to me, "You have an X factor in your play which all the great attacking players have. The problem with you is that you can either win a game or lose a game. You are a little too at either end of the spectrum for me." That was hard to hear then. I was playing well for Leinster at the time and there were Leinster supporters saying I should be on the Irish team. When I look back objectively, there was no reason for me to be on the Irish team.

'After beating England that season, when all the madness had died down, I went to meet my dad and my uncle. All the fans had gone home but there was an Irish fan who had flown in especially for the game from somewhere in Africa and was flying back immediately. He recognised me and came over to us and said, "Thanks very much." It is little things like that which stay in the mind for ever, because you could tell it meant so much to him. You just can't put a price on an experience like that.'

A series of injuries would disrupt D'Arcy's career but he announced his comeback in 2009 when he came off the bench to score a crucial try to set up a famous victory over France. 'The main thing I remember was being picked up by three or four lads and thinking I must have scored! It meant a lot on loads of different levels. Those are the moments that you play rugby for.'

11

DEANO
PAUL DEAN

When it came to a running, 15-man game, Paul Dean was peerless. His genius was the way he took attention off his centres, his backline alignment and speed of delivery. Few Irish players have ever been better able to straighten a backline, but Deano was able to run incredibly straight and he was also a beautifully balanced runner with an outstanding hip movement which he used to great effect in beating the opposition and to create space for those around him. He had magnificent hands, and was rarely, if ever, seen dropping a pass. He was also an exceptionally good tackler.

Ireland's summer tour to South Africa in 1981 marked Dean's initiation into the Irish set-up. It was to prove an education for him in every sense of the term: 'I am still learning what happened on that tour. There were three young lads in the squad: Michael Kiernan, John Hewitt and myself. We were going to bed very early at night, getting up early to go training, and we couldn't understand why the older players were so tired in the mornings. We were on different clocks. They had a different agenda.

'The three of us were so naive and innocent. To give you an example, I roomed with one very senior player, who shall remain nameless, for four nights, but I never saw him at night-time and I was so naive I thought he didn't want to room with me because he was afraid I'd be snoring!'

The next year, Dean found himself at the centre of Ireland's first Triple Crown victory in 33 years. He is surprisingly downbeat about it: '1982 was a great year for Irish rugby but not a great year for me. I was only a small cog in a very big machine. Of course, I know I was lucky to be there. I played very averagely. Ollie Campbell played fantastically behind a very efficient pack. I was doing a lot of chasing and tackling. It was workmanlike stuff rather than being creative. You don't realise at that age how fantastic it was until afterwards. Yet I wasn't playing the type of game I wanted. I was fulfilling other people's dreams but not my own.'

Dean believed Mick Doyle's appointment as Irish coach transformed his career: 'Doyler had been a fan of mine since I played my first game for Leinster on tour in Romania. He was the coach and before the match I jokingly said to him, "The first ball I get, I will score." The problem was that the first ball I got was on the halfway line but I did score. He liked the way I ran with the ball and played the game.

'The Scottish game in '85 was the high point of my career. It wasn't just that we won the Triple Crown but the way we played that season. Doyler had the guts to let us play the game we wanted to play. We felt we could have taken on the world. I was 25 and at the peak of my career.'

Sadly, what should have been the crowning glory of Dean's career became the nadir. 'My goal was to play for all the teams I could possibly play for: Ireland, the Barbarians and the Lions. I succeeded but the pity for me was that my Lions adventure in 1989 only lasted eight minutes. It was so frustrating because I was going to be playing alongside the best backline in the world with the likes of Rory Underwood, Ieuan Evans and Gavin Hastings. In training, I constantly reiterated that I was always going to pass the ball, and that if somebody was going to kick the ball, it wasn't going to be me.

'Before the Lions team was announced, we all knew that there were three candidates for the two out-half spots: Craig Chalmers, Rob Andrew and myself. When we were playing in the Five Nations, Rob Andrew was very confident he was going to get selected, and, in fairness to him, he was playing quite well. The rumour was that he had planned to bring his girlfriend with him and had even bought an apex ticket for her. When the squad was announced and he wasn't selected, I rang him and said, "I'll look after your girlfriend while she's out here and you're not!" When I got injured, he was brought out as a replacement so he had the last laugh.

'I was 29 years old and had had almost 10 years of international rugby and my body was shaky. It was a simple injury. I was putting too much pressure on my knee on an uneven part of the pitch and my cruciate snapped. I was in tremendous pain. It was like having a knife cut through my knee; I was almost in tears. I knew immediately I was going home and it nearly killed me in the circumstances to miss out on the opportunity to play with such great players.'

12

THE PLAYER'S PLAYER
SHAY DEERING

When Ireland drew 9–9 with Wales in 1974, the late Shay Deering, 'Deero', made his international debut. His selection continued a great family tradition. His father Seamus was a distinguished Irish forward of the 1930s, and his uncle Mark (both from Bective Rangers) had also played for Ireland. Deero was a colossus of a forward, with awesome power, who had the honour of captaining his country. Few people have made a greater impression on those who knew him both on and off the field.

A new range of emotions comes into Tony Ward's voice and facial expression as he talks about the man who was, and is, his inspiration, and he speaks with even more intensity than normal: 'For me, the best Irish player by far in his position was Shay Deering. He was the ultimate personification of bravery. His biggest problem was his lack of fear. He would stick his head in where most people would stick their boot. Fergus Slattery would be the first to admit that the way he and Shay complemented each other for UCD and Leinster was a significant factor in Slats's progression to the top.

'His caps were a paltry return relative to his ability and commitment. He was one of those players who oozed – and I mean oozed – physical presence and charisma. He was the original gentleman off the pitch, but, boy, was he a hard man on it. He particularly loved showing a gap to an outside-half or scrum-half and then, when the player took the bait, he pounced on him. My favourite rugby player of all time is Gerald Davies, but my all-time hero is Shay Deering. He will always have a special place in my heart.

'He won eight caps for Ireland between 1974 and 1978, captaining his country in his final appearance. He won Munster and Leinster Cup medals and a Leinster League medal and was capped for both provinces. He had a most distinguished career, but – long after the cups and caps have been counted – it is the friendships he made along the way that mattered the most. Shay was quite simply the player's player.'

Ward's admiration for Deering is almost matched by Mick Quinn's: 'He was such a charismatic man. His smile signalled friendship, but, when he hit you in a tackle, friendship went out the window. He was a great teacher and leader and you would have died for him. We all knew about his medical condition so we organised a golf classic to help him out a bit. Four days before he died, he carried around his bag and played nine holes of the course. I remember Stewart McKinney, who was his rival for the Irish jersey, was in tears and how upset Slats [Fergus Slattery] and people like that were. His funeral will live with me for ever. I gave the homily at the Mass. Gracer [Tom Grace], who wouldn't be my biggest fan by any means, told me afterwards that it was the best speech I ever made. I think it was for the emotion as much as the content.'

For his part, Tom Grace finds it very difficult to talk about his great friend's death, but his respect for Shay both as a player and as a man knows no limits: 'If someone asked me for a definition of the player's player, I would simply have two words to say – Shay Deering.'

For Johnny Moloney, Deering was a brilliant constellation in an otherwise gloomy sporting sky: 'He was a very sympathetic personality off the field but hard as nails on it. In 1995, I saw his son Shane helping Westmeath win the All-Ireland minor football title. At one stage, he brought off a rugby tackle which his father would have been proud of.'

Like so many others, Mick English was totally bemused that Deering only won eight caps, particularly since Ireland were languishing at the rocky bottom of international rugby that had been their all-too-familiar habitat when he was in his prime: 'He was one of the best forwards I ever saw. No one could surpass his commitment. He was one of the few genuinely unforgettable people I ever met.'

Deering's heady mixture of athleticism, speed, aggression, power, skill and bravery won him incredible respect from his peers, but in his final years it was his bravery that provided an enduring memory for Tony Ward.

'That he was brave on the field is beyond dispute, but in his final years his bravery was stretched to the limits in the face of his battle against a terminal illness. In recent years, I think of him regularly, particularly whenever I hear the Bette Midler song "Wind Beneath My Wings", from the film *Beaches*, because of the line: "Did you ever know that you're my hero?" Every time I hear that song, Deero flashes into my mind.'

13

DEMPSEY'S DEN
GIRVAN DEMPSEY

It was supposed to be Mission Impossible, but Girvan Dempsey guaranteed himself a place in Irish rugby immortality when he scored the try that beat England in 2004. Against all the odds, Ireland ended England's 22-match winning streak at 'Fortress Twickenham', which stretched back to the 1999 World Cup when they were beaten by New Zealand. It was England's first Championship home defeat under Sir Clive Woodward, whose coaching regime began in November 1997. To put the icing on the cake, the English were parading the Webb Ellis trophy at Twickers for the first time since their World Cup victory in Australia. Dempsey's try immediately entered the pantheon of greatest Irish touchdowns of all time alongside both Kevin Flynn's try in '72 and Ginger McLoughlin's try in '82 at the same venue.

The try came after 51 minutes when Gordon D'Arcy made a classic break through the field and the ball was taken on down the left then stitched back to the right, where the pack took up the charge. After the ball was recycled, both D'Arcy and Brian O'Driscoll threw long passes across the field, and Tyrone Howe passed to Dempsey, who scythed over.

Girvan feels that the only people who were not shocked by the turn of events were the Irish team: 'Although nobody gave us a chance, we went into the game with a lot of self-confidence and felt we could take the scalp of the world champions. All week, Eddie O'Sullivan had been asking, "Why can't we beat England?" Training had gone well all week. Going on to the pitch, the noise from the English fans was incredible. They got a try from Matt Dawson early on. Brian O'Driscoll called us together and said, "Right, lads. This is a big game. Let's buckle down." I know it is a cliché but the try was straight off the training ground. We had worked that move again and again in Naas and everyone played their part perfectly.'

Many Irish fans were very annoyed by the rash lunge Ben Cohen made at Dempsey as he scored the try. 'I know some people were very unhappy about it but I bear no ill will towards him. You have to do everything you can to stop a try. The problem was that I had to go off with a damaged right knee because of the incident. While I was not angry with him, I was livid that I had to leave the pitch on what was to be one of the greatest days in the history of Irish rugby.'

After beating England, there was still unfinished business for the Irish team. 'It was great then to go on and win the Triple Crown against Scotland in Lansdowne Road. Down through the years, Scotland had given us many a beating in the Six Nations, even on days when we were expected to win. They had performed poorly in the competition up to that game, but, with Matt Williams in charge of them and with his intimate knowledge of so many of our players, we knew they would raise their game. It was such a fantastic feeling once the final whistle went. Nobody wanted to leave afterwards. We felt it was a tangible reward for all the hard work we had put in down the years. The previous year, losing the Grand Slam decider against England had been such a massive disappointment. We felt the distance between us was nowhere near as great as the scoreboard suggested. Jonny Wilkinson produced the greatest display of rugby I have ever seen that day and the margin of their victory flattered them, so it was doubly nice to win the Triple Crown in Lansdowne Road 12 months later. Once Gordon got the try, we just knew it was going to be one of those great days.'

Since he retired, Girvan has been on the coaching staff with Leinster, working with the assembly line of promising players the province is producing, such as Ian McKinley.

Dempsey doesn't count scoring the try that beat the World Cup champions or winning the Triple Crown as the high point of a career that saw him win 82 caps. For him, a bigger moment came when, having played for the Irish Under-21 squad, he was first called into the Irish senior squad for the game against Georgia in November '98. He sat on the bench that day but won his first cap when he replaced Conor O'Shea.

He recalls that day with pride: 'During the second half, I was warming up with Ciaran Scally. I hadn't really thought I was going to be brought on but then Donal Lenihan, who was the manager at the time, turned to me and said, "Get your kit off. You're going on." When you are a kid, you dream of winning your first cap, but at that moment my dream was coming true, which was an unbelievable thrill. My parents were in the crowd and I knew how proud they would be. To add to the occasion, I scored two tries.'

14

DOYLER
MICK DOYLE

In 2004, the news broke that Mick Doyle had been tragically killed in a car accident. It is difficult to comprehend that this man who gave new meaning to the phrase 'larger than life' is no longer with us.

Mick made his international debut against France in 1965 and scored a try on his debut. He retained strong memories of his international career: 'Noel Murphy and Ray McLoughlin were a great help to me in adjusting to the demands of international rugby. I always looked up to Bill Mulcahy. He always made you aware of what it was to be an Irish player and the standard you had to reach to do justice to the green jersey. I loved every single game I played for Ireland. The highlights for me were beating South Africa in 1965, playing against England with my brother Tommy also playing on the other flank for Ireland, scoring a try against Wales in the ninth minute of injury time in 1968 and touring with the Lions to South Africa in the same year.'

The year 1968 marked his retirement from international rugby, a decision prompted by non-rugby factors: 'I was 28. I had been a perpetual student up to that time. It was time for me to settle down and to build up my veterinary practice.'

As Leinster coach, Mick took them to five interprovincial titles between 1979 and 1983 (1982 shared), although there was controversy about the manner in which he was appointed as Irish coach, with Willie John McBride being cast aside after just one year. What prompted him to throw his hat into the ring for the position?

'After Ireland lost to Scotland in 1984, Moss Keane and Willie Duggan came to me and persuaded me that I should run for the job of Irish coach because they felt we were going nowhere fast.'

There was no disguising the pride in his voice as he talked about the Triple Crown in 1985: 'I had built up a huge dossier of information about each player. I had made up my mind, if I ever was made a coach of a representative side, I would give players responsibility for their own performances. The only thing I would not tolerate is players not trying. I think it is fair to say I gave straight answers to players and there was honest selection, which helped to build up the right spirit.'

The highs of 1985 were, dramatically reversed the following year when Ireland were whitewashed in the Five Nations Championship, and 1987 was also a year of missed opportunities, amid some rumours of discontent within the Irish camp.

'We should have won the Triple Crown in 1987. We let the game against Scotland slip through our fingers. Things were sometimes misinterpreted. After we lost that match, the then chairman of the selectors, Eddie Coleman, asked if he could sit in on our team meeting. I told him I would have preferred it if he didn't, but because he was chairman of selectors I couldn't stop him if he really wanted to. During the meeting, I was very critical of the players' performances and told them so in forthright terms and what I expected of them. I also said that what I had said was not for repeating outside. Some people obviously thought I was putting on a macho display for Eddie's benefit and was trying to show them up. Within a week, a journalist, David Walsh, had the story. I didn't think the "affair" did lasting damage. The mood was brilliant after we beat Wales in Cardiff, and the guys in a show of affection threw me in the bath!

'I think that it's probably fair to say that I was less tolerant towards the end, particularly during the World Cup in 1987. My period as Irish coach cost me about £750,000. Before we left for that tournament, my business was going down the tubes. I didn't have time to keep my eye on the ball in terms of my business. I had never experienced stress until then, but, literally up to the last minute before going Down Under, I was frantically trying to salvage my business. I was also hitting the bottle too hard and it wasn't doing me any favours. It was the darkest hour of my life because everything I had worked for was disappearing before my eyes. Of course, what made it much worse was that I was worried about not being able to provide for my family.

'I suppose we didn't have the same off-the-cuff attitude we had in 1985. On the rugby side, things were not going right in the build-up. We lost Nigel Carr in that horrific bomb blast, which was a huge blow. I always take too much on and I was trying to do everything I could for the players on the organisational side. Philly Orr told me I was doing too much.'

Doyler was not without his critics – Neil Francis was the most high-profile one – but he also had his champions. Mick Galwey has a special place in his affections for Doyle: 'Maybe it was the Kerry-mafia thing but he was always very kind to me in his articles in the paper.

I suppose, as we both were from Kerry, we had a special connection. I think anyone who recalls the way we won the Triple Crown will know that he left a unique legacy to Irish rugby. It's a cliché to speak of someone as larger than life but in his case it is completely true and the world is duller without him.'

15

THE SMOKER
WILLIE DUGGAN

A sport played by women and men with odd-shaped balls is bound to produce great characters and moments of mischief and mirth. In any roll of honour of the characters in Irish rugby, Moss Keane and Willie Duggan are at the top of the list.

Hence the story told at a Lions reunion dinner: 'Moss and Willie read that drink was bad for you. They gave up reading.'

Stories abound about Duggan, who won 41 caps for Ireland. A man with little enthusiasm for training, his most celebrated comment was: 'Training takes the edge off my game.' Duggan was one of a rare group of players who always made a point of bringing a pack of cigarettes with them onto the training field. Asked once in a radio interview if this was a major problem for him fitness-wise, he took the broadcaster by surprise by saying that it was a positive advantage: 'Sure, if it was not for the fags, I would be offside all day long.'

Another time, he was having a fag in the dressing-room in Twickenham before Ireland played England. The time had come to run onto the pitch but Duggan had nowhere to put out his cigarette in the dressing-room. He knew that if he ran out in the tunnel with the fag in his mouth, the cameras would zoom in on him straight away. The Scottish referee, who was making his international debut, was in the dressing-room, so the Irish number 8 went over to him and said, 'Would you hold that for a second, please?'

The obliging referee said yes, but Duggan promptly ran out onto the pitch – leaving the ref with no option but to put out the fag. The ref went out to face the glare of the cameras and the first sight the television audience had was of him holding a cigarette!

Willie was never too concerned about tactics. Asked by a journalist for the reason for a vintage Leinster performance, he answered, 'We had decided to go out in the first half to soften them up and kick the proverbial s**t out of them. And it went so well for us that we had a quick word at half-time and decided to kick the s**t out of them in the second half!'

WILLIE DUGGAN

Fergus Slattery tells a story about Willie, his partner in the back row. In 1983, some of the guys played in a match against the Western Province in South Africa. The match was played in mid-July. Typical of Willie, all he took with him on the trip was a small bag with his toothbrush and cigarettes. Willie was never too bothered about training at the best of times, but in the middle of the summer he was totally unfit. The game passed right by him. At one stage, Fergus saw him stamping on the ground. 'Slats' went over to him and asked him what the hell he was doing. Willie answered, 'Oh, I'm stamping that bloody snail which has been following me around since the match started!'

Donal Lenihan was a key member of the Triple Crown-winning sides in 1982 and 1985, and he has fond memories of many of the players who soldiered with him in various triumphs: 'The best Irish forward I ever played with was Willie Duggan. He was the Scarlet Pimpernel of Irish rugby because he was so hard to find for training! Having said that, he wouldn't have survived in international rugby so long without training. Willie took his captaincy manual from a different world. His speeches were not comparable with anything I'd ever heard before or since.

'One of my clearest memories of Willie's captaincy is of the morning after the Scotland game in 1984; the papers all had a picture of Duggan with his arm around Tony Ward and speaking to him. Willie was not known for his gentle words of encouragement to his players. It was just before Wardy was taking a penalty. It appeared that Willie was acting the real father figure, but, knowing him as I do, my guess was he was saying, "If you miss this penalty, I'll kick you all the way to Kilkenny!"'

John O'Driscoll, Willie Duggan and Fergus Slattery firmly established themselves as the most effective Irish back-row combination since the days of the 1948 Grand Slam side. So how does O'Driscoll evaluate Duggan?

'Fergus and Willie played hard on and off the pitch. The difference was that, whereas Fergus never seemed to show any ill-effects the next day, Willie did! It was an accepted fact that Willie was last for every exercise in training. Our recurring nightmare was that Duggan would beat one of us into second-last place! This would suggest that we were totally unfit and almost certainly lead to our demise on the Irish team.'

Ned Byrne, Willie Duggan's cousin, won an All-Ireland senior hurling medal with Kilkenny in 1972 playing at top of the left. His uncles Eddie and Podge Byrne also won All-Ireland hurling medals with Kilkenny in the 1930s. Later, as a prop-forward, Ned won six caps for Ireland. In one match, Duggan was playing for the Public School Wanderers when Byrne was clobbered in the eye. Byrne turned to his cousin for comfort, but was instead given the benefit of Willie's wisdom: 'I told you, when you hit a guy, don't be watching him. Watch the guy who's coming in behind him.'

16

THE BEST OF THE WEST
ERIC ELWOOD

Having initially shown great promise as a Gaelic footballer, Eric Elwood turned to rugby and scored 293 points for Ireland in his 35 internationals. He was first capped against Wales in 1993 and played his last Test against Romania in 1999, having played in both the 1995 and 1999 World Cups. His 8.37 average points per game is all the more impressive when you consider that Irish rugby was generally in the doldrums for most of his international career. Eric will probably be best remembered for his role in two great moments in the history of Irish rugby: the 17–3 victory over England in 1993 and the 13–12 victory over the old enemy the following year. To win there in 1994 was a massive achievement, given the slump in Irish rugby's fortunes at the time.

One of Elwood's biggest fans is Tony Ward: 'The first time I saw Eric play was for Connacht against New Zealand in 1989 in the Sports Ground. I watched his career develop over the years with Galwegians, with Lansdowne, with Connacht and Ireland. The one thing that always struck me about him as a player was the sheer presence he brought to the position. There is a gravitas to him, in that you always knew he was there. Even when he was not on top form, he would always make an impression on a game. That is the way it should be. You knew from the way he played that he was the man in charge. You always knew he would take responsibility for calling the shots, and, when he got it wrong, he always held his hands up. I would like to think that in my playing days when I made a mistake I forgot about it and got on with the match and Eric was always like that. When John Giles is analysing games on TV, he often describes a player who hides when the going gets tough as a "sunshine player". Elwood was never in that mode and never shrunk from any challenge, even when the odds were stacked against him.

'Apart from his presence dictating a game, he was also the playmaker-in-chief and a wonderful kicker. He did not have a great left foot but what a right foot! Like myself, he perhaps lacked a little bit of pace to accelerate through the gap. Whenever he got into trouble, it was because he got caught in two minds: he tried to make a break but got cut off. Unlike Ronan O'Gara, who, when he gets caught making a break from time to time, does not have the physical presence to hold on to the ball and a turnover ensues, such was Elwood's physical presence that, when he got caught in the tackle, he was able to ensure that his side retained possession.

'The Connacht star was almost robotic in the way he worked so hard on the bread-and-butter basics of the game: kicking off and restarting. He was a master of what we call in the modern game "hang-time", where you put the ball high in the air to give the forwards time to get underneath it. It was a skill he really honed to perfection.

'His work ethic was second to none and I know he particularly impressed the Connacht players in that respect. He played his last game for the province in April 2005 but probably stayed on a year too long as a player, as I did myself. With the advent of professionalism, he was finding the going tough in his last year. He maximised his career through hard work and sheer graft. He was a model pro, albeit having come through the amateur age. He epitomised how a player can adapt to a professional environment in the modern age.

'He represented his province a record 177 times. I was delighted that in 2005 he was inducted into the Irish Rugby Union Players Association's Hall of Fame. Connacht has produced some exceptional players down the years like Ray McLoughlin, Ciaran Fitzgerald, John O'Driscoll and Mick Molloy, but I know if I had to pick my Connacht player of all time it would be Eric Elwood.

'The great Gareth Edwards once claimed, "Rugby football is really a simple game; it's only the coaches who make it complicated." This remark should be treated with caution because such was Edwards's talent that he could make things look easy which other mortals would have found impossible. Although it may contain more than a grain of truth, the reality is that coaches exert a huge influence in the modern game. That is why I am delighted that at the end of his distinguished career Eric has turned his attention to coaching. Having made such an enormous contribution to Connacht rugby in particular and to Irish rugby in general, it is wonderful that future generations of Connacht players will have the benefit of his wisdom and vast reservoir of experience.'

17

NATURAL BORN THRILLER
MICK ENGLISH

In his full life, Mick English had three claims to fame. First, he was an accomplished Irish out-half, succeeding no less a person than Jack Kyle in the number-10 jersey.

Second, he has been immortalised around the world in after-dinner speeches by Tony O'Reilly. Playing against Phil Horrocks-Taylor during a Wolfhounds match in Limerick, English was asked what he thought of his opponent, who had scored a try that day. English replied, 'Well, Horrocks went one way, Taylor the other and I was left with the hyphen.' In the O'Reilly version, this exchange happened after an Ireland–England international at Twickenham, although, in fact, English never played opposite Horrocks-Taylor in an international.

Third, and perhaps most surprising, he might be said to be the architect of Richard Harris's acting career. When the actor Anew McMaster was touring Limerick, he stayed in English's home. He required some extras for his stage production of the Dickens classic *A Tale of Two Cities*. English supplied him with some of his friends, including Harris and the horse trainer Teddy Curtin. They were paid half a crown each per performance to do the mob scenes. Subsequently, Harris was badly bitten by the acting bug and spent hours talking about acting in Mick's kitchen with McMaster. McMaster persuaded him to go to London and join an acting school. Appropriately, Harris went on to win an Oscar nomination for his role in a film called *This Sporting Life*.

English was close to Harris: 'At Rockwell College, I was fortunate to be on a Junior Cup-winning team in 1949 and also played against Crescent College in the senior final that same year. We lost 8–0 and, having started at out-half, I moved to first centre, second centre and wing – not a good day! Richard Harris played in the second row for Crescent that day. We became good friends after we left school. We met on a daily basis at Sarsfield Bridge and walked together to work. I went to my clerical job at the Insurance Corporation of Ireland and Dickie to his father's flour store in Henry Street, where he was chief mouse catcher! He was always an actor and the centre of all "divilment". We played junior interpro for Munster together, and I have no doubt that if he had not gone to London, he would have gone all the way in rugby. After he left to pursue his acting career, the next time we met he was on stage in Brendan Behan's *The Hostage*. Free seats for the pals from Limerick!'

English won final trials in '56 and '57, but had to wait until 1958 for his first cap for Ireland. Ireland lost 9–6 after John O'Meara retired injured, in a match that was the final curtain call for Cliff Morgan's distinguished international career.

English was tickled by a letter written to him by the late Mai Purcell of the *Limerick Leader* when he won his first cap. The letter read:

> Mick. I should like to impress on you that I'm spending a whole week's wages to visit Dublin just to see you play and I beseech you not to make an idiot of yourself on this occasion.
>
> I furthermore request that on this auspicious occasion mindful of your duties and responsibilities not only to your club and the people of Limerick but to your country as a whole, that you keep your bloody eye on the ball. Good luck and God Bless.

The following year came the highlight of his career when he dropped a goal to help seal a 9–5 victory for Ireland over France and book his place on the Lions' tour of New Zealand and Australia.

English's international playing career from 1958 to 1964 had many interruptions, some through injury, some by being out of favour. He was capped in every season of his six-year international career. However, in that period, seven other out-halfs were also capped for Ireland: W.J. Hewitt, Seamus Kelly, Ken Armstrong, Dion Glass, Gerry Gilpin, Gerry Hardy and John Murray. Which Irish out-half impressed him the most?

'It has to be Ollie Campbell. He's as close to perfection as you get. He had it all – a superb tactical brain, wonderful place kicking, great tackling ability, an outstanding team player and his kicking for touch was first class. In my view, a close second was my good friend Barry McGann who was an extremely accomplished tactical player.'

In 1962, English moved from Limerick to Dublin and joined Lansdowne chiefly through the influence of the late Gordon Wood and Paddy Berkery. He has a unique record with the club. After winning a cup medal in 1965, he played on all teams right down to 3rd Ds.

'My last match was for Lansdowne 3rd Bs in Maynooth in 1977 at the age of 44! The field was a converted Gaelic pitch and surrounded with barbed wire to keep the sheep away. After the game, I gashed my leg on the barbed wire and ended up in hospital for anti-tetanus injections – not the finale I would have wished for!'

18

THE FLYING FINN
MOSS FINN

Moss Finn earned his 14 caps for Ireland in the golden age of amateurism, at a time when players had few of the perks expected by today's sportsmen. For one home match, he was rooming with Michael Kiernan in the Shelbourne Hotel, and one of them went down for a haircut and charged it to their room. Shortly after, the IRFU billed both players for half a haircut each.

In 1982, after Ireland won the Triple Crown, the team travelled to France hoping to win the Grand Slam. The Irish team bus entered the stadium and was surrounded by French supporters who were going crazy, thumping the side of the bus and shouting abuse at the team. The Irish team were very tense and everyone was silent. Donal Lenihan was sitting beside Moss Finn. The French fans were screaming, *'L'Irlande est fini! L'Irlande est fini!'*

Moss stood up and said, 'Christ, lads. Isn't it great to be recognised?'

Irish rugby in the past has sometimes been accused of being too insular. In compiling this book, I thought it would be useful to get a more detached perspective, so I spoke with one of the stars of the great Welsh team in the 1970s, Ray Gravell. I spoke to him initially as a total stranger, but, as soon as he heard my accent, he launched into a glorious recitation of lines of Irish poetry, before dazzling me with his knowledge of Irish history. He gave me his views on the greats of Irish rugby.

'On the pitch, I have been fortunate to play with and against some of the greats of Irish rugby. Straight away, I think of Willie John McBride. I played against Willie John during his last game for Ireland in the centenary year of the IRFU. We beat Ireland well, though Willie John scored a try. Late in the game, Phil Bennett chipped through and I was chasing it. You don't think in the clamour of Cardiff Arms Park you will be able to hear any voice in the crowd but I could hear perfectly this marvellous Irish accent shouting, "Kick a-head Ireland. Kick any f**king head." In that moment, I realised that, despite the intensity of the competition, it is really only a game.

'I got to know a number of the Irish players well on the Lions tour in 1980. In Wales, we had two great out-halfs at more or less the same time in Barry John and Phil Bennett. The difference between the two is that Phil made space, whereas Barry made time. In Ireland, you had the amazing situation where you produced two great out-halfs in Tony Ward and Ollie Campbell, who I got to know well on that Lions tour. Tony I would describe as a big man with short legs. I would describe Seamus Oliver Campbell as the bravest of the brave. He was so pale and slight-looking, but he really put his body on the line in the tackle. People talk about his kicking but there was so much more to his game than that. Another superb kicking out-half I came across for Ireland was Barry McGann. Barry was the fastest out-half I've ever seen over five yards. The problem is that he was completely f**ked after five yards!

'John O'Driscoll was incredibly brave on the field. I kept in touch with him. I will never forget that, on the Lions tour, we played a match a week before the first Test and they sprung this amazing kicker who could kick the ball 80 yards and was really crucifying us. Bill Beaumont said we must do something about him. The next time he kicked the ball, I tackled him ferociously and broke his shoulder. John said to me, "Grav, what the f**k are you doing?"

'I replied, "I caught him a late one, early."

'Of course, he is Brian O'Driscoll's cousin. Brian is a world-class player and I would have loved to have played with him. I'm not sure if I would have enjoyed playing against him as much, because he would be whizzing by me and I think I would be spending a lot of my time looking at the back of his jersey! Gordon D'Arcy is another great new talent to have come on the rugby stage and it is great that Ireland have two such classy players in their backline.

'Fergus Slattery was a brilliant player and a great mix of the verbal and the physical. Mike Gibson is a complex man but he formed a great centre partnership with Dick Milliken. Because he was such a star of the Lions tour in 1971, Welsh rugby fans have huge admiration for Seán Lynch. Every time I come over to Ireland, I head to York Street to visit Seán in the Swan Bar. He never lets me buy a drink, though. Willie Duggan was another awesome player and a great man to knock back a pint! I would probably say the same thing about Moss Keane. These guys were legends on the pitch and legends in the bar! Sometimes too much drink is not enough! It only took one drink to get them drunk. The problem was they could never remember was it the 24th or the

25th! I always remember playing against Leinster in a club match and they had a 17-year-old in the centre who just flew by me at one such stage. Already he was a class act and Brendan Mullin certainly became a great player after that.

'When I think of the greats of Irish rugby, though, I have to reserve a special place for Shay Deering. He was *the* man for me. He was a superb wing-forward and a wonderful leader because he led by example. He was so brave. I always felt very comfortable and secure in his company. I just loved Shay and it was such a sadness when I heard that he passed away. Not just the rugby community but the world at large is a much poorer place without him.

'If I was to pick someone, though, who is the unsung hero of Irish rugby, I would say it was Moss Finn. Everyone knows what a great character he is but what some people forget is that he was a hell of a player. The strange thing is, because of the two great tries he got against us in 1982, we have a greater appreciation for his playing abilities in Wales than many people do in Ireland. He fully deserves his place in the greats of Irish rugby.'

19

CAPTAIN'S LOG
CIARAN FITZGERALD

The beauty of television coverage of sport is that it can occasionally capture an image which offers a telling insight into a sporting hero. For the Irish rugby fan, an enduring image will always be Ciaran Fitzgerald's efforts to rally the Irish team as they appeared to be letting the Triple Crown slip through their fingers in 1985 against England in the wake of their dazzling and stylish victories away to Scotland and Wales. Even those who had no experience of lip-reading could clearly make out his plea from the heart (as he temporarily put aside the good habits he acquired as an altar boy with the Carmelites in Loughrea): 'Where's your pride? Where's your f**king pride?'

Fitzgerald's record speaks for itself – Triple Crown and Championship in 1982, a share of the Championship in '83 and the Triple Crown again in 1985. He first made his mark captaining the Irish B team in the 1977–78 season. Then, on the controversial tour to Australia in 1979, he made his international debut, playing in both Tests, although he went out as number two to Pat Whelan.

'At the time, there was an incredible fuss about the fact that Tony Ward had been dropped and Ollie Campbell was chosen in his place. I was totally oblivious to it all. I heard my own name mentioned when the team was announced and nothing else registered with me. A tour is a great place to win a first cap because you were sheltered from all the hype, press attention and distractions that you get at home. I was able to hold my place the following season. I never felt threatened but I never felt comfortable. All you can do is perform to your very best and forget about the lads who are challenging for your position.'

In the 1980–81 season, Fitzgerald sustained a serious shoulder injury in a club match.

'A bad situation was made worse by a doctor during the match. Immediately after the injury, he tried to "yank" my shoulder back into place. Then I was assisted off the pitch. He put me on the flat of my back on the sideline and tried a second time. As a result of the injury and the "cure", I missed the entire international season.'

In 1982, he found himself taking over the captaincy from Fergus Slattery. What was the secret of his success?

'I think I'm very sensitive to people and curious about them. I was still a relatively inexperienced player in comparison with most of my pack. I knew there was no way I could use my army style to deal with these guys. You have to remember there were a lot of world-class players in the forwards like Orr, Keane, Slattery, O'Driscoll and Duggan. The previous year, Ireland had won no match and those guys were fed up hearing from people who knew virtually nothing about rugby: "You're only a shower of . . ." That really annoyed them and they were fired up to prove just how good they were.'

The following year also saw Fitzgerald selected as captain of the Lions. 'It was like a whirlwind. I first heard about the captaincy when I got a call from a journalist. I was very surprised to hear the news because the strong rumour, coming from the English press, was that Peter Wheeler was getting the job. It was a tremendous honour and I didn't give a tuppenny damn about who was disappointed. There was so much media hype, it was hard to focus. It was like getting a first cap multiplied by ten with all the receptions and media interest. I had to take ten days off in Mayo to regain my focus and kept in shape by training three times a day.

'I underestimated the ferocity of the campaign that would be waged against me. I couldn't influence what was said about me, so I just tried to do all I could to get the best possible performance out of the team. It's part of the psychological war that goes on when the Lions tour New Zealand that both media "talk up" their respective squads. In New Zealand, though, they were stunned to see that the British media were trying to outdo each other in terms of rubbishing me. By the time we arrived, everybody wanted to know who this fool of a hooker was. It got to the stage where I expected the first question of every interview to be: "What kind of ape are you?" I was amazed that the New Zealanders knew everything about me. It shows how fanatical they were about the game. Gradually, they discovered that, in my case, what you see is what you get and they largely turned on my side, so we ended up with a bizarre situation of the British press against me and the Irish press and sections of the home press for me.'

Fitzgerald was appointed coach to the Irish team in 1991, although he did not match his success as a player. 'If I had the chance to do it differently, I would in terms of my time as coach. I was reluctant to take the position but the IRFU pressed me. There was a good buzz early on, in that we brought in a lot of new players and we played an exciting, expansive game. Although we played an attractive brand of rugby, we were always nearly winning. That's not good enough. Eventually, you have to win, otherwise morale and confidence start to sap. The tour to New Zealand in 1992 was a bit of a disaster. We faced an impossible task because so many key players were unable to travel. For business reasons, I shouldn't have travelled, but out of loyalty I went because there were so many defections. We made a superhuman effort and again nearly won the first Test, but it was downhill all the way after that. Later that year, I had to step down for business reasons. It was not the ideal time to go, because I would have liked to go out on a winning note.'

20

FATHER AND SON
DES FITZGERALD

Des Fitzgerald lost out on a place on Ireland's Triple Crown-winning team to Jim McCoy because of Mick Doyle's running-game philosophy. Although Fitzgerald was without doubt the better scrummager, Doyler told me he picked McCoy because he was better in the loose. Nonetheless, Fitzgerald went on to have a distinguished Ireland career and won 34 caps for Ireland.

Phil Orr had good reason to remember Des Fitzgerald: 'The low point of my career came in 1986. I lost my place for the Welsh match to Paul Kennedy of London Irish, I think more because of the final trial than because of the drubbing we got from France in our opening match of the campaign. I was up against Dessie Fitzgerald on one side of the scrum and Jim McCoy was up against Paul Kennedy. Jim was pretty secure in his place and I don't think Paul thought he had any real chance of getting into the side, so they weren't trying too hard, but Dessie was mad keen to get picked and was wired to the moon that day so I didn't give the "commanding performance" I would have liked. Des was a very tough opponent and was very unlucky to miss out on our Triple Crown.'

Behind the scenes, Fitzgerald would play a big role in the Irish squad. In the build-up to the World Cup in 1991, Fitzgerald, Philip Matthews and Brendan Mullin formed a triumvirate which negotiated with the IRFU over the way players were to be remunerated for their efforts. The IRFU wanted the squad to sign a participation agreement where they would sign over all rights about the use of their photographs and image rights to them. In effect, the players were being asked to give them a blank cheque. The players believed that the Union wanted to squeeze everything out of their commercial appeal but to give them nothing in return. It was a bitter pill for officials to swallow but the players said no.

In 1991, it was touch and go whether the Irish players would take part in the World Cup. A deal was only worked out at the eleventh hour after some frenetic contacts with Ronnie Dawson. In fact, at the time of the inaugural dinner of the tournament, Fitzgerald and co were still meeting Ken Reid to negotiate an agreement. It was probably the first evidence of player power in Irish rugby, because the players secured a deal that was to their satisfaction. They put themselves under pressure but that made them more determined. In the end, Fitzgerald and his colleagues think they could and should have done even better. They lost narrowly to Australia because they did not slow down the game after Gordon Hamilton's try.

It is funny the things that go through players' minds. The squad were speaking to Australia's Tim Horan after the match. He told them that, after the Hamilton try, he thought it was all over for them and they would be on the plane home the following morning. He had put a lot of his clothes in the laundry that morning and his big fear was that the clothes wouldn't be ready for the following day! Then Michael Lynagh intervened and got Australia out of jail with his try.

One of Fitzgerald's greatest legacies to Irish rugby is his son Luke, who is gifted with extraordinary levels of natural ability. Not only does he have great pace but he also has a wonderful change of pace and he kicks well too. He has a unique capacity to launch an attack for a teammate, but, with his light footwork, to pop up somewhere else later at pace and take the attack on to the next level.

GOAL's John O'Shea was happy to tell me his views on current Irish players even though I never asked him: 'Jamie Heaslip is the greatest rugby player to have worn the green jersey since the Second World War; Johnny Sexton is out and away our most talented and brilliant number 10, while Luke Fitzgerald is a player of consummate skill who, when he moves to full-back, will become arguably the greatest attacking number 15 in the history of the game.'

Tony Ward is well placed to assess the career of both Fitzgeralds: 'I played with Des and he was a fine scrummager. I was at his 50th birthday party and some people were speculating that it was a genetic miracle that someone not known for his speed like Des could father a son with such blistering pace as Luke! Now that the so-called "golden generation" are coming towards the end of their careers, Luke is the future for Irish rugby. I have no doubt that, if he can avoid injury, he will go on to become one of the greats of Irish rugby.'

21

CENTRE OF EXCELLENCE
KEVIN FLYNN

Kevin Flynn was capped 18 times in the centre for Ireland, initially between 1959 and 1966. After a gap of six years, his good form in Leinster's win in the interprovincial championship catapulted him back into the Irish side. He was capped a further four times in the 1972 and '73 seasons, becoming part of an elite group of Irish players to play in three different decades, following Syd Millar and Tony O'Reilly.

'After I left school, I played for Terenure College Past for a year and then moved on to Wanderers, and in my first year there won my first cap when I was 19. The great Ronnie Kavanagh was a huge influence on me. Although I played in the final trial and there was a good bit of talk about me knocking at the door, my international call-up came as a surprise to me.

'Of the match itself, I particularly remember the Lansdowne Road roar. You hear about that but you have to really experience it first-hand to appreciate how special it is. The whole thing had a dreamlike quality. The thought flashed across my mind: "What am I doing here?" I probably remember more about that game than any other. Everything went well for me personally and for the side and we won 14–9. It was a dream debut. I made a break which set up a try for Niall Brophy.

'As the game went on, my confidence grew and we were on top but nobody would pass the ball to me. I kept shouting for the ball to Mick English. Eventually, he turned to me and told me in no uncertain terms to "f**k off" and that there was no way he was going to pass the ball to me. It was nothing personal but he was not going to take the chance of losing possession.

'There was a postscript to the match that I hadn't expected. A week or so after, I got a bill from the Union for sixpence for a phone call I made to my family after the match!

'I came on the scene for the last game of the season, which meant I was too late for consideration for a place on the Lions tour. Hamstring injuries restricted my appearances for Ireland.'

These injuries made it difficult for Flynn to feel he was a settled international but simply being in the company of so many great players was a very enriching experience for him. 'Of course, there was A.J.F. O'Reilly, who was a class player and had an aura about him. In my first game against France, one of their wingers, who was O'Reilly's opposite number, came through like a rocket between David Hewitt and myself and scored a try. O'Reilly came up to me afterwards and said, "He was your man!" I was lucky in that my partner in the centre, David Hewitt, was an exceptional player and had great pace.

'The most satisfying win was against England in 1964 when we ended a 16-year losing sequence at Twickenham. We hockeyed them by playing a running game and so did they.'

Flynn neglects to mention that he scored two tries himself on that occasion.

'Another clear memory for me is that in 1962 our game against Wales was postponed due to the outbreak of foot-and-mouth disease. Up to that time, Irish sides concentrated on frustrating the opposition by preventing them from playing their game, though it was more subtle than the boot, bite and bollick approach. When you think about it, we were normally up against bigger, more powerful sides but we coped with them because we always had some very intelligent players. Later, we introduced more sophisticated ploys, like calling our passes. To fool the opposition, we would call short which really meant long.

'Ray McLoughlin brought a new dimension to the job of captain – almost bringing in a coaching style. He was perhaps the first of the deep thinkers of the game. It was the first time we seriously discussed the game in advance and tactics came into it. He decided that initially we had to be defensive. There was a fair amount of analysis of the opposition and closing down players – Jack Charlton style.

'The regret of my career is that we never won a Triple Crown. We should have won one but let a victory against Wales slip through our fingers by missing our kicks.'

Of Flynn's five international tries, he is best remembered for his grandstand score against England in Twickenham in 1972. Ireland trailed 12–7 when Barry McGann dropped a goal. Then, when everyone thought the final whistle was about to be blown, from an Irish scrum close to the English 25, Johnny Moloney fed McGann, who passed to Flynn, and the evergreen centre, like a prisoner suddenly bursting the confining bonds of a strait-jacket, cut through the English defence like a knife through butter for a superb try. To rub salt in the English wounds, Tom Kiernan added the conversion and Ireland won 16–12.

22

FRANNO
NEIL FRANCIS

Since his retirement from rugby, Neil Francis has drawn on his experience as a player at the highest level to become a match analyst and rugby columnist with Setanta television and the *Sunday Tribune* and the *Sunday Independent*. His forte is his ability to highlight technical aspects of play which might go unnoticed to the casual observer, as well as his self-confidence in articulating his views honestly and in a forthright manner.

An analyst offers a great service to the viewer, particularly in a sport such as rugby because rugby codespeak lends itself to much confusion. 'There's some discussion between Brian O'Driscoll and the touch-line', for instance, does not actually mean what it suggests. An analyst like Francis can draw on his vast reservoir of experience to educate the audience. He points out things the armchair fan will not be aware of, like the fact that when there is a penalty, it is when there is complete silence that the kicker is conscious of the crowd, not when there's noise. It is easier when you have a din around you. For the viewer, Francis provides a privileged vantage point greatly enhanced by his inside knowledge. He can interpret, analyse and speculate with the insight that only seasoned internationals can bring to a game. He also brings a waspish sense of humour, such as in his description of Bernard Jackman's shortcomings with the throw-in: 'He wouldn't hit water if he fell out of a boat.'

During his playing career in the Irish second row, Francis himself was the subject of a vintage piece of rugby punditry from retired Scottish international Ian McLauchlan, who was acting as a summariser for BBC television when Scotland played Ireland in Murrayfield. The diminutive Scot had been capped as a loose-head prop 43 times and captained Scotland in 19 major internationals, and there is a famous picture of Ian, on tour with the Lions in 1974, lifting one huge South African prop clean off the ground in a scrummage. Ian's attitude to the game, though, was probably most starkly revealed in his match commentary. When Francis swung a punch but missed his intended target, Ian expressed his concern – but not about the violence. With millions of viewers watching, he warned Francis that he was in serious danger of getting the name of a softie because: 'There isn't much point in having a go at somebody unless you make sure that you connect.'

Victor Costello has another memory of Francis. While his first cap was the highlight of Costello's career, it also left him with an enduring legacy. 'The tradition is that when you win your first cap everybody buys you a drink. When I won mine, I took a knock on the head and had to go to bed for a while, but I met up with the lads later on that night. When I got back to the hotel, I was starving. The problem was that it was three in the morning. I asked the receptionist how I might get some food. She told me that I could ring out for pizza but that it was very slow. Just after I dialled in my order, though, a guy walked in with a pizza. I was rooming with Neil Francis at the time and I quickly realised the pizza was for him. I pretended it was for me, though, and I brought it to the tea-room and scoffed it all down. When I went up to our room, Franno was watching television. I was absolutely stuffed but I pretended to be starving and asked him how I could get some food. He told me that I could ring out for pizza but he told me not to bother because it was so slow and that he had rang for a pizza over an hour earlier and it still hadn't arrived. I was very sympathetic and I asked him if he would mind waking me up and giving me a slice when his pizza finally arrived. He generously agreed.

'The only problem was that the next morning he found the pizza box in the tea-room and he discovered it was me that ate it. He actually was really annoyed and to this day he has never forgiven me! In fact, whenever he writes about me in his column he will never call me "Victor" – he insists on referring to me as "the pizza robber".'

Francis's contribution to Irish rugby was not always positive, as Simon Geoghegan can testify. He was rooming with Francis the night before the Fiji game in November 1995, which was Murray Kidd's first outing as team coach. Francis got thirsty during the night and drank a glass of water in the bathroom. The next morning, when Geoghegan went to retrieve his contact lenses, he discovered that Francis had unwittingly drunk them and the glass of water.

23

THE WEST'S AWAKE
LEO GALVIN

What makes an Irish rugby great? While this book features players like Jack Kyle and Brian O'Driscoll who are renowned worldwide because of their exploits on the rugby field, it is important in these pages to acknowledge the contribution of the many players who have made a lifetime commitment to their club, province and country, and who have continued to quietly dedicate themselves to the game behind the scenes after their retirement without getting huge accolades. One such man is Leo Galvin, whose career playing for Connacht spanned three decades. A former captain and president of Athlone RFC and Connacht, he was one of the driving forces behind the club's amalgamation with Ballinalsoe to form Buccaneers. Galvin occupies a unique place in the annals of Irish rugby – he is the only man from Roscommon to have played rugby for Ireland.

Born into a farming family in Taughmaconnell, his immersion into rugby only began when he went to secondary school at Garbally College.

Galvin is currently one of two Connacht representatives on the IRFU committee, and, on a bitter-cold Thursday evening immediately after attending a committee meeting, he recalls his lifelong involvement in Irish rugby: 'I have great memories of my time playing for UCD, where I played with great players like Fergus Slattery, Tom Grace and the inspirational Shay Deering. Playing for so long with Connacht, I had a number of great days – the outstanding one was when we played against the All Blacks and I found myself trying in vain to catch some of the greatest legends in rugby history, like Grant Batty and Sid Going. The highlight of my career was playing for Ireland against Argentina in an autumn international in 1974. It was an incredible experience to line out in the second row with a player of the stature of Willie John McBride.'

Galvin is one of a small group of players – the most famous of whom is Frank O'Driscoll (Brian's father) – who played for Ireland but who never received a cap. At the time, Argentina was not recognised by the International Rugby Board and so caps were not awarded for internationals played against them. Does this omission upset him?

'It would have been nice to get a cap but it was such an honour to have played for Ireland and donning the Irish jersey, and that honour was all I needed. It is nice to see that the jersey I wore that day is hanging on the wall in the rugby club in Athlone.'

Given his role with the IRFU, where does Galvin see the future for Connacht rugby?

'There has been, in recent years – thanks to the great work of the Connacht Board and the many volunteers through the province – a great expansion of the game at grassroots level in Connacht. This manifests itself in the number of newly formed clubs and the growth in player numbers coming through our youth, school and academy structures.

'The IRFU are generally recognised as having done a great job with the Irish game in general and have steered Irish rugby very successfully through the stormy waters of professionalism. I welcome the IRFU's recent reaffirmation of that commitment to support professional sides in Ireland.'

Asked about his sporting heroes, Galvin shopped local and selected a fellow Roscommon man: 'I had massive admiration for the late Dermot Earley because he had such great sportsmanship. I played against him a number of times while he played for the army team – despite the Ban!'

In 1887, one of the GAA's founding fathers, Maurice Davin, had called for a ban on rugby and soccer. The political leanings of the GAA had been clearly manifested in 1902 when Rule 27, 'The Ban', was introduced. It prohibited members of the GAA from playing, attending or promoting 'foreign games', such as soccer, rugby, hockey and cricket. In 1938, the GAA controversially expelled its patron, Ireland's first President Douglas Hyde, for attending an international soccer match. The Ban was clearly shown to be out of step with the times in 1963 when Waterford hurler Tom Cheasty was banned for attending a dance sponsored by his local soccer club. The ban cost him a National League medal.

When Dermot Earley played for the army, it would have been folly for him to be seen playing rugby from a GAA perspective. As a result, the team could only have 14 players in the team photograph. Sometimes, the referee might stand in for him. This became something of a recurring joke in rugby circles. On one occasion, a referee walking onto the field said, 'Let's get the photograph over, because I know I have to stand in here for your man.' The press officer of the rugby team came up with an assumed name for Dermot – Lieutenant Earley became Lieutenant Late.

Galvin enjoys the camaraderie of rugby: 'One of the benefits of being involved in rugby has been the opportunity to make so many great friends and to meet many interesting people. One person I got to meet a few times was the former England and Lions captain Bill Beaumont. He is a very down-to-earth guy who is really easy company. I also had the opportunity to meet with the great Philippe Sella when he came to Athlone. He was a joy to spend time with. The late Moss Keane was a great friend of mine and a great supporter of rugby clubs throughout Ireland. He was a great storyteller and was always so entertaining and told stories as only he could!

'Another fabulous character is Mick Quinn, who, like Ollie Campbell, does great work with the Charitable Trust who help players who have been seriously injured or disabled. He is a great storyteller also. One of his most popular in Athlone dates back to 1974 when Ireland faced England at Twickenham. Although they were underdogs, Ireland won 26–21. Before the game, the Irish players were running onto the pitch when they were stopped in the tunnel by an official in a blazer who had the archetypal RAF moustache. He said, "Tally ho, boys. Tally ho. The BBC cameras are not ready for you yet." The Irish lads were just itching to get on the pitch and found the waiting a pain, particularly when they were joined in the tunnel by the English team. The English were led by their captain, John Pullin, who was shouting at his team about Waterloo. The Irish players couldn't understand what Waterloo had to do with them. The English players looked bigger and stronger than their Irish counterparts. As they were always on television, they were all huge stars and had mega names like David Duckham and Andy Ripley. The Irish players were studiously trying to avoid eye contact with them, as they planned to rough them up a bit on the pitch. However, Tony Neary went over and tapped Moss Keane on the shoulder and said, "Moss, best of luck. May the best team win." Moss growled back, "I f**king hope not!"'

24

GAILLIMH
MICK GALWEY

Mick Galwey could have been one of the Kerry GAA greats, but in his native county he chose 'the road less travelled' and opted for rugby as his main game. His decision was vindicated by his 41 caps for Ireland, captaining his country in 4 of those games, over 130 appearances for Munster, a place on the Lions tour in 1993 and the award of an honorary doctorate in law from Trinity College in 2002 for his services to rugby.

The roots of his interest in the oval ball came from Moss Keane, another noted Gaelic player: 'As Moss Keane was from Currow, he was my hero. There was massive interest in the area when he started to play for Ireland. The first time I saw him play, though, was in a Gaelic match in Currow. He was their full-forward and target man and he did the job well, though I think rugby robbed him of his athleticism. Then there was the whole Moss legend which added to the glamour of rugby.'

Gaillimh believes that his training as a Gaelic footballer was a big help to his rugby career, primarily in terms of his having an eye for the ball. However, he feels that the primary benefit of his association with Kerry was not on the playing field. Former Irish rugby coach the late Mick Doyle's first love was the GAA, though when he began his secondary education as a boarder in Newbridge College, rugby exploded into his life. He trenchantly aired his views about the state of Irish rugby through his weekly column in the *Sunday Independent*. His criticism was such that Moss Keane once said to him, 'Thanks be to Jaysus I don't play any more. Otherwise, I'd be afraid to open the paper on Sunday because of what you'd say about me!'

Doyle was not a man to lavish praise on the Irish team with wanton abandon, so, when he described an Irish victory as an 'eighty-minute orgasm', one had to sit up and take notice. Gaillimh's finest hour in the green jersey was in Ireland's victory over England in 1993. In a team performance in which all the boys in green were heroes, it is difficult to single out one player for special attention, but Galwey deserves special mention. Six weeks before that match, he was lying in a Dublin hospital with his neck in a brace, and his rugby future was shrouded in uncertainty. At one point, he was even told that his playing career was history. A shadow on his X-ray cast an ominous cloud on his prospects. For four fear-filled days, he waited for the all-clear. Then it was out of hospital and on to the training field. A week later, he played for Ireland against France – a game that offered the promise of better things following total embarrassment at Murrayfield. The next match saw Ireland overcome the Welsh in Cardiff, with Eric Elwood making a hugely impressive debut. The win was sealed with Galwey scoring a fine try – helping him to become one of only two Irishmen able to secure a place on the Lions' tour to New Zealand with Nick Popplewell.

Mick Quinn tells a story about Galwey and Will Carling. The famous English captain was not loved universally by his teammates. When Ireland played England, it was a typically robust match. After a heated ruck, where boots were flying with more frequency than planes at an airport, everyone picked themselves off the muddy pitch to reveal the man at the bottom of the pile of bodies. It was Carling. He had a huge gash under his eye. The referee, slightly shocked that the English captain should be the victim of such thuggery, asked, 'Right, own up, who did this?'

Immediately, Galwey piped up, 'Take your pick, ref, it could have been any one of twenty-nine of us.'

Mick is one of rugby's great diplomats, and he is loath to criticise anybody. As with many Kerry people, you have to read between the lines to figure out what he is saying. When asked his opinion about Brian Ashton's tenure as Irish coach, he kicks for touch. Galwey denies that, towards the ignominious end of Ashton's reign, one of the Irish squad said to him, 'Tell me, how long have you been with us, not counting tomorrow?'

25

NOT SIMPLE SIMON
SIMON GEOGHEGAN

Simon Geoghegan spent much of his international career waiting for a pass. Indeed, it is surprising that he never got the nickname Cinderella because it often seemed nobody wanted to take him to the ball. David Campese once remarked, 'The only thing you're ever likely to get at the end of an English backline is chilblains.' Geoghegan again would have empathised with this scenario.

After making his mark with London Irish in 1991, Geoghegan won his first cap for Ireland. Great tries that season against Wales and England established him as the rising star of Irish rugby. However, the following season, as Ireland lost every game, he had no chance to impress. Things went from bad to worse the following season when he hoped to make the Lions' tour to New Zealand. His ability as a defender was not just questioned, it was positively derided – particularly after Derek Stark scored a soft try on him in Murrayfield.

'Yes, 1993 was a bad season for me. My club form was poor and that probably affected my confidence when playing for Ireland.'

His problems at the time were not just on the field, as he was temporarily suspended from the Irish squad. What prompted this exclusion?

'I'm not the most diplomatic person in the world. When I give my opinion, I tend not to mince my words. I was unhappy with the way the team was playing and the fact that I was getting so few opportunities, and I made my views known in a public way – but that's all water under the bridge now.'

A prominent rugby journalist openly questioned his commitment to the Irish team because of an incident in which he threw his Irish jersey on the ground. Did this type of criticism hurt him?

'Not in the least. Anybody who knows me knows of my commitment to Ireland and judges me by what I do when I am wearing my green jersey on the pitch, not by what I do with it in the dressing-room.'

In 1993, it was the victory – and more particularly the manner of the victory – against England which confirmed that Irish rugby was on an upward curve. The win was sealed with Mick Galwey scoring a fine try. For Geoghegan, though, it was a turning point because he had regained his best form. The pity was that it was too late for him to claim a place on the Lions tour. When injury struck, it was his partner on the wing, Richard Wallace, and not the golden boy of Irish rugby that got the call to go south as a replacement.

Still basking in the glory of their win over the All Blacks, the English expected to exact retribution in 1994 in Twickenham, but a splendid try from Geoghegan helped Ireland to secure another shock win – this time on a score of 13–12. During these years, the Underwood brothers played on the wings for England. Whenever either scored a try, the director of the BBC coverage of the English game always cut to the stands where invariably their mother was dancing a jig with elation. After scything past Tony Underwood to score that try, Simon is said to have turned to Underwood and remarked, 'I hope your mother saw that!'

The same year saw Geoghegan departing from his club London Irish for the spa town of Bath. The area around Gloucester, Bath and Bristol is the hub of a hotbed of English rugby, with Bath's status in English rugby during the 1990s comparable to that of the great Kerry team of the 1970s and early 1980s. This is largely due to the work of one man, Jack Rowell, who transformed Bath from a team of virtual no-hopers into the cream of the crop.

Rowell also thought big. Although Geoghegan was a big-name acquisition, Rowell had earlier tried to bring David Campese to Bath from Milan. He had somebody investigate how much it would cost to get Campese to sign on. When he heard the figure £200,000, he gulped but immediately did his sums and speculated that, over three years, it worked out at £67,000 per annum, which just might be possible. The plan was abruptly shelved when Rowell was told that Campo's contract with Milan was not for three years but for five months!

Joining Bath was a move Geoghegan made with his eyes open: 'I knew I was taking a risk. There was no guarantee that I would get my place on the team. Reputations mean nothing at Bath. You either performed to the highest level or you were off the team. That was not a problem for me. In fact, it was the reverse. I knew that if I joined Bath, I would be playing consistently at a higher standard. Basically, I had the confidence in my own ability to believe I could hold my own at the highest level, but, believe me, the work ethic was very strong in the club.'

26

GLORY DAYS
MIKE GIBSON

When Ireland toured Australia in 1979, press attention centred on the elder statesman of Irish rugby, Mike Gibson, the most capped international of all time. Gibson was then 36 but still feared because, although his flesh was not as willing as in the golden days of his prime that made him one of the most outstanding players in rugby union, his keen brain and polished skills still functioned unimpaired. It was widely expected that the tour would mark his swansong and the press looked forward to one last hurrah, in which he would weave his magic just one more time. He made two Test appearances on the tour, which, added to his twelve Lions' Test appearances, edged him one ahead of Bill McBride (sixty-three and seventeen) on the overall international match list with eighty-one (sixty-nine Irish caps).

For Mick Quinn, Mike Gibson was Ireland and the world's greatest player: 'When we trained with the Irish squad, Mike Gibson, John Robbie and I were always at the front when we ran. Once Gibbo invited me up North to train with him at the Mary Peters Track. I considered it a great honour. When you are training with rugby players, you only get as fit as the unfittest player on the team. When you have finished running, you have to wait for the slowest runner to complete his run before starting again. When I went to train with Gibbo, I learned that if you wanted to be really fit, you had to train like an athlete and on your own.

'The one thing we didn't do then that players do today was to be very careful about our diet. I was a steak man. I never smoked nor drank, which helped. I had to train very, very hard myself because the competition with Tony Ward and Ollie Campbell on the scene was so intense. I even trained on Christmas morning. The thought that kept me going then was that the two lads were in bed and I had one up on them! Today, I hear players talking about all the sacrifices they make. I don't begrudge them the money they get in this professional era but I really get sick when I hear it suggested that the current players are more committed than we were. I doubt if any player today, professional or not, trains harder than Gibbo did. I certainly learned a lot just by watching him train, and playing with him was an education in itself.

'I like to think th,at I played my part in Gibbo's great displays for Ireland. I always blessed myself with Lourdes water before matches. The only players who would come looking for some off me were Moss Keane and Willie Duggan. Moss would sneak over when he thought no one was looking and ask me for some of that "firewater". I always splashed some on Gibbo's legs when he wasn't looking and he went out and played like a genius!

'Gibbo was such a meticulous single-minded player. I think the only player who could match him in that respect was Ollie Campbell.

'Gibbo had a great temperament. The only time I ever saw him rattled was on the tour to New Zealand in 1976. We were really up against it in some of the matches. I remember Tom Grace saying at breakfast, "Quinner, do you think we'll get out of the place before they realise we're afraid of them?" We laughed at the time but I wonder! Barry McGann did not share the general concern. He was playing at out-half that day and was kicking everything, and I mean everything. At one stage, Gibbo yelled for a pass but Barry said, "Listen, Mike, when I meet a player who can run as fast as I can kick it, then I'll think about passing it!"'

Asked about the Irish players he admired most, Fergus Slattery's reply is immediate: 'I loved playing with Mossie Keane because of his great commitment. I would much rather play with somebody who has very little talent but total commitment rather than the reverse. I also admired Ollie Campbell's wholesome commitment to making himself what he was – a top-class player. He is the role model you would want to hold up to younger players because of his endurance and because he developed his skills to the very maximum. However, the great of Irish rugby is C.M.H. Gibson. The rest are also-rans.'

27

THE YEAR OF THE TWO MIKE GIBSONS
MIKE GIBSON

Ireland's opening match of the 1979 season was a home game against France. A new star was born with a famous name in the tall, lean Mike Gibson. He dominated the lineout on his debut as he ranged along the line to deny France the platform to launch penetrating attacks.

After that, it was off to Cardiff Arms Park, where Gibson was to learn that the Irish team's preparations were somewhat on the unconventional side. Captain Fergus Slattery brought the team to see *Adventures of a Window Cleaner* and *Adventures of a Taxi Driver*. Those films certainly took the players' minds off the game!

A n unfortunate postscript to the match came in a subsequent article written by the Welsh flanker Paul Ringer for a tabloid newspaper after his defection to rugby league. Commenting on the dual standards over dirty play in rugby union, he cited the example of an instruction five minutes before the kick-off in that match to 'sort out' Tony Ward:

> The meaning was clear and I set to it. Trouble was he was so good I couldn't lay a finger on him until late in the game but I eventually flattened him off the ball and we went on to win. I got such a booting from the Irish forwards afterwards that I couldn't get out of bed for two days. After I'd laid out Ward that time, he turned up late at the after-match reception with a massively swollen eye.

Tony Ward was a big admirer of Gibson's: 'Mike played at full-back when he was at school and many would argue that he played there as a number 8! He was a very underrated player whose best years at the highest level coincided with mine. One of my happiest memories in the green shirt was when we beat France in Auch in 1988 when he gave one of the best displays of number-8 rugby that I have ever seen. He was brilliant. Although he was seen by some as a bit of a glamour boy, when Gibbo got stuck in, he was a great player. That night, he took the game by the scruff of the neck and was physically involved, which was an aspect of the game he was often accused of avoiding.

He and Willie Duggan were, in many ways, in the rugby context, polar opposites, with Donal Spring somewhere in between.'

With his giant frame and exceptional lineout abilities, Gibson seemed destined for a great career in the Irish shirt, but his career was cut short because of injuries.

Gibson also made his mark in the Leinster shirt but his time with the province was not without incident. One night before a big match for Leinster, Terry Kennedy, Ronan Kearney and Gibson came in at an ungodly hour after a night on the town. The Leinster coach at the time, Mick Doyle, decided to crack the whip. The next morning, the three players were summoned to attend Doyler's room at 11 a.m. Doyle was sharing with Ken Ging. The problem was that, the previous night, the selectors had had a right old party themselves and the room was covered with empty bottles. Ging was told to tidy up and he hid them under a chair in the corner.

The three lads arrived at the appointed hour and Ollie Campbell, who was captain that year, was asked to attend. Doyler proceeded to tear into the three miscreants using every cliché in the book about how they were a disgrace to Leinster and how they had let themselves down. Ollie was very uncomfortable about witnessing this tirade. He pulled out the chair from the corner to sit down and bottles went spinning all over the floor. Terry Kennedy and Mike Gibson burst out laughing and said, 'F**k off, Doyler.'

Gibson also features in one of the stories told to me by Mick Doyle. Jonathan Davies, Gibson and Rob Andrew are all in Saudi Arabia, sharing a smuggled crate of booze when, all of a sudden, Saudi police rush in and arrest them. The mere possession of alcohol is a severe offence in Saudi Arabia, so, for the terrible crime of actually being caught consuming the booze, they are all sentenced to death! However, after many months and with the help of very good lawyers, they are able to successfully appeal their sentences down to life imprisonment.

By a stroke of luck, it was a Saudi national holiday the day after their trial finished, and the extremely benevolent Sheikh decided they could be released after receiving just 20 lashes each of the whip. As they were preparing for the punishment, the Sheikh announced, 'It's my first wife's birthday today, and she has asked me to allow each of you one wish before your whipping.'

Jonathan Davies was first in line; he thought for a while and then said, 'Please tie a pillow to my back.' This was done, but the pillow only lasted ten lashes before the whip went through. When the punishment was done, he had to be carried away bleeding and crying with pain.

Rob Andrew was next up. After watching the Welshman in horror, he said smugly, 'Please fix two pillows to my back.' But even two pillows could only take fifteen lashes before the whip went through again and the Englishman was soon led away whimpering loudly (as they do!).

Gibson was the last one up, but before he could say anything the Sheikh turned to him and said, 'You are from the most beautiful part of the world and your culture is one of the finest in the world. For this, you may have two wishes!'

'Thank you, Your Most Royal and Merciful Highness,' Gibson replied. 'In recognition of your kindness, my first wish is that you give me not 20 but 100 lashes.'

'Not only are you an honourable, handsome and powerful man, you are also very brave,' the Sheikh said with an admiring look on his face. 'If 100 lashes is what you desire, then so be it. And your second wish, what is it to be?' the Sheikh asked.

'Tie the Englishman to my back.'

28

URBI ET ORBI
JIM GLENNON

Although he is not an arrogant person, Jim Glennon does make one proud boast: 'Nobody used his arse better in the lineout than I did!'

Glennon was never a great lineout winner but was very hard to get a lineout ball from. He formed a very effective second-row partnership with George Wallace for Leinster and they were christened *Urbi et Orbi* by Mick Doyle. In 1996, Glennon was chosen as the Philips manager of the month for his work with Leinster – guiding them to the interprovincial championship and to the European Cup semi-final.

Strangely, Glennon's memories of being capped for Ireland are not as happy as his memories of playing for Leinster: 'Tragedy struck the club just after I won my second cap in 1980 when one of our players in Skerries, Bernard Healy, got a bad neck injury which devastated the club. In 1987, I broke A.J.F. O'Reilly's record for the longest gap between internationals when I got my third cap. But, by the weirdest of coincidences, the joy of being recalled for me was shattered when another clubmate, Alan Boylan, sustained a serious neck injury on the eve of the game.'

In 1980, the year Jimmy Carter had arranged a boycott of the Moscow Olympics because of Russia's invasion of Afghanistan, Glennon toured Romania with Leinster, under Mick Doyle and Mick 'The Cud' Cuddy, for an eventful tour.

'A vivid memory for me is of going to see Romania play Russia with Phil Orr and George Wallace. The Russians were staying in the same hotel as us but on a different floor. That night, the three of us met up with the Russian captain and we invited him and his colleagues up to our room for a jar. We had stared disaster in the face earlier when we discovered that there was only one bottle of whiskey in the hotel! Worse still, that bottle was in the Cud's room and not intended for public consumption. The Cud was annoyed, to put it mildly, when he discovered it missing. He had to be restrained by Doyler. Usually it worked the other way around.

'We had a great night conversing with the Russians in French and exchanging razors for Moscow Olympic badges! The next morning, the manager of the Russian team came into the lobby, asked to speak to "the leader of the Irish delegation" and invited Leinster to tour in Russia. It was a pretty strange spectacle because the Russians had KGB types following them everywhere, watching their every move. I thought this invitation might provide the key to our rapprochement with the Cud, so I headed in before the Russian delegation to explain the situation. The Cud was not impressed. He said, "Look, Glennon, would you ever bleep off and tell them Russians to bleep off, and while you're at it tell them to bleep off out of Afghanistan as well!"'

Glennon was involved in Mick Doyle's first and last representative games as coach: in 1979, when Leinster played Cheshire, and in 1987, when Ireland played Australia, respectively. He lays claim to an unusual distinction – he once saw Doyle speechless: 'After his heart attack during the '87 World Cup, Doyler rejoined us after a ten-day stay in hospital. We were staying in a motel-type place. A few of us, known on the tour as the "amigos", were out late one night and sneaking furtively in. There was an uncarpeted stair outside Doyler's room and he was woken up by the activity. He recognised one of the voices. The next day the culprit was given a right ticking off in front of the whole squad. As Doyler delivered his attack, the player in question stood and listened, but when the coach had finished the bad boy said, "Jaysus, Doyler, there's none so pure as a converted hoor." Doyler was left too stunned to speak.'

After winning two caps for Ireland in 1980, Glennon spent seven years in the international wilderness. He came out of retirement to win his final four caps. 'I had genuinely given it up in 1986. Then a barman asked me how many caps had I won. I said, "Three, two in 1980 and one in 1987." No doubt I would have forgotten about that pledge, but when we got home Phil Orr and his wife called to see us. Phil bet me a tenner that I wouldn't play for Leinster that season. A weighing scales was produced and I was the wrong side of 20 stone. I later learned that Phil's approach had been semi-organised because Roly Meates, who was coaching Leinster at the time, was looking for an extra bit of power in the scrum. I can tell you it wasn't for my lineout ability! The season with Leinster went really well and I found myself back in the Irish team and flying off to the World Cup.'

Asked about the greatest character he played with, he does not hesitate for a second: 'Phil O'Callaghan. I toured with Philo to Zambia in 1977. I learned more about touring in those five days with Philo than I learned in the remainder of my career – though I'm not prepared to elaborate!'

29

GOOD SHOW
KEN GOODALL

Ken Goodall was an outstanding number 8 forward and made an immediate impact on the Irish team when he made his debut against Australia in 1967. He was capped nineteen times for Ireland between 1967 and 1970, scoring three international tries, before turning to rugby league with Workington. His celebrated hoof-and-chase try in Ireland's 14–0 win over Wales at Lansdowne Road in 1970 will forever be recognised as one of the greatest tries in Irish rugby history. He also toured South Africa with the Lions in 1968. He joined the tour as a replacement but was injured in the first match he played and was unable to take any further part in proceedings.

For Willie Anderson, Goodall was one of the greats of Irish rugby: 'The players I most admired were Ken Goodall and Mervyn Davies. I even grew a moustache to look like Mervyn!'

When I asked the voice of rugby, Bill McLaren, for his opinion of Goodall, he began with a long preamble: 'My own rugby playing career with Hawick came to an abrupt end in October 1948 when it emerged that I had contracted tuberculosis of the lungs. As a player, I was no shrinking violet. My father delighted in recalling an incident when he was watching me play against Kelso and was seated beside a large farmer supporting Kelso. Outraged by my robust tactics, the farmer referred to "that big, dirty, black-headed bugger McLaren". Discretion was the better part of valour and Dad decided that was not the right moment to profess his connection with his son.

'My favourite story goes back to the build-up to a Scotland versus Wales match in 1962. The day before the game the leader of the Scottish pack, Hugh Ferns McLeod, gave his view of the game. He was a reluctant leader because he wanted to concentrate on his own job as a prop, but once he was persuaded to do so by a Scottish selector, Alf Wilson, he wanted to do it properly. As Hugh was giving his team-talk, he noticed the forwards weren't paying him attention and were talking among themselves. He was 5 ft 10 in. and he walked up to the forwards, who were all towering over him. Undaunted, Hugh said,

"Come here, ma wee disciples." When they all gathered around, he continued, "Now, ah want tae tell ye that ah've been asked ti lead this pack tomorrow, that ah'm no very keen on the job and that's what I'm going to do, and if any of you lot want to be pack-leader, just let me know and ah'll put a word in for ye at the right place. The next one who opens his trap, I'll bring my boot right at his arse."

'One of the Anglo-Scots in the group said, "Well, I didn't understand a word of that but it all sounded damned impressive." They listened and the next day beat Wales off the park, their first win in Wales for 25 years, and their first win in Cardiff for 35 years.

'The following year, before Scotland played France in Paris, Hugh went up to his fellow forward Frans ten Bos and said, "Frans, ye think ye're a guid forrit but really ye're jist a big lump o' potted meat. Ah'm going ti tell ye somethin'. If ah was half yer size, ah'd pick up the first two Frenchmen that looked at me the morn and ah'd chuck them right over the bloody stand."

'The next day, Frans had the game of his life and Scotland won by 11 points to 6.

'From these incidents you can gather I am a big fan of people who give 110 per cent to the team and really put their body on the line. Ken Goodall did that but why I admire him was that he married intense commitment with great skills – both in terms of his technical ability as a scrummager and in terms of his excellent handling skills. That famous try in 1970 showed that he had speed of thought and speed of foot, which is a great combination in a rugby player.'

Willie John McBride was another big admirer of Goodall: 'He was one of the players I wanted in my corner if I went to war, because he would never let you down and always give his very best. With his fierce will to win, he was my kind of number 8.'

Mick Doyle was also fulsome in his praise of Goodall: 'How would I sum up Ken? There were good Irish forwards, there were great Irish forwards and then there was Ken. He ranks up with the great number 8s. Only Willie Duggan could come close to him in the green jersey in my opinion. What made him special was his football intelligence. The famous try against England would not have come had he not some speed of foot, but the ability to see what was on was what made him a player apart and that was because his brain worked so quickly.'

30

AMAZING GRACE
TOM GRACE

In 1972, Tom Grace won the first of his 25 caps in the high-pressure zone at Stade Colombes in Paris. To soothe his frayed nerves, he sought consolation from an old hand: 'Team captain Tom Kiernan traditionally spoke at the team-talk with each player individually. I recall that he spent a lot of time talking with the wingers. The froth was coming out of his mouth, he was so fired up. He warned us about the way the French would bombard us with high balls. The consoling thing, though, was that he assured us he would be there beside us to take the pressure off us. The match was barely on when the French out-half kicked this almighty ball up in the air between Kiernan and myself. To my horror, I heard Kiernan shouting, "Your ball." So much for all that brothers-in-arms talk, but that's the captain's prerogative! I caught the ball and nearly got killed!

'After the match, I didn't realise how significant our victory was. I could see that players who to me were heroes, like Willie John and Tom Kiernan, were very emotional about the whole thing. Now I understand why. My second match was in Twickenham. I remember seeing the number of big cars going into the ground and the smoked salmon and the champagne parties and how that was used to motivate the Irish side. It was also stressed how important it was for the Irish community in England for us to win. If there was any doubt about that, the Irish fans in the crowd's reaction after Kevin Flynn scored that famous try said it all.'

Grace collected his third cap against the All Blacks in January 1973 when he scored a dramatic equalising try in the right-hand corner to tie the match at 10–10. Some moments live in the memory and that try is one, when like a salmon-leap he sailed in a great arc through the air and scored a try in the corner with a split second to spare.

'There was a lot of speculation afterwards about whether the ball had crossed the dead-ball line or not. Thankfully, the *Irish Independent* had a photographer on hand to show it hadn't. Barry McGann always says if it wasn't for him, I would have been famous. After I scored the try, he narrowly missed the conversion which robbed us of our part in rugby's hall of fame.

'I will never forget our match against England that season. The Troubles were at their height and it was a brave gesture on the part of the English team to travel to Dublin. The reception they got when they went out on to the pitch was amazing, with a standing ovation. The emotion ran through the whole Irish team. To the credit of our coach Ronnie Dawson, he was able to channel that emotion into performance and we won the match.'

Grace toured with Willie John McBride on the all-conquering Lions tour to South Africa in 1974. However, despite scoring 13 tries, he looks back on the experience with mixed feelings: 'I was very disappointed not to get a place in the Test side, but before going on that tour I had sprained my ankle. For three months, we were treated like superstars. It was very hard when I got back home just to have beans and toast for my tea!'

Following a crushing 26–3 Irish defeat at the hands of the French in 1976, Grace succeeded Mike Gibson as captain of the Irish side. He has mixed feelings about the experience: 'I don't think playing on the wing is the best place to captain a team from. Also I think my game suffered from the captaincy.'

That summer, Ireland took on a formidable task with a tour to New Zealand and Fiji under Grace's leadership in the hope of helping the development of the young, inexperienced players. In the circumstances, Ireland put up a creditable performance.

Initially, Grace admits, he felt the pressure of the media: 'When we arrived, there were two television journalists waiting for me to set up one of the interviews. I liked one of them immediately but not the other. So much for my judge of character. When we got to recording the interviews, the guy I hadn't liked turned out to be extremely nice and the bloke I liked was, in fact, the very opposite. He began by quoting John O'Shea at me. He had written that we would have been much better off training in the hills of Kerry than going to New Zealand. Somebody must have been praying for me because I heard myself saying, "Our philosophy is that there is no better way than to learn from the best." I still don't know where I got that answer from.

'We lost the Test against the All Blacks 11–3. I think we lost the game because both Barry McGann and I missed a string of kicks. As captain, I also blame myself for not instilling sufficient belief in the players that we could win. That game was there for the taking.

'Another memory of that tour typifies the power of rugby friendships. I had marked Grant Batty when we played the All Blacks in Lansdowne Road. Grant was not involved with the Blacks in 1976 but he sent me on a bundle of New Zealand dollars to buy a round of drinks for the Irish team.'

31

THE BULL
JOHN HAYES

Nicknames are an integral part of rugby culture, some flattering, some less so. Rob Andrew earned the nickname 'Squeaky' because he never did anything wrong, while Stuart Barnes, whose waistline was less than trim, was known as 'The Barrel'. Jason Robinson, one of the stars of England's 2003 triumph, is often called 'Bible Basher' because he is a 'born again' Christian and because of his hatred of bad language. Mind you, others call him 'McDonald's' because of his love of junk food. Austin Healey was called 'Melon Head' when he was young because of his big forehead and Shane Byrne was known as 'Mullet' because of his trademark hairstyle. Scott Gibbs, a key player for Wales and the Lions, was nicknamed 'Car Crash' because he did not just tackle people, he obliterated them. The English hooker Steve Thompson is called 'Shrek' because of his . . . distinctive features.

Eddie O'Sullivan has three nicknames. He trained as a PE teacher in Limerick and played a lot of indoor soccer there. As he was a very incisive player, he got the nickname 'The Dagger'. People have used that against him since he 'replaced' Warren Gatland as Ireland coach! When he went to Garryowen as a player, he did a lot of weight training, which was very unusual in the 1970s, although it's now par for the course in rugby. As his teammates did not believe he was doing weights for rugby reasons, they called him 'The Beach Boy'. He played on the wing with Garryowen and he was pretty quick, so some people called him 'Fast Eddie'.

The best-known nickname in Irish rugby, though, is that of John Hayes, 'The Bull', because of the deep affection in which he is held by Irish rugby fans. Donncha O'Callaghan provides the most revealing insight into the Bull's personality: 'The rest of us would be looking forward to a 100th cap, but John would rather get off the pitch, get home and milk his cows.'

He has witnessed glory days but also some major disappointments. A case in point came as the 2003 Six Nations reached its climax, when Ireland faced England in a Grand Slam decider at Lansdowne Road.

JOHN HAYES

It is a match which is embedded into the Irish psyche, following the English captain Martin Johnson's unwillingness to yield to President Mary McAleese on the red carpet. The Irish public were outraged by the 'snub' to the President. In the event, it was probably the only excitement all day, as England outclassed Ireland.

Hayes believes that the following year, though, Ireland took an important step forward: 'People said we were a "nearly team" before we won the Triple Crown. I remember Brian O'Driscoll saying when we beat Australia in 2002, "Let's not be the nearly team, let's not get the good win now and again, but let's strive to beat the big guns consistently." I think we did that winning the Triple Crown. We had beaten France in 2000, England in 2001 and Australia in 2002, but we hadn't strung enough good results together against top opposition. Winning the Triple Crown took that monkey off our back and gave us a base to build on. When we went on to tour South Africa after winning the Triple Crown, a good performance was no longer to lose by only ten points. A good performance was nothing less than a win.'

Tony Ward is one of the many big fans of Hayes: 'For twenty-seven years, I had the great good fortune to bask in the glory of one of the great moments in Irish sport when Munster beat the All Blacks in 1978. It is now time for us to take our rightful place in the shade and pass the torch to the new high kings of Munster, Ronan O'Gara and company. As Tom Kiernan, coach in '78, so rightly said when throwing his arm around me in Heathrow on the way back, "Ward, we're buried." Saturday, 20 May 2006 became the high point of Munster rugby when the red army finally claimed the holy grail of European rugby by defeating Biarritz 23–19 in the Heineken Cup final at Millennium Stadium in Cardiff. Bear in mind that, from conceding seven points in the opening few minutes, Munster went on to outscore Biarritz 17–3 in the remainder of the half to the break. It represented their most convincing half of rugby in the three finals to date. As Mick Galwey said to me at the break, they were converting pressure into points, unlike in their previous finals. They pushed the bounds of fitness, conditioning and most of all commitment beyond anything they had in the past. This was new territory and, given its context, the biggest single achievement yet in the long and proud history of Munster rugby. It takes a good team to win one Heineken Cup but Munster showed they were a really great team to win it a second time. I was thrilled for all the Munster players, but none more so than John Hayes, who has given so much for so long – not just for his powers in the scrum but for the incredible lifting work he has done in the lineout for both Munster and Ireland. Arguably, he was more indispensable than even Brian O'Driscoll to the Irish team at certain stages, which is a hell of a tribute to John. I know many Munster fans felt that the Claw could never be replaced in the front row but John has taken on that mantle.'

For his part, Hayes enjoys the story told about Clohessy – which he stresses is apocryphal – involving the referee who decides that he has to make a quick getaway after an Irish international against England at Lansdowne Road in which he sends off three Irish players and awards two controversial penalties. He drives too quickly, crashes coming round a bend and is thrown through the windscreen onto the road. By coincidence, the car following him is driven by one of the players he sent off, Peter Clohessy, and he stops to see if he can help. He finds that the referee is in a bad way and makes a 999 call on his mobile.

'I think the referee's dead,' he shouts down the phone in panic. 'What can I do?'

'Calm down,' says the operator, used to dealing with emergencies. 'First of all, go and make sure the referee is dead.'

The operator hears a choking sound and the cracking of neck bone.

Then the Claw returns to the mobile. 'OK,' he says. 'I've made sure he's dead. Now what should I do?'

32

ON THE OUTSIDE
NOEL HENDERSON

Noel Henderson, who won forty caps for Ireland at outside centre between 1949 and 1959, is responsible for one of the most famous quotes in the Irish sporting vernacular: 'The state of British sport is mostly serious, but never hopeless. The state of Irish sport is usually hopeless, but never serious.'

In the course of a radio commentary on an Irish international, Henderson was being slated by the commentator – his father was so outraged at the stream of insults that he threw the radio out of the window!

Jack Kyle's voice betrays the nerve-tingling excitement as the great moments of the 1940s and 1950s are unreeled before the vivid mind's eye of memory, particularly of Noel Henderson and his fellow internationals: 'There is a big advantage in being a small country, if that isn't a contradiction in terms, in that it is difficult for good players to slip through the net because of the interpros, the matches between the combined provinces and the rest of Ireland and the final trial. If you were any good at all, somebody saw you play somewhere!

'I was not a great tackler. If I had to play rugby as a forward, I would never have played the game! Our back row of Jim McCarthy, Bill McKay and Des O'Brien was so strong that I didn't have to bother too much with the normal defensive duties of a fly-half. McCarthy was like greased lightning and an incredible forager and opportunist. I could virtually leave the out-half to our two flankers. I just stood back and took him if he went on the outside.

'I was doubly blessed in that I also had Noel Henderson playing alongside me in the centre. He was a marvellous defender performing many of my defensive duties and I'm not just saying that because he was my brother-in-law!'

It was his brother-in-law who was to cause Kyle's greatest surprise in rugby: 'Noel caused a major shock one day at our team meeting. He was a very quiet man and normally was not very loquacious at those sessions. As was his custom, Karl Mullen concluded by asking if there were any questions. Noel asked, "What I would like to know, captain, is there any way of knowing will the out-half be taking his man for a change?"

'Noel is the father of four daughters. I met the former Scottish centre Charlie Drummond once, who also has a lot of daughters. When I told him about Noel, he said, "We're raising good stock for future rugby players."

'There's a man who takes the long-term view!'

Kyle always enjoyed the good-natured banter between backs and forwards. He tells the story of the time Noel Henderson walked into a restaurant in Limerick, ordered a drink and asked the waiter if he would like to hear a good joke about rugby forwards.

'Listen, mister,' he growled. 'See those two big guys on your left? They were both second rows for Shannon. And that huge fella on your right, he is the number 8 for Young Munster. And I am the prop-forward for Garryowen. Now, are you absolutely positive you want to go ahead and tell your joke here?'

'Hah, guess not,' Henderson replied. 'I wouldn't want to have to explain it five times.'

Jim McCarthy was another big fan of Henderson: 'I was on the Lions tour with Noel in 1950. We were two of nine Irish players on the tour as well as George Norton, Michael Lane, Tom Clifford, Jack Kyle, Jimmy Nelson, Bill McKay and the captain of the Lions, Karl Mullen. Noel was a great character like Tom Clifford, who was a larger-than-life figure, especially when he sang his party piece "O'Reilly's Daughter". His only rival in the character stakes was probably Cliff Davies, a Welsh coalminer. Cliff was greeted by the New Zealand Prime Minister, S.G. Holland, who said, "Glad to meet you, Cliff." Cliff retorted: "Glad to meet you, Sid."'

Former Irish captain Des O'Brien was keen to correct the stereotype of his Irish teammates: 'One of the images a lot of people have of rugby players is that they are ignorant buffoons. On that great Irish side, Noel Henderson, Jack Kyle and myself had a great interest in poetry. It broke the tedium of many a train journey for us. Jack was particularly interested in the poetry of Yeats and he's also a great Patrick Kavanagh fan. We swapped poems and read poetry to each other. We even wrote our own poems. Mind you, if our rugby was the same standard as our poetry, we would never have won the Grand Slam!'

THE WIZARD OF OZ
ROB HENDERSON

During his playing days with London Irish, Rob Henderson came under the stewardship of Clive Woodward. As well as getting to know him as a coach, they got to know each other socially: 'I've spent some time with him. I've even had Christmas dinner with him. I invited myself! We had a delightful Christmas. He's a lovely fella and he's very smart. He was as good at business as he was at organising the England team. The guy is focused to the nth degree. I expected that he would do a great job coaching the Lions. I told that to everyone I could think of who knew him before the tour in the hope he might pick me! He got the results he did with England because he got the best out of people. He did that by giving everything he had himself to it. He doesn't do anything unless he does it wholeheartedly.

'I played golf with him one day. I'd started playing two or three months beforehand but I'd got all the gear from a sponsor. We came to the first tee and I hit one down the middle, which was a miracle. I was really keyed up, but by the time I got to the eighth hole I had lost all the balls in my bag and about 14 of Clive's. He loves his golf and when I hit another ball into the woods, he just looked at me sadly and said, "I think we better go in now."

'I gave him the green jersey I wore when I won my first cap for Ireland. I presented it in a grand manner, as befits Clive – in a Tesco bag! He wasn't there when I dropped it into his home so he wrote to me and said when I eventually grew up he would return it to me!'

Henderson's reaction took me by surprise when I suggested that the high point of his career must have been the Lions tour of 2001: 'No. Without question, the high point for me was when we beat France 27–25 in the Stade de France in 2000, the first time in 28 years. It was an unbelievable atmosphere. It obviously helped that the fella next to me [Brian O'Driscoll] scored three tries. These are memories that I will never forget. Obviously, the Lions tour was also a real highlight. To make the trip in the first place was fantastic, but to play in all of the three Tests was wonderful.'

Hendo's awesome power was the perfect foil for Brian O'Driscoll's sublime skills, and together they provided the coach, Graham Henry, with the perfect midfield combination of strength and flair.

For most players, their first cap is an unbelievable thrill. Henderson is an exception: 'My first cap was against Samoa in November 1996. I'd been playing well that season. I'd played in the Peace international that April and scored a try. Against Samoa, I didn't play particularly well and we got thrashed. As a result, the team got slagged to the high heavens and I didn't get capped for another year – against the All Blacks.

'Another bad time was the New Zealand Development tour in 1997. Oh my God, was that a low point! Terrible. We played eight games on that tour – lost seven and won one. I played in seven games and each of those we lost. The side we beat, when I wasn't playing, was New Zealand's equivalent of Ballybunion rugby.

'Being dropped for the World Cup in '99 was another low point. Ever since that day, I tried to drive myself forward and push my career on. I've been blighted with injuries. Every single one of them was a low point. Just ask my wife. Fortunately, rugby has provided me with a lot of opportunities to meet people and to travel to interesting places.'

Rob's wife, Angie, discovered the legendary status of one player in the Irish set-up: 'Peter Clohessy left more than just a hole in Irish rugby when he retired in 2002 – he left his seat at the back of the bus vacant too! I was amused to find, like a school bus, the team coach had the naughty big boys who always sat on the back seat. The "usual suspects" included Claw, Woody, Axel Foley and Rob. In 2003, after joining the team on their coach to travel the short journey across town for a celebratory dinner, I found a spare seat that just happened to be next to the man I married. The conversation unfolded as follows:

'Me: "Oh, that's nice, darling, you saved me a seat . . ."

'Rob: "That's Claw's seat . . ."

'"But, Rob, Claw's not here, he didn't play, he's retired."

'"Yeah . . . but it's still his seat."'

34

DENIS THE MENACE OF THE WING
DENIS HICKIE

Rugby is in Denis Hickie's blood. For years, his father, Tony, was one of Ireland's most distinguished full-backs, and, like his father, Denis attended the acclaimed rugby nursery St Mary's College in Rathmines, Dublin. He played his first game for the school when he was only eight. He also played other sports, such as badminton and tennis, and really excelled at athletics. He was also a choirboy with the Dublin Boys' Singers but, as his rugby career developed, the other commitments had to be sacrificed, although his dedication reaped a handsome reward: 'My fondest memory is of winning the Schools Cup with St Mary's. People who don't understand the magic of schools rugby will find this hard to believe, but anyone who has ever won a Leinster Cup will know exactly what I mean. At the time, winning it was on a par with winning the World Cup.'

Success for Denis at St Mary's was followed by success with Ireland: he won the Triple Crown with the Irish Schools Side coached by Declan Kidney, and the Irish Under-21 side coached by Eddie O'Sullivan. In 1997, at the age of 20, he made his senior debut for Ireland, and, with his blistering pace, quickly caught the eye, especially with a number of stunning tries, notably against France in Paris. Then, in 1998, a combination of injury and a perceived below-par performance in a Test match in South Africa saw him fall out of favour for two years.

In 2000, Ireland were humiliated by England at Twickenham. Radical surgery was needed and Hickie found himself back in the fold. In his second coming on the Irish team, Denis was an immediate success. Irish rugby fortunes took a dramatic turn for the better, and climaxed in a stunning win against France in Paris, a match that will always be remembered for Brian O'Driscoll's three tries.

'I was only 20 when I made my debut for Ireland. When I came back into the side, I was 24. By then, I was much wiser. The press had written me off but I was always confident in my own ability. I had a better perspective about life because I had matured as a person.'

The highlight of any player's career is to be selected for the Lions, and in 2001 Denis Hickie seemed set to join that elite club. Ireland opened the season brightly, but then the foot-and-mouth outbreak intervened, and Irish players were no longer in the shop window. Denis Hickie was controversially omitted from the Lions squad.

Naturally, it was a tough time for him: 'I was very disappointed when I was told that I was left out. I had really wanted to play for the Lions. I knew that a lot of Irish players would be making the trip, and I wanted to be there with them. I think I learned a lot from the experience. At the start of the season, people had spoken of me as a certainty for selection but I didn't make it on the plane. You can't take things for granted. Thankfully, I got the chance to play for the Lions in 2005.'

Hickie is philosophical about his disappointments: 'The best bit of advice I've ever got is both rugby-related and life-related. It was: "It's not the mess you're in but how you deal with it." In other words, no matter what you do, you will have problems in life, and the real issue is not the problems themselves but the way you deal with them.'

Despite that setback, Denis feels very fortunate to have played with Leinster and Irish teams that have had so many characters and great players. Hickie and Brian O'Driscoll enjoyed a good-natured rivalry as they yo-yoed in the race to be Ireland's recordbreaking try scorer. O'Driscoll grabbed the record off Hickie with his 24th try for Ireland against Italy in 2004. After the match, Drico received a text message from Hickie: 'I suppose I should maybe, perhaps, congratulate you on your new record. Bol**cks!'

His Ireland career has left Denis with 62 caps and many happy recollections: 'I have had so many great memories, but three stand out: my first cap against Wales, beating France in Paris in 2000 and beating England in 2001. I have been lucky enough to score over twenty tries for Ireland but my first one is the one that stands out.'

Who was his most difficult opponent?

'In my first season, things had gone really well for me against Wales and I thought I had arrived. Then we played England and they trounced us. I was up against Tony Underwood, who was then in the prime of his career. Tony is probably not the best player I ever played against but he really showed me what international rugby is all about.'

35

THE STAR OF DAVID
DAVID HUMPHREYS

On the way to winning his 72 caps, David Humphreys amassed a number of records, becoming Ireland's record point scorer, Ireland's most prolific drop-goal scorer and the first Irish player to score more than 500 points in international rugby.

Humphreys is keen to pay tribute to two of his earliest coaches: 'Shortly after I moved to London Irish, I was coached by Clive Woodward, who was excellent. It is very difficult to pinpoint what made him so good, because in pure technical ability he probably wasn't the best but his man-management skills were excellent. His greatest achievement was to get the best out of all of us. At London Irish, I was later coached by Willie Anderson. Willie has been a big factor in my career there and he was a huge factor in my decision to come home and play for Dungannon and Ulster. He was a wonderful coach because of his enormous technical ability, but above all for the strength of his passion for the game.'

The highlight of Humphreys' career came in January 1999 when he captained Ulster to victory in the European Cup: 'We didn't have a very good team but we got on a roll. There were just a few hundred people at our first match but our success struck a chord initially across the province and then throughout the whole of Ireland. Driving down to Dublin for the final in Lansdowne Road, all the flags of support for us really inspired us. All of Ireland got behind us as we were bidding to become the first Irish side to win the competition. I suppose it was all the sweeter for me as I was captain.'

It is often said that a week is a long time in politics but Humphreys was to learn the hard way that seven days can also be a long time in rugby. Exactly seven days after the zenith of his career came the nadir, as he describes: 'Unquestionably the low point of my days in an Irish shirt came against France at Lansdowne Road. I had a chance to win the game with a penalty very close to the end of the game but I missed it. It was just such a horrible feeling when the final whistle went. To go from top of the world to being the villain was a very sobering experience and I suppose it highlighted just how cruel sport can be.'

Humphreys was faced with the chance to redeem himself with another penalty which was to give Ireland their first victory in Paris in 28 years. 'It wasn't like it was the last kick of the game so the pressure wasn't weighing as heavily on me as the year before. There was still a few minutes to go, so if I missed there was another chance. It is for situations like those that I spent hours and hours practising, so that I would be able to slot the ball between the posts, and that helped me to relax as I faced up to the kick.'

From a personal point of view, another highlight for Humphreys came in 2002 when he scored a record thirty-seven points in a European Cup tie against Wasps in a 42–3 victory, scoring a try and four drop goals in the process.

Humphreys is one of the most amiable and articulate people in rugby. Yet, at the mention of one name, he is uncharacteristically reticent. After a series of uncomplimentary comments about him on RTE television from panellist George Hook, Humphreys allegedly refused to be interviewed by RTE television. What, then, is his attitude to 'The Right Hook'?

'The one subject I have never spoken on the record about is George Hook. I have no plans to change that policy.'

One incident is forever imprinted on Humphreys' brain: 'Probably my favourite rugby story, though, goes back to 2003 just before the World Cup. The international players were away with the Irish squad and Johnny Bell was made captain of Ulster for a Celtic League match. Just before the game, Johnny gathered all the players around him, brought them into a huddle and said, "Right, lads, there's just two things I want from you in this game." He paused dramatically. You could have heard a pin drop as the lads were hanging on to his every word. You could almost cut the tension with a knife as he said, "Honesty, commitment and work rate." The lads almost fell on the floor laughing at his gaffe. Ulster lost badly and Johnny's career as a captain came to an abrupt and undistinguished end!'

36

THE KEANE EDGE
MOSS KEANE

The entire Irish nation was in mourning in 2010 with news of the death of Moss Keane. Few sports personalities were more loved.

Speaking to me about his funeral, Ollie Campbell observed, 'I've never experienced anything like it. It must have gone on for a few hours. Despite his innate modesty, Moss would have loved it. When his wife Anne spoke, she received a standing ovation. I thought of the line: "Anyone who lives in the hearts of those they leave behind will never die." Those words could have been written for Moss.'

It was only when you met someone like Moss Keane that you really understood the phrase 'great of Irish rugby' – he was a huge hulk of a man, with a penchant for straight talking and a treasure trove of stories and jokes, although surprisingly few about rugby, more about matters agricultural.

Moss had originally made an impact as a Gaelic footballer. However, he was not known for being 'fleet of foot'. According to folklore, after a less than resoundingly successful career in Gaelic football, his conversion to rugby came when he overheard a friend saying in a pub, 'A farmer could make a tidy living on the space of ground it takes Moss to turn.'

Stories about Moss are more common than showers in April – though few are printable in our politically correct times. Some are even true! Moss had a nice line in self-deprecating humour: 'After I left university, I found I had no talent for anything, so I joined the civil service! I won 52 caps – a lot of them just because they couldn't find anybody else.'

One of Tony Ward's most vivid memories of Moss goes back to Munster's victory over the All Blacks in 1978: 'We were leading 12–0 with only minutes left and there was a scrum close to the sideline. Our lads wheeled the scrum and drove the Blacks over the sideline right up against the wall. The All Blacks were not very pleased about this and a scuffle broke out. One of their players, Andy Hayden, swung out his arm to have a swipe at Brendan Foley and Moss grabbed him by the arm and said, "Don't. You'll lose that one as well." Hayden turned, smiled and accepted it. The meaning was clear.

'Moss is one of the great characters of Irish rugby. On the pitch he was a tiger, but off the field a pussycat. I'll never forget when we played England in 1979, he took off on a run and the crowd started chanting: "Mossie, Mossie". He was one of those characters who lifts the whole crowd and that in turn lifts the team.'

Mick Quinn was another huge fan: 'Whenever we played for Ireland on the Saturday, Moss and I would still turn up for the match with Lansdowne on the Sunday, even though we wouldn't be in the best of shape. For Moss, though, it would be a case of the morning after the night before. You don't get that kind of dedication to the club as much today.'

Tony Ward and Mick Quinn both got 18 points in a final trial for Ireland, but Quinn felt he had outplayed Ward on the day and was feeling pretty good. Later that night, Moss came up to Quinn at the reception and told him that he was the best out-half he had ever played with. He was pretty chuffed with his compliment and told him so. Shortly after, he was going to the toilet and he saw Mossie talking to somebody but he couldn't make out who it was at first. As he passed them by, he realised it was Wardy and he heard Mossie tell him he was without doubt the finest out-half ever to play for Ireland. Quinn gave him a kick in the backside for his dishonesty. Mossie followed him into the toilet, put his arm around him and said, 'Don't worry, Scout. I was only being diplomatic.'

Folklore about Moss grows with every day and distinguishing fact from fiction is not easy. Moss was playing for the Wolfhounds, and in the side was Charlie Kent, the big blond English centre. Charlie is a diabetic, and at half-time this rather puffed-up ambulance man arrived in the players' huddle and tapped Moss on the shoulder. The man asked Moss if he was the man who wanted a sugar lump. Moss said, 'Arra, Jaysus. Who do you think I am, Shergar?'

One of Moss's most famous trips was to Dubai, where he had a speaking engagement. According to legend, he required so much Dutch courage before taking off that he had to be lifted off the plane. As he was carried off, people watching thought it was part of the ritual of a Muslim funeral. When he returned home, he was asked about his most striking impression of life in a Muslim country. He replied, 'If you steal anything, they cut off your hand. If you tell a lie, they cut off your tongue. I didn't see one flasher in the whole place.'

He was also asked about the food and drink.

'The drink was fine but the food was mad hot. No wonder these people are called the Shiites.'

The definitive verdict on Moss came from Mick Doyle: 'For the first half, Moss would push in the lineouts and in the second he'd jump in the scrums. That would always confuse the English.'

37

HOOKERS
KEN KENNEDY

When Ireland launched their Championship campaign against France in Dublin in 1965, the team's fortunes were entrusted to Ken Kennedy, a young medical student from Queen's University, Belfast. It was the start of a long international career. In 1974, Kennedy became Europe's most capped hooker when he won his 41st cap and in total he won 45 caps for Ireland between 1965 and 1975. Kennedy was central to Ireland's Championship win and was one of seven ever-presents that season with Mick Quinn, Dick Milliken, Seán Lynch, Terry Moore, Fergus Slattery and Willie John McBride.

Rugby tours could be said to have a number of striking similarities with religious pilgrimages, such as uniformity in dress codes, the chanting of familiar songs and a feeling of community and fellowship throughout. Lions tours, in particular, are the stuff of legend – as much for their off-field activities as all the epic games on the field. A Lions tour is a journey into the unknown, particularly for a novice. One player, who shall remain nameless, on the Lions' tour to Australia in 2001 was told he would be 'dirt-tracking' – a well-known rugby term for not being in the first team on tour – but, rather than being downcast, he was excited by the news, declared that he loved BMXs and asked where the track was! Another was to learn, much to his embarrassment, that, on tour, when a player expresses an interest in having a 'blow job', he is merely after a short!

Ken Kennedy had a dramatic introduction to his involvement on the Lions' tour to South Africa in 1974. Although travelling as a player, it was Kennedy's medical skills that were first called for, when Bobby Windsor was taken ill with food poisoning. He was so ill that he was taken to the back of the plane and told to suck ice-cubes to help him cool down. As team doctor, Kennedy came to take his temperature without knowing about the ice-cubes. When he looked at the thermometer, he shouted out, 'Jaysus, Bobby, you died 24 hours ago!'

Inevitably, when talking of front rows, the famous Pontypool front row of Charlie Faulkner, Bobby Windsor and Graham Price – celebrated in song and folklore by Max Boyce – looms large for Kennedy. The camaraderie between front-row players is amazing, especially among the Pontypool gang. It is a strange fact of rugby life that people in the same positions on the field tend to pal around together off it. It was said that Windsor's tactic with novice opponents was to bite them on the ear early in the match and say, 'Behave yourself, son, and nothing will happen to this ear of yours.'

Windsor is one of the game's great raconteurs. One of his favourite stories is about a Welsh Valleys rugby club on tour in America. On coming back from a night on the town, two of the players could not find their rooms. They decided to check for their teammates by looking through the keyholes. At one stage, they came across an astonishing sight. There in her birthday suit was a Marilyn Monroe lookalike. Close by was a man who was chanting out with great conviction, 'Your face is so beautiful that I will have it painted in gold. Your breasts are so magnificent that I will have them painted in silver. Your legs are so shapely that I will have them painted in platinum.' Outside, the two Welsh men were getting very aroused and began jostling each other for the right of the keyhole. The man inside hearing the racket shouted out, 'Who the hell is out there?' The two Welsh men replied, 'We're two painters from Pontypool.'

Kennedy had a memorable moment after the third Test in Port Elizabeth. The Lions had gone into the game two down, and so it was the decider. In shocking weather, the Lions lost 12–10, and thereby the series. The Lions were very disappointed – it was a game that had been won everywhere but on the scoreboard. Still, there was no sulking. In the best tradition, the Lions decided to drown their sorrows and so a monumental piss-up was held. A few equally drunk South African fans had got into the hotel's off-limits area, and a bit of a skirmish developed. At one stage, the Lions manager Jack Matthews chucked a couple of the intruders down the stairs from the floor. He picked up a watch off the ground and flung it down after the guys, with a cry of: 'And take your blasted watch with you!' Then he saw his bare wrist: in the excitement he had flung his own watch down the stairs.

Mick Doyle was one of the many former players who paid homage to Ken Kennedy: 'The great thing about my rugby career was that it gave me the opportunity to meet so many great characters like Ken Kennedy. He has a great irreverence. I would describe him as a macho David Norris. I have great respect for him as a person and he was an incredible player.'

38

RATSKINSKI
TERRY KENNEDY

As everybody in rugby knows, Terry Kennedy's nickname is 'The Rat', but very few know its origins. On St Mary's tour to Russia in 1977, J.B. Sweeney, who was a great stalwart of the club, christened Kennedy the Russian-sounding 'Ratskinski', and it was then abbreviated. Hence 'The Rat'.

His international teammate Johnny Moloney has many happy memories of that trip: 'We toured Russia in 1977 but I have no recollection of where the invitation came from. I was captain of the touring side and I was recently reminded by some of my colleagues on the trip that I was a very strict one. There was a lavish dinner in our honour the night before one of the matches, with all kinds of delicious food on the menu, but I insisted that our players have the healthiest diet. What was worse, from their point of view, I wouldn't let them near any drink before the match.

'I did let them relax after the games. One of our colleagues, J.B. Sweeney, was less than impressed, at the reception the Russians had provided us with, with the news that the bar was closing ridiculously early. He was in the FCA and was well up on military matters. He went for a walk over to the American embassy and got talking to one of the soldiers outside. The result was that he got an invitation into the "mess" in the embassy. Word trickled back to the rest of us and we joined him. That became our regular social outlet and at one stage we were invited there for breakfast.

'It was a strange environment at the time because we had two Russian police going everywhere with us, keeping tabs on everything we did. One of them was Nikita, who spoke perfect English but with an American twang, and the other was an older man, with no English, who was calling the shots. At no stage could we escape the feeling that "big brother" was watching us.

'We did a lot of fundraising before the trip and it really cost us nothing to travel out. It was the pre-Glasnost, pre-Perestroika era and everybody out there was mad for Western goods, especially jeans. We had all our team blazers and jumpers and O'Neills playing gear, so we were able to sell off our jeans for a nice sum in today's money. But our masterstroke was to convince the Russians that O'Neills was the Irish for Adidas! That tour cost us virtually nothing as a result of our blackmarket activities. It was ironic that in the embassy mess we could buy European beer with the local currency but in the hotel we could only buy the local brew, which tasted horrible, and that with American dollars. We were flush with Russian currency following the sale of our "wally" jeans supplied by J.B. and Terry Kennedy.'

Kennedy won the first of his 13 caps on the wing for Ireland against Wales in 1978, and went on to tour South Africa with Ireland in 1981. Before the 1981 tour, John Robbie was called into his bosses' office (he worked for Guinness) and was told that he was not allowed to go. Robbie resigned, although he was married with a young child to support.

Fortunately, he did retain his sense of humour through this difficult time enough to wind up Terry Kennedy: 'The great departure day arrived, and then we learned about the cloak-and-dagger methods that we were going to use to get to South Africa. I suppose it was necessary, and we were getting worried about running the gauntlet at Dublin airport, as we'd heard that a massive demonstration had been planned. I rang Terry Kennedy and in my best Peter Sellers Indian accent I told him that I was Kader Asmal, the high-profile leader of the Irish anti-apartheid movement, and could I talk to him? Terry was very worried and, when I asked him to confirm some secret arrangements for our departure, I could almost see the beads of sweat pouring from his brow. He was gibbering like an idiot and nearly collapsed in relief when I told him it was me.'

Mick Quinn has vivid memories from that tour: 'John "O'Desperate" O'Driscoll is the consummate gentleman but he liked to enjoy himself on tour. He was a very committed, driving player but a real Jekyll and Hyde character. His party piece was to hang out of windows late at night. During Ireland's tour of South Africa in 1981, this got a bit boring after a number of weeks. For the sake of variety, he decided he would hang someone else out of the window, so one night he dangled Terry Kennedy by the legs as he held him outside the hotel window – seventeen storeys up. It's the only time his teammates ever saw Terry quiet. Then Willie Duggan came into the room, puffing his cigarette, with a bottle of beer in his hand and with his matted hair that hadn't been combed since the tour started. As Willie was such a senior player and a close friend of John's, people assumed he would talk some sense into him. All he said to John before turning and walking out was: "O'Driscoll, you don't have the guts to let him go." He was right too!'

39

KEYES TO THE KINGDOM
RALPH KEYES

Ralph Keyes made quite an impression on the 1991 World Cup, and was finally recognised as the class player he assuredly was when he became the top scorer in the competition, coming out ahead of such luminaries as Grant Fox, Gavin Hastings and Michael Lynagh with 68 points. Keyes is one of the many Irish internationals produced by the Cork Constitution assembly line. In his eight caps for Ireland, Keyes scored ninety-four points, a very impressive return by any standards.

Tony Ward was a rival for Keyes in the latter stages of his career, and is ideally placed to appraise Keyes: 'I do think Ralph was sold short by the system, and because of the Brian Smith situation he did not get the number of caps he should have. When I started back in the late 1980s as a regular columnist with the *Evening Herald*, I pulled no punches when it came to dealing with the issues of the day. One of the areas where I nailed my colours to the mast most visibly was the area of Brian Smith's brief "flirtation" with the Irish rugby team. Whatever faults may lie with soccer's rules in relation to qualification to play for one country or another, the situation in relation to Brian Smith on the Irish rugby team was indefensible. If a player has declared and played for his native place of birth, unless there are extraordinary circumstances, then that should be his lot. To think that Smith, having played for Australia against Ireland in the '87 World Cup, could have ended up playing for Ireland against Australia in the World Cup in 1991 if he had hung around a bit longer does not bear thinking about. The entire principle was wrong. It must be said that the fact that Smith did not exactly set the world of Irish rugby alight had nothing to do with my feelings.

'It was clear that Ralph and myself were battling for the second out-half spot for the World Cup squad, but thankfully I made it on the plane to Sydney. After the World Cup, Doyler stepped down as Irish coach and Jimmy Davidson replaced him. Given Doyler's affection for Deano, it was always going to be hard to wrestle the number-10 shirt from him while Doyler was in charge. With Davidson at the helm, I felt I might have a better chance to claim my place for the 1988 Five Nations. The key fixture for me was going to be the final trial on 19 December 1987. If I could pull something special out of the hat, I could achieve the perfect Christmas present – a recall to the Irish side. The problem was that I went into the game hampered by a thigh injury and was forced to withdraw 20 minutes into the second half. Dusk was descending as I walked off. It was a metaphor for my career. There was a slightly farcical element to the proceedings, appropriate to the pantomime season, when I had to take off my blue jersey and hand it to the young pretender, Ralph Keyes. The gesture said it all. Ralph was on the fast lane and I was on the way out.

'I found it extraordinary that the selectors continued to choose Brian Smith ahead of Keyes for the Irish team when Paul Dean retired, as Keyes was such a great all-round player. After Smith switched to rugby league, the door opened for Ralph in the 1991 World Cup to show his talents to the rugby world. I was genuinely thrilled for him that at last he had the proper stage to showcase his talents. He grabbed the opportunity literally with both feet. Ralph secured his place in rugby history by becoming the highest scorer in the World Cup with 68 points. The fact that this distinction went to New Zealand legend Grant Fox in the opening tournament underlines the elite club he joined.

'Another thing about Ralph was the great combination he had with Michael Bradley for Cork Constitution, Munster and Ireland. It was as good a combination as ever played for club, province and country.

'I would go so far as to say that he was the best two-footed player we have ever had, certainly in my lifetime. We have had great kickers of the ball. Barry McGann is an obvious example, but he was very much a right-footed kicker. I, like Ollie, favoured my right foot but could kick with my left. Today, Ronan [O'Gara] can kick with his left foot, but only uses it to get himself out of a pickle. Ralph, though, could kick with equal ability and conviction off either foot and could feel comfortable whether he dropped the ball on the left or the right, and, of course, this asked different questions of the back rows. They never knew which foot he would kick from, which meant that he had time to clear the ball. In terms of kicking the ball out of hand, Ralph was up there with the very best and a superb place kicker to boot.'

40

UNCLE TOM'S CHAMPION
MICHAEL KIERNAN

Michael Kiernan comes from solid Irish rugby stock – not only was his uncle Tom an Irish rugby legend, but his maternal uncle, Mick Lane, was also part of the golden era of Irish rugby. Lane was first capped in the centre in the Triple Crown decider when Ireland lost to Wales at Swansea in 1947, though he played most of his rugby on the wing. Contrary to the perception that, apart from the wizardry of Jack Kyle, the Irish backs of that period were not up to much, Lane and Noel Henderson, his colleague in the backs, were chosen with Kyle on the Lions' tour to New Zealand in 1950. Jim Kiernan, Michael's father, was an international selector from 1984 to 1987. Yet, despite this illustrious background, Michael was not brought up amid rugby fanaticism, and the seeds of a promising running career were sown at school. As he recalls, 'The highlights of my running career were winning the national 200m title in 1981 and representing Ireland against Scotland that same year. At that stage, though, I had to make a choice between athletics and rugby – and rugby won.'

That same year saw Kiernan touring South Africa with the Irish rugby team. He played for the Munster side that beat Australia 15–6 at Musgrave Park in 1981 and was selected as substitute for the international against the Wallabies, although tonsillitis forced him to cry off.

However, all his Christmases would come at once in 1982. Kiernan exploded onto the international scene when he came on as a replacement for David Irwin, who broke his leg in Ireland's 20–12 victory over Wales. Irwin's partner in the centre, Paul Dean, was also injured and replaced by John Murphy.

'The first match of the International Championship was called off because of snow. I was 19 then but had turned 20 for the Welsh game. It was such a thrill for me, particularly as I was so young, to be in the company of such classy players as Ollie Campbell. I was happy just to be on the bench and felt so honoured to be wearing an Irish tracksuit. If I had been there 15 or 20 times, it would have been very different. I had enough belief in my own ability to know my chance would come sooner or later. It's very easy to make your debut coming on as a sub because you miss out on the anxiety of the night before and all the hype and distractions.

'The Triple Crown happened very fast. It was a kind of fairy tale and a little bit unreal. In hindsight, the senior players like Fergus Slattery, Moss Keane and John O'Driscoll had been toiling away for years without any success. I was only on the scene for four weeks and had won a Triple Crown. In the later years of my career, I appreciated the memories of the good times much more. Although we didn't win the Triple Crown in 1983, it was as good a year as 1982 because we won the same number of matches and we beat France.'

There were a handful of begrudgers who hinted that he might have got his place on the team because his uncle Tom was coach. Was he troubled by this kind of talk?

'Not in the least. Anyone who knows my uncle understands that I got my place on merit. If anything, the fact that I was his nephew made things even harder.'

Kiernan toured with the Lions to New Zealand in 1983, and has mixed emotions about the experience: 'As a young man, it was a great elation to be chosen for the Lions. It was a fantastic experience on a personal level but it was not a happy tour because we lost too many matches. The tour probably took its toll on me because I was dropped for the opening two internationals in 1984. Having said that, I don't think I deserved to be dropped.'

Another Triple Crown beckoned in the crunch match against England in 1985. The sides were tied at 10–10 in the final minute. Then Kiernan dropped a goal following a pass from Michael Bradley – who subsequently admitted that he thought he was, in fact, passing to Paul Dean – to give Ireland victory.

'My kicking was only one factor that season. A number of new players came on the scene in 1984–85, which created a great buzz. Mick Doyle was very refreshing in his attitude. We felt we could try anything, even when we weren't fully sure it would come off. In that first season, he was crucial to our success, though perhaps his contribution drifted a bit in the following years. Having said that, there were a number of essential elements that combined to give us the Triple Crown in '85. Our back row was incredible and Paul Dean was a genius at finding space. If you could write the script, you couldn't have come up with a more dramatic conclusion.'

MICHAEL KIERNAN

Many rugby fans felt Michael Kiernan left the Irish team prematurely. For the first time, Paul Dean can exclusively reveal the real reason for Kiernan's retirement. 'He left because of illness. The truth is, everyone was sick of him!'

41

THE GREY FOX
TOM KIERNAN

Ireland has produced many players who were noted for their commitment to the green jersey. In this category are people such as Jack Macauley, who was said to be the first married man to be capped in international rugby in 1887 – according to rugby folklore, he got wed just to get leave of absence to play for Ireland! A well-known Kerry man to play rugby was the peerless Con Houlihan, who lined out for his beloved Castleisland. He took his fair share of heavy tackles: 'I never got capped for Ireland, but I got kneecapped for Castleisland.'

However, few Irish players showed the same commitment to Ireland as Tom Kiernan. Kiernan was first capped at full-back against England in 1960. In 1970, he eclipsed the hallowed Jack Kyle's tally of 46 caps in the victory over Wales. He won his 54th and final cap against Scotland at Murrayfield in 1973, having established 2 other milestones at the time: scoring a record 158 points for Ireland and captaining his country for a record 24 times. Kiernan took over as coach of the Irish national team in 1980, succeeding his cousin and Cork Constitution clubmate Noel 'Noisy' Murphy.

Cork Constitution have produced Irish rugby legends down through the years, including Kiernan and Murphy. The two former internationals have entered rugby folklore in a story from the day they were on a trip to England. They passed a shop and saw a notice on the window which read: 'Trousers £2. Shirts £1.50.' Tom and Noel were thrilled. They decided they would make a killing and buy them cheaply in England and sell them off at proper prices back home in Ireland. They decided to play it cool and speak in English accents. When they went in, they calmly walked up to the counter and said to the manager, 'We'll buy all the trousers and shirts you have.'

The manager looked at them with astonishment. Despite their feigned accents, he asked, 'Excuse me, gentlemen, are you both from Cork?'

Noel and Tom asked in unison, 'How did you know?'

'Oh, call it an inspired guess. You probably didn't notice but this is actually a dry cleaners!'

Kiernan was a great motivator. He coached Munster to their win over the All Blacks in 1978 and Ireland to their Triple Crown win in 1982. Before Munster played Australia in 1967, the team met in the Metropole Hotel. Noel Murphy limped in before the match and said, 'My leg is shagged and I can't play.' A sub was duly called for and informed of his selection. Then Kiernan cut loose with his motivational speech, and everyone was ready to tear into the Aussies afterwards. Noel Murphy was so caught up by Kiernan's emotion that he said, 'Arra, f**k it, Tom, I'll play.'

Although Dick Spring's international record is not the one he would have wished for, he still has many happy memories of his rugby days: 'Barry McGann and I had been out for the night. The next day, we were training for Munster and neither of us were feeling the best. Tom Kiernan was training the side at the time. An awkward, high ball was pumped in between us and both of us shouted, "Yours." Tom intervened immediately and said, "Gentlemen, there's only one call in rugby: 'Mine'!"

'Tom is an accountant by profession and has a great head for figures – most of the time at least! After the All Blacks were beaten by Munster in 1978, Tom, as their coach, was asked by a local journalist if it was a one-off. In all earnestness, Kiernan is reputed to have replied: "You could play the All Blacks two or three times and they would beat you nine or ten times!"'

Ciaran Fitzgerald believes that Kiernan was pivotal to Ireland's Triple Crown success in 1982: 'Tom was always two moves ahead of you. I often heard myself saying things and I would later get a flashback and see that Tom had discreetly planted the thought in my mind either the previous day or a week earlier. He was a great man manager. He was always prompting you because he wanted the ideas to come from the players themselves because they took more responsibility for their own decisions. Tom was not called "The Grey Fox" for nothing.'

42

THE PERFECT 10
JACK KYLE

The former BBC commentator Cliff Morgan – himself one of the all-time great fly-halfs – once said, 'Jack Kyle was the very best, the loveliest of players and the loveliest of men.'

That says it all.

Cliff often talks about his first international for Wales against Ireland. He had heard so much about his legendary opponent Jack Kyle, and was all set to take him down a peg or two. As the match progressed, Kyle was not featuring prominently and Morgan relaxed, believing that the Irishman did not live up to his reputation. Suddenly, Kyle made a break and scored a stunning try. That was an eloquent testimony to Kyle's genius. He only needed one opportunity and he stamped his class all over a match.

Jack Kyle OBE was the undisputed star when Ireland won their first Grand Slam in 1948, as well as three International Championships in four years in 1948, '49 and '51. Those years are known universally throughout the rugby world as 'the Kyle era'. His arsenal of gifts was amazing: tactically astute, razor sharp in decision-making and with great pace off the mark that made him a very difficult target to nail down. At 5 ft 9 in. and 12 st. 6 lb, he was a lightweight who packed a heavyweight tackle. He first played for Ulster as an 18-year-old and made his official Ireland debut against France in 1947. He went on to win 46 caps between 1947 and 1958, when he made his final appearance in a 12–6 victory over Scotland at Lansdowne Road. That may not seem a lot by today's standards, but they spanned eleven seasons in the days when there were only four regular internationals a year.

It is no accident that his time in the green shirt coincided with perhaps the greatest-ever era in Irish rugby. He also captained Ireland on 6 occasions and in the course of his 46 caps he scored 24 points from 7 tries and a drop goal. In addition, he toured with the Lions in Australia and New Zealand in 1950, starring in 16 of their 23 games, including all 6 tests, and scoring 6 tries. One of these, a startling effort of individual brilliance in the first Test, is still talked about in New

Zealand, in the same way that Brian O'Driscoll's wonder try in the first Test in 2001 is still talked about in Australia. The legendary All Blacks full-back Bob 'The Barefoot Boy' Scott went as far as to describe him as 'the best player in the Lions team, and, in all the years since, I have never seen a better first five-eighth'. He was the conductor of the orchestra in the golden era of Irish rugby.

Yet, for all his achievements and all the plaudits heaped upon him, he is the personification of modesty, claiming, 'Tony O'Reilly famously said, "The older I get the better I used to have played." I am in the same category!'

At school at Belfast Royal Academy, he won an athletics cup for sprints: 'When I was starting off, I had the benefit of the advice of Dickie Lloyd, who played for Ireland before and after the First World War. He told me, "Practise always with the ball in your arms – walk 25, sprint 25, walk 25 and sprint 25." To be fast off the mark is as vital for an out-half today as it was then; Daniel Carter shows that. Things have changed so much in other areas, though. In our day, we were trying to avoid the opposition; nowadays, they're deliberately running into people. It's a much tougher game. You need to be able to take the knocks today.'

Kyle came of age during the Second World War, and recalls his father building an air-raid shelter in the back garden of the family home in Belfast. Jack is keen to acknowledge his debt to his dad: 'My father was a great believer in education and I am eternally grateful that he passed that on to me. As boys, we were told, "Sport is about the friends you will make," and now I'm an old guy I realise how true that was. Our fathers, mind you, would tell us that studying was the thing and we couldn't be wholly ruled by rugby football. And I don't think we were: rugby then, even at the highest level, was a recreation for a passage or two, and when it was over we went happily enough back to our textbooks.'

Yet his father also knew how to put him in his place: 'When my late father read that I had been selected to head off on a six-month tour with the Lions, his words across the breakfast table were: "Does that young fellow ever intend to qualify in medicine?"'

A revealing insight into Kyle's integrity came in 1958 after his last game, a 12–6 victory over Scotland, when he was dropped for the next one. The then chairman of selectors Ernie Crawford suggested that he make a retirement speech at the post-match meal, to make it seem his decision. The offer was spurned with characteristic politeness. 'My response to Ernie was: "Everyone knows I'm being dropped. I don't want to stand up and say I'm retiring. I've had a great innings. No one could ask for a better time in the game than I've had."'

Jack lives now in a 'wee village' on the County Down coastline. He is a gentleman in both senses of the term and someone who places a high value on friendship. One of his friends had always wanted to visit Paris, and Jack brought him there for his 90th birthday. His friend was suitably impressed by the wonders of one of the great cities in the world. At one stage, they were sitting by the Seine sipping coffee, during which time many beautiful women passed by. Jack's friend turned to him and shook his head sadly: 'Ah, Jack, if only I was 70 again!'

43

THE CORK EXAMINER
DONAL LENIHAN

Donal Lenihan cuts an imposing figure. He was born into a GAA-mad family, and his Kerry-born father, Gerald, played with the hurling immortals Jack Lynch and Christy Ring, but still found time to become an Irish heavyweight international boxer. His heroes were not rugby players but the stars of the 1973 All-Ireland-winning Cork side such as Jimmy Barry-Murphy and Billy Morgan.

Donal recalls his first full cap against Australia in 1981: 'I usually roomed with Moss Keane. He was coming to the end of his career at that stage. Our room was like an alternative medical centre with pollen, garlic tablets and a half-dozen eggs. The mornings of internationals I woke up to see Moss eating three raw eggs. It's not the sort of sight that you want to wake up to! Having said that, Moss was an enormous help to me in the early days. I especially appreciated that he let me make the decisions about the lineout.'

When the Ciaran Fitzgerald era ended, Lenihan stepped into the breach and took on the mantle of captaincy: 'I struggled a bit during my first term as captain but was much more comfortable in the role second time around.'

He led Ireland to the inaugural World Cup in 1987. It was not a happy experience for him as he saw his side struggle to make any impression. Ireland's slide accelerated the following season, culminating in a humiliating defeat at Twickenham, when Jimmy Davidson succeeded Mick Doyle.

Injuries forced Lenihan to depart from the international stage slightly ahead of schedule. He puts it succinctly: 'I knew it was time to retire when the bits and pieces started falling off my body.'

During the 1989 Lions tour to Australia, the Wednesday team acquired the nickname of 'Donal's Doughnuts' – Donal's, of course, because they were captained by Lenihan and Doughnuts because they played to 'fill the hole in the middle of the week'.

Lenihan's ready wit was to the fore on a number of occasions on that tour.

At one stage, Bridgend's Mike Griffiths asked, 'Can I ask a stupid question?'

'Better than anyone I know,' answered Lenihan.

Another time, the touring party were driving through Sydney when they passed a couple coming out of a church after being married. In all earnestness, Jeremy Guscott asked, 'Why do people throw rice at weddings?'

Lenihan replied immediately, 'Because rocks hurt.'

Scott Hastings grew impatient when his brother Gavin seemed to prefer playing tennis or going windsurfing with Ieuan Evans rather than with him. Lenihan commented, 'Ieuan's like the brother Gavin never had.'

'What about me?' asked Scott.

'You're the brother he did have,' responded Lenihan.

Lenihan was a victim of one of the great wind-ups in Irish rugby. In the 1980s, at the height of the apartheid era, there was a lot of money being offered under the table for players to play in exhibition games in South Africa. Hugo MacNeill has a great ability to do African and Australian accents and he often used them to great effect to tease his Irish teammates. When Lenihan was captain of Ireland and Munster, Hugo rang him and pretended to be a chap called Fritz Voller from the South African Rugby Board. He said, 'I'm ringing you in connection with permission we got from the IRFU to allow you to play in a special match we've arranged between the Springboks and a world selection. The match will be played on 14 October.'

Donal replied, 'I'm sorry. I'm totally committed to my responsibilities with Munster and Ireland and I'm unable to make the trip but thank you for the kind invitation.'

'But we would like you to captain our world selection.'

'I'm sorry, I can't make it because of my commitments to Munster and Ireland.'

'But you could have a nice holiday and your wife could come with you and stay on for an extended holiday when you return to Ireland.'

'No. I can't because of my commitments to Munster and Ireland.'

'OK, I hear what you're saying. I don't want to put you under undue pressure. Thanks for listening. I suppose there's no point in saying that your match fee would be £30,000 sterling.'

There was a pregnant pause.

'Sorry?'

'Oh, I was just mentioning your match fee would be £30,000 sterling. It would be lodged into a Swiss bank account. But I wouldn't want to compromise your commitment to Munster and Ireland.'

'That's OK. Sorry, what date in October did you say again? Let me recheck my diary. Now that I think of it, my poor wife, Mary, needs a little holiday!'

At which point, Hugo rapidly reverted to his own accent and said, 'Lenihan, I've got you by the balls.'

44

THE LYNCH MOB
SEÁN LYNCH

In 1971, Colin Meads prematurely dismissed the Lions forwards as 'too many sweat bands, not enough sweat'. Seán Lynch was one of the men who made Meads eat his words. Although capped 17 times for his country, Lynch is not a player to take himself too seriously. Success at club level provided the platform Lynch needed to step onto the international stage. As he recalls fondly, 'Denis Hickie and I were capped for the first time against France in 1971, becoming the first current Mary's players to play for Ireland. Jimmy Kelly and George Norton had played for St Mary's and Ireland but were not Mary's players during their international careers. It was a wonderful achievement for the club. When the side was announced, there was a great club celebration.'

After just one season at international level, Lynch was chosen by the Lions on the historic tour to New Zealand. He was to play a more central role than anybody could have foreseen at the start of the tour. The week before the first Test in Dunedin, the Lions had lost their two first-choice props, Ray McLoughlin and Sandy Carmichael, with long-term injuries in the infamous 'battle of Christchurch'. The match confirmed an old adage: 'New Zealand rugby is a colourful game – you get all black and blue.'

Willie John McBride warned his fellow forwards after this bruising encounter, 'You have not seen anything yet. They will throw everything at you, even the kitchen sink.'

Lynchie's prop partner was the squat Scot Ian McLauchlan, 'Mighty Mouse'. One of his opponents scornfully dismissed him with the words: 'You'll be Mickey Mouse by the time I've finished with you.'

Yet it was the Lions who had the last laugh, winning 9–3. The crowd's silence after the game bore eloquent testimony to the scale of the shock. From that moment, a win in the series was a distinct possibility, although the All Blacks restored parity in the second Test. The Lions won the third Test 13–3 in Wellington, thanks in no small measure to a vintage display by Barry John, and the final Test at Eden Park, Auckland, ended in a 14–14 draw.

For Lynch, it was do or die: 'We were getting very tired at that stage and were anxious to return home but at the same time we didn't want to squander a 2–1 lead. We were determined to prove that we were the best. Our mood had changed during the tour. When we arrived, we probably believed deep down that the All Blacks were invincible. By the finish, it was us who thought we were almost invincible.'

Before the match, the captain, John Dawes, simply said to the players, 'We have come this far. We're not going to throw it away now.'

Dawes looked each player in the eye. Further words were unnecessary. Each player knew what they had to do. The joke later among the players was: 'We were so fired up, when the referee ran onto the pitch, three of us tackled him.'

Spurred on like a wounded animal by the ire of a fanatical nation, the All Blacks started like a whirlwind, taking the lead after just four minutes courtesy of a soft try from Wayne Cottrell. The tension got to the Lions and they under-performed. However, when they were trailing 14–11, J.P.R. Williams dropped a goal from about 40 yards to tie the match.

Lynch is eternally grateful to the coach's role in the Lions' success and to two coaches who had a big impact on his development into a top-class player. 'Carwyn James, the Lions' coach in 1971, was one of the great visionaries of the game. Ronnie Dawson was Ireland's first coach and was very instrumental in bringing Ireland into the modern era.

'On the non-playing side, my greatest memory of the Lions tour is of visiting a vineyard. I think it was run by a religious order. I had red wine, white wine, blue wine and everything that was going. At the end, I didn't know where I was or who I was! I wasn't moving very sprightly the next morning.'

The definitive Seán Lynch story is told by Mick Quinn: 'Lynchie was on the Irish tour to Argentina in 1970. All the players were attending a dinner. A Lord somebody was to be the main dignitary. Before he arrived, the players were told that he had Parkinson's disease and to be patient as it would take him a long time to walk to the dinner table. After what seemed a half an hour, the Lord eventually made it to the seating position. He was sitting beside Lynchie and said, "Well, Mr Lynch, are you enjoying your tour?"

'Lynchie replied, "Yes, Mr Parkinson, I am!"'

45

THE LION KING
WILLIE JOHN McBRIDE

It is inconceivable that a discussion on great Irish forwards should begin without reference to Willie John. The fact that it is unnecessary to use his surname says it all. To say his rugby CV is impressive is an understatement: 63 caps, 5 Lions tours, 17 Lions Test appearances, captain of the most successful Lions side of all time. In the 1972–73 season, he surpassed the record of Scottish prop-forward Hugh McLeod when he made 43 consecutive appearances in international rugby.

Born one of six children in Toomebridge, Co. Antrim, he lost his father aged four and was brought up by his mother on a small farm. The hardships he experienced give a lie to the perception that rugby in Ireland is a game only for those born with a silver spoon.

Gareth Edwards has gone on record to say that Willie John McBride was his sort of captain because of his creed of total commitment and he would have followed him anywhere. Willie John was wont to say: 'I hate small men.' Each match was rugby's high noon for him. He believed in all or nothing – 'lay down your life or don't come with me'. He is spoiled for choice when asked about the highlights of his career.

'Beating Australia in the Test in Sydney (11–5) was a great achievement particularly as we had to strap up three players because of injury to get them onto the field. Our win over Wales in 1970 was also a magic moment. We had an amazing pack of forwards then, with world-class players like McLoughlin and Slattery. The team was probably at its peak in 1972 but politics probably cost us the Triple Crown. It was great towards the end of my career to lead Ireland to the Championship in 1974.'

There was no doubt, though, that his finest hour was the Lions tour in 1974, when he was an inspirational captain, and he remembers it fondly: 'I was a Lion at 21 but losing became a habit. I'd had a baptism of fire in my first Test because I was up against two of the all-time greats in Johan Claassen and Colin Meads. I had to wait nine matches for a win with the Lions.

WILLIE JOHN McBRIDE

'The 1974 tour was like all my Christmases at once. When the tour was finished the players presented me with a lovely engraved silver water-jug which read: "To Willie John. It was great to travel with you." That is my most treasured rugby possession. There is a bond between that team that will never die.'

In his final home international, Willie John scored his first try for his country when Ireland defeated France 25–6. Such was the emotion generated that the crowd ran onto the pitch to celebrate the try. To mark the centenary season of Irish rugby, the IRFU arranged a match between Ireland-Scotland and England-Wales in April 1975. It was to be the last time the Ballymena man would lead out a side at the home of Irish rugby. Events took an unexpected turn after the match when he was hijacked by the late Eamonn Andrews and whisked away to become the subject of an episode of *This Is Your Life*.

When asked about his most difficult opponent, McBride does not hesitate for a second: 'Colin Meads was as hard a man as I ever came across, though I also played against his brother Stan, who was another tough nut. Colin (nicknamed Pinetree) was the best, most aggressive and perhaps the most totally committed player I ever played against. [A small indication of his rugged indestructibility was his remarkable recovery from a horrific car crash, in 1971. His back was in plaster after the accident but he was playing rugby within six months.] There were so many other great players, like Gerald Davies, who was the greatest winger I was fortunate to play with.'

He is less than enchanted by all the trends in the coaching of players: 'We played by vision. Today, players have to be led. They watch so many videos. I'm not sure what you can learn from watching videos because every game is so different.'

Listening to Willie John talk, it is striking to observe the contrast between his vocabulary and value system and that of the current breed of players. His word is his bond. The idea of a player requiring a contract to play rugby is completely alien to him.

How would he like to be remembered?

'I'm a very boring person. I've only had the one employer, I've only had the one club and I've only had the one wife. To me loyalty is paramount and I'm worried about the rugby supermarket that is developing where players are moving like commodities on a shelf. I don't like the idea of the cheque book running Irish rugby. I would like to be remembered as a man of loyalty and as someone who always gave his best.'

46

JIM'LL FIX IT
JIM McCARTHY

Dolphin's Jim McCarthy won Munster Cup medals in 1944, '45 and '48. He was capped twenty-eight times for Ireland between 1948 and 1955, captaining the side four times in 1954 and 1955, and scoring eight international tries. He was also omnipresent in the Irish team which won the International Championship in 1951, and toured Argentina and Chile in 1952 with Ireland.

He is best remembered as a breakaway forward of the highest quality, playing in all four matches in the 1948 Grand Slam year, and for the entire season of 1949. He brought a new dimension to wing-forward play, particularly in relation to helping the out-half breach the opposing half. A flying redhead, he was an invaluable ally to Jack Kyle, combining with him to devastating effect. His back-row combination with Old Belvedere's Des O'Brien and Bill McKay in those years is among the finest in Irish rugby history.

Ireland's Grand Slam victory in 1948 prompted McCarthy to engage in what the IRFU saw as extravagant behaviour: 'After we won the Triple Crown in Belfast, I sent in my expenses to the IRFU. I claimed four pounds and ten shillings but only got four pounds and seven shillings. They deducted three shillings because I had rung my family to tell them we had won the Triple Crown and because I had gone outside the *table d'hôte* menu. I had ordered two raw eggs to eat the morning of the match. That was part of my ritual. I also took glucose. It probably did me no good physically but psychologically it gave me an extra edge.'

McCarthy toured with the Lions to Australia and New Zealand in 1950. 'Looking back, there were some great players on that team. Scotland's Graham Budge was a peculiar case. He had come from nowhere to play in the final Scottish trial, in the four matches in the Five Nations, and then went on the Lions tour and after that was never heard of again. In 1980, I was holidaying in Pebble Beach in America and I went to a local rugby tournament. My eye was caught by a headline which read: "Rugby player dies with his boots on". It reported how the previous year a player had dropped dead playing a match on the same ground. It was Graham. He would have been in his fifties then but was still playing rugby when he grabbed the ball and made a run. He dropped dead on the halfway line.'

The following year saw McCarthy touring with Ireland to South America. 'It was a total success off the field and a disaster on it. We were the first international team to be beaten by Argentina. When we got there, we were told we couldn't play any rugby because Eva Peron had just died. They sent us down to Santiago, Chile, to teach the cadets how to play. After eight days, they beat us!

'The players didn't take the playing side very seriously. At one stage, Paddy Lawler went missing for a few days and nobody had a clue where he was. When he returned, a team meeting was hastily called. The team manager solemnly announced that he had been talking to Dublin, which was a big deal in 1952, and then looked around menacingly and said, "I'm deciding whether or not to send some players home." Paddy stood up straight away and replied, "We've been talking among ourselves and we're deciding whether or not we should send you home!"'

McCarthy became the record try scorer for Ireland for a forward. What was the secret of his success?

'Wherever the ball is, you be there. When I was playing for Ireland, the best place to be was two feet behind Jackie Kyle.'

McCarthy always had a special relationship with Tony O'Reilly: 'Tony came down to take up his first job in Cork and joined us for afternoon tea, which led him to stay a few days, which became two years and in the process he became one of the family. When he first came, he would say "your house, Jim, and your children and your wife", but he quickly changed the "yours" to "ours". I had no problem with "our kids" and "our dog", but when he started saying "our" wife I showed him the door!

'I knew the first time I saw him that he would be a success in anything he turned his hand to. He had it all and more. Having said that, I don't envy him. I believe he was never fully exploited on the Irish team. I think he should have been selected at full-back to get the best out of his attacking abilities. There are two sayings which I think apply to Tony: "The bigger the reputation, the smaller the gap" and "To be good, you've got to be twice as good". Everybody wants to cut the guy with the big reputation down to size.

'I was best man at both his weddings! I only played one season with Tony at international level. When he arrived on the scene, he was the darling of the media and could do no wrong. After his first match against France, the *Irish Independent* said that I had played poorly and had not protected Tony well enough, even though I wasn't playing in the centre! I was dropped for the next match after that report and never played another international. Twenty-five years later, Tony put me on the board of Independent Newspapers just to make up for their injustice to me all those years ago!'

47

WHERE WE SPORTED AND PLAYED
BARRY McGANN

Although Barry McGann won 25 caps for Ireland between 1969 and 1976, he has an ecumenical background in a sporting sense. His brothers, Seán and Diarmuid, played Gaelic football for Cork.

'I'm the son of a Galway man, a Tipperary mother and, being born in Cork, I couldn't but be interested in sport! I played everything in Cork – golf, cricket, soccer, Gaelic football and hurling. I grew up at the back of the Mardyke. It was the golden half-mile because it produced so many sports stars, like former Irish soccer international Noel Cantwell and, of course, Tom Kiernan.

'I played soccer for Young Elms. We won the Under-15 and Under-18 national titles, which helped me get a place as inside-forward on the Irish youths side. I was the only Cork player on a side which included Mick Leech and Terry Conroy. We were one of twenty-four teams for the UEFA finals and finished sixth in the tournament. The highlight for me was when we beat Holland. It was a major achievement since the Dutch side included no less a person than Johan Cruyff!

'Our manager was the late Gerry Doyle. Around the time I was first capped for Ireland, I moved to Dublin. Gerry was managing Shelbourne then and persuaded me to play for them. They had some tremendous players at the time, like Ben Hannigan and Eric Barber. What I most remember is the slagging I used to get whenever I went back to play in Cork. One time, we were playing Cork Celtic. As I ran on to the pitch, I heard a voice saying on the terraces: "Who's that fella?"

'"That's McGann, the rugby player."

'"Oh, wouldn't you know it by his stomach!"'

An even more damning indictment of McGann's bulk was subsequently provided by Tony O'Reilly's quip: 'Twice around Barry McGann and you qualify as a bona fide traveller!'

McGann's rugby education began at Presentation College. 'I started playing with the junior side at twelve and had three seasons as a junior player and two as a senior, captaining the winning Munster Schools Senior Cup side in 1966.'

Within three years, McGann was making his international debut. 'The tradition was that the team was announced on Sunday morning. I heard about it on the half-one news on the car radio. I was travelling to Donnybrook, where Lansdowne was to play Bective. The first indication I had that I had entered a new phase of my career was that, as soon as I got out of the car, a journalist rushed up to me for my first interview. The match was cancelled because of the weather and we adjourned to the bar. I was the last one to leave – around midnight. I did get down to hard work after the game. My first international season was my best.'

McGann grabbed his opportunity with both hands and feet, contributing a drop goal in Ireland's 17–9 victory, their first victory over the French in 11 years. The big question was whether McGann would hold his place because surely he could not hope to displace Mike Gibson when he recovered from injury. A solution was found by bringing Gibson back into the centre. McGann laughs at the memory: 'I gave Mike Gibson a whole new career as a centre.'

There are a number of matches which still evoke a warm glow on McGann's face: 'Beating France in Paris was a great thrill. I especially remember Ray McLoughlin's try. He was in the wrong place at the wrong time and fell over the line with the ball! Playing against the All Blacks was also a magic moment. We drew with them, 10–10, in 1973. Tom Grace got a try in the last moment in the right corner. I missed out on rugby fame because I officially missed the conversion that would have won the game for Ireland. The kick was so high that it was difficult to see which side of the post the ball went but, to this day, I'm convinced that the ball did not, in fact, go wide. Earlier that week, the All Blacks had got out of jail against Munster in Musgrave Park with a penalty in injury time when we drew 3–3. Another chance of being part of history snatched away from me. Not a lot of people know this but I was part of the Munster squad that defeated the All Blacks in 1978. Every rugby fan knows the name of the Munster team but no one knows the name of the subs. I was sub to Wardy.'

A decline in form deprived McGann of participating in Ireland's victory in the 1974 International Championship, as he admits: 'I got Mick Quinn his ten caps for Ireland because I was his only competition and I wasn't up to much at the time!'

McGann does not harbour many regrets about his career: 'I don't allow myself to give in to the "if only" syndrome, but I would have loved to have toured with the Lions. I was on stand-by for the 1971 tour to South Africa. They didn't bring a second out-half because they had a number of utility backs who could slot in at number 10. Barry John was the first choice.'

How does he react to the perception that he never properly fulfilled his potential because he was not dedicated enough?

'Rugby was never more than a recreational activity for me. Having said that, I didn't lack application. I trained hard when I needed to but I enjoyed the social side. My business career was also important, so rugby was never the only thing in my life.

'The rugby scene was very different in my time. There were no real stars until Tony Ward came on to the scene. I missed out on the beauty contest! I do recall, though, that at one stage the ladies' column in the *Evening Press* referred to me as "our chubby hero". My own mother was delighted with the final line in the feature: "Every mother should have one." Now, because of Sky Sports and so on, rugby stars are treated almost the same way as Madonna!'

48

CROWNING GLORY
ROBBIE McGRATH

Scrum-half Robbie McGrath had his first taste of the green jersey in Ireland's win over Southland in Invercargill on Ireland's tour of New Zealand in 1976. The Wanderers player had been flown out as a replacement when Donal Canniffe broke an ankle in training. In an ill-tempered match, McGrath's head was badly cut by a petulant opponent.

That tour created so many stories it deserves a book of its own. Phil O'Callaghan had been recalled for the tour, and he looked a bit older than the rest of the team. A journalist asked him who he was. Philo answered, 'I'm Ireland's secret weapon.'

There was a lot of surprise that he was selected but he played a very significant role on that tour, and he earned his cap on merit. He could be described as 'the traditional Irish rugby tourist'. When Ireland were being intimidated on the pitch, he was not found wanting.

Ireland had other great characters in the squad, and none more so than Brendan Foley, whose son Axel became a star with Munster and Ireland. At one stage on that tour, Foley came down to the foyer of the hotel which had a big fountain. He went in to the middle of it to do some fishing. He didn't catch anything! After that he was known as 'Foley never caught a fish'.

On that tour, Jimmy Davidson was called in to the Irish side as a replacement. He was so happy to be selected that he jumped for joy when he got on the team bus for the first time. He jumped so high that he smashed his head against the roof and needed six stitches.

For his first game on the tour, the Irish were worried about things getting out of hand on the pitch. At one stage, there was a melee in the ruck and Pat Whelan mistakenly stamped Davidson on the head. Initially, the Irish lads thought one of the New Zealand guys had done it and there was bedlam for two minutes. When order was restored, the first thing the Irish players heard was Davidson shouting at his own teammate who had been responsible for the injury: 'You f**king idiot, Whelan.' After the game, Davidson needed multiple stitches.

ROBBIE McGRATH

John Robbie was the youngest player in the Irish party and he looked it. On one boat trip during the tour, some New Zealander glanced at him and remarked in all seriousness that it was nice of the New Zealand Rugby Union to allow the Irish manager to bring his son along on tour.

That tour concluded with a match against Fiji, which is an intimidating venue to play in, but Ireland defeated their hosts 8–0. There were heavy areas of the pitch, so much so that frogs were jumping on the playing surface during the match. Normally, there are shouts of joy after an Irish team is announced. The Fiji game was no exception. However, so humid was the climate that this time all the hurrahs came from the players not selected. They were much more interested in looking out on the most beautiful ocean in the world than watching the match.

The Fijians were lovely people but after the game there was a bit of an incident between an Irish player and one of theirs. When asked about the resolution of the incident, the Irish player who shall remain nameless said in all earnestness, 'I gave him a black eye!'

The Irish team travelled throughout the island in an old bus with no glass in the windows. John Robbie got a bit drunk after the game. He had told the team about the craze at the time of 'lobbing moons' – pulling one's trousers down, bending over and displaying the bare backside to all and sundry. The trick was to choose the time and the place with the most care to get the greatest effect. The Fijian bus was too much of a temptation, and so Robbie lobbed a moon. The locals were totally amazed. Suddenly, the Irish players heard an anguished scream. It was Robbie shouting, 'My God, I've lobbed my wallet.'

It had fallen out the window and Christmas had come early for some lucky local.

Robbie McGrath won the first of his 17 caps against Wales in 1977 and drank from the keg of glory as the boys in green won the Triple Crown in 1982. Ciaran Fitzgerald believes that McGrath has never been given the credit he merits in Ireland's success in those years: 'Ollie Campbell, apart from being an outstanding player, had a great rugby brain and I relied on him to control the game for us. His partner at scrum-half, Robbie McGrath, also played a crucial role. He was a very underrated player who never got the acclaim he deserved.'

Ollie Campbell also acknowledges McGrath's contribution in the green jersey: 'Robbie was an integral part of our success in 1982. He did his defensive duties very well but was also a good link man to release an attack. People remember that we won the Triple Crown decider against Scotland that year by kicks, but it is sometimes forgotten that we played thrilling rugby against Wales that year and scored great tries. Robbie had a large part to play in that and I was certainly very grateful for all the support he gave me, which made my job a lot easier.'

49

STEWARDSHIP
STEWART McKINNEY

Moss Keane made his debut in the Irish scrum in the cauldron of the Parc des Princes in 1974. He was stamped on and was feeling very miserable. His colleague Stewart McKinney offered his own brand of consolation: 'Cheer up, Moss, it could have been a lot worse. You would have suffered brain damage if you'd been kicked in the arse.'

McKinney was a great player who was capped 25 times for Ireland. He had many party pieces, the best-known being his ability to eat all the flowers on the table at a rugby dinner. He was constantly requested to perform and generally obliged.

Philip Orr has vivid memories of rooming with McKinney for his international debut against France in Paris in 1976: 'My clearest memory of the whole weekend was breakfast the morning of the match. I was rooming with Stewart McKinney and he ordered breakfast in bed for both of us, scrambled egg and toast. We were waiting for ages and ages but with no sign of any service. Stewart went out in the corridor and saw a few waiters walking up and down with trays of food. He simply grabbed one from a very surprised waiter and exchanged pleasantries and brought in the tray.'

McKinney was on the 1974 Lions tour. An important shift had taken place in the Lions' approach to touring three years previously, when they were transformed into a more professional outfit by Carwyn James, the Welsh coach who took charge of the side on their tour to New Zealand in 1971. He saw rugby as a piece of opera and famously said, 'It is something that can flow like music and opera and can be beautiful to watch.' He wanted his players to play, to enjoy the experience, to take responsibility and to have the courage to make decisions for themselves. He really brought the players together as a squad and got them to be the best they could be, which is what the great coaches do, and as a result the Lions won that series.

Although McKinney was sceptical about the opera analogy, he and his colleagues bought heavily into the philosophy of togetherness, courage and taking responsibility.

McKinney was at the centre of a revealing incident with 'Mighty Mouse', Ian McLauchlan. The famous Scottish prop asked McKinney which was the greater honour: to play for Ireland or the Lions? Stewart thought for ten seconds before saying Ireland, upon which Mighty Mouse slapped him on the face.

'Did I say the wrong thing?' asked McKinney.

'No, you gave the right answer.'

'Then why did you slap me?'

'Because it took you ten seconds to find it,' replied McLauchlan.

As a noted compiler of amusing rugby anecdotes, that Lions tour fixture provided McKinney with many stories. His favourite was when a celebratory dinner was organised in Rhodesia after the tour. The then Rhodesian Prime Minister Ian Smith arrived to make a speech. Shortly after, two Irish players, Dick Milliken and Fergus Slattery, decided to return to their hotel. Having consumed beverages rather stronger than orange juice, they were feeling particularly adventurous. As they walked out, they noticed just outside the entrance to the club was a beautiful black-tinted-window Cadillac. They decided to borrow the car and go for a drive. After driving around for a few minutes, the partition behind the front seats slid across and the Prime Minister asked, 'Are you gentlemen looking for a job?'

A constant source of amusement on the tour was the Welsh prop Bobby Windsor. In the golden age of amateurism, the manager of the Lions was Alan Thomas, who had a tendency to lose things, especially room keys. He had a phone in his room but each player on the team was only allowed one phone call a week. Windsor spotted Alan's key and held on to it. Every evening, he used it to sneak into Alan's room and phone his wife. As the tour concluded and the team were leaving the hotel, Alan came into the foyer and addressed the entire squad in a crestfallen voice, 'I'm very disappointed. I have been handed a phone bill for a thousand rand. One of you guys has been using the phone every night behind my back. The Lions are supposed to be the cream of rugby but one of you has let the side down in this way. Sadly, the guy who did this is a countryman of my own. He's been ringing Pontypridd.'

At this point, Bobby Windsor jumped up from his seat and started waving his fists menacingly, as he said, 'Which of you bas***ds has been phoning my wife?'

STEWART McKINNEY

Johnny Moloney played with McKinney on that Lions tour: 'South African rugby players like to keep their friends close and their enemies closer. You have to man up to face them, especially in the scrum. It is said that forward play is like a funeral – you have to get in front, with the family; not behind with the friends. When the going got tough, Stewart was not found wanting.'

50

MIGHTY MAC
FREDDIE McLENNAN

Freddie McLennan was an outstanding attacker for Ireland on the left wing. He won eighteen caps between 1977 and 1981 and was one of the great personalities of Irish rugby.

Phil Orr has never forgotten McLennan's unique sense of humour: 'One of the clearest memories I have is of touring Romania with Leinster in 1980. It was like entering a time warp. Most of the time we were starving because there wasn't enough food, largely because it all went up to Moscow. There was nothing in the shops except bare shelves. If you wanted an orange, for example, you had to order it the day before. One incident stands out for me. We stopped for a meal of sorts in a halfway house. As we got off the bus, what struck me most was that there wasn't the sound of a bird to be heard. I learned later that DDT had killed all the insects and the birds had migrated.

'The belief at the time was that one in every four people in Romania was an informer for the Securitate. It subsequently emerged that this was a lie deliberately put about by the Securitate to keep everyone in line, lest anyone they were talking to would report them back for subversion or, perish the thought, making a joke about the dictator, Nicolae Ceausescu.

'On the tour, we were soon fed up with the food on offer. On a bus journey, the two big jokers in the side, Paul McNaughton and Freddie McLennan, walked up the bus with a list, taking the lunch orders. We were told we could choose between T-bone steak or grilled chicken, and we had to indicate whether we wanted chips, baked or sautéed potatoes, and select from a choice of vegetables, as it all had to be ordered in advance. All the players got very excited, and great care was taken over the menu. We arrived at an impressive-looking restaurant for a big meal. There was a buzz of expectancy – which turned into a stunned silence when the food arrived. Each dish was the same: a big bowl of clear, greasy soup and in it was a huge fish head complete with eyes. Nothing was eaten. McNaughton and McLennan had to be led out – they were laughing so much they couldn't walk.'

FREDDIE McLENNAN

McLennan also showed his flair for a joke on Ireland's tour to South Africa in 1980. One Saturday, he was 'duty boy' (the player in charge of informing players about travel arrangements, etc. for a particular day during a tour abroad – each player takes it in turn). The squad had been given the day off and had to decide how to spend it. Freddie, himself a keen golfer, offered two choices. They could either go for a game of golf or take a trip around Johannesburg harbour. Eighteen players favoured the harbour trip on the basis that they could play golf at any time but would not always get the chance to do some sightseeing in Johannesburg. The next morning, the players were ready at 8 a.m. for their trip around the harbour only to be told that, since the city was 5,000 feet above sea level, it did not have a harbour and that the nearest seaside was a massive bus trip away.

However, Johnny Moloney once saw the tables turned on McLennan: 'Mick Quinn would sometimes involve me as his partner-in-crime. He had this trick he played on every player gaining his first cap. A lot of players before their debut start to feel that they are a bit sluggish and not at their best. Quinny would pretend to be very sympathetic and tell them he had the solution. He would inform them in the strictest confidence that the top players always took a freezing-cold bath to give them an edge in a big match. The only reason why this was not generally known was that it was a trade secret.

'The biggest casualty in all of this was Freddie McLennan. We put him in a cold bath and added buckets of ice. We told him he had to wait in there for 20 minutes, otherwise it was no good. He was squealing like a pig. When his time was up, he couldn't move and had ice on his legs.'

Colin Patterson was a big fan of McLennan: 'Freddie is a great personality. Once when we played England, Freddie and John Carleton were having a real jousting match. At one stage, John sent Freddie crashing to the ground in a tackle. As he was going back to his position, Freddie shouted at him: "John, John. Is my hair all right?" If you watch the video of the game, you'll see John cracking up with laughter and Freddie straightening his hair.'

51

GINGER
GERRY McLOUGHLIN

The late film star Richard Harris, one of Limerick's best-known sons, was so swept away by the euphoria of Munster's victory over the Lions in 1978 that he wired the following message from a movie set in Johannesburg.

> Your historic victory over New Zealand made roaring headlines in every South African paper. I've been on the dry for 10 months, but I can't think of a better occasion or excuse to re-acquaint my liver with the drowning sensation of a drop. I wish I was there. I rang Richard Burton and, although he extends his congratulations, I detected a tinge of jealousy.

Prop-forward Ginger McLoughlin was one of the Munster stars on that famous day. In Ireland's opening match of the 1979 season, a home game against France in which Tony Ward kicked three penalties to tie the score at 9–9, one of Ireland's debutants had reason to be proud of himself. Gerry McLoughlin, the carrot-haired Shannon prop, came through his baptism of fire against the hallowed French front row very much with an enhanced reputation. He went on to win 18 caps.

In 1982, Ireland's 20–12 victory in the opening Five Nations game against Wales raised hopes of a Triple Crown, and the away fixture against England was going to be crucial to achieving this ambition. The match is best remembered for a moment from Gerry McLoughlin, who scored a try after he was driven over the line by the sheer weight of Irish players who were up in support. 'Ginger' claimed that he pulled the other players over with him.

Ciaran Fitzgerald played beside McLoughlin in the front row and is ideally equipped to appraise Ginger's career: 'Moss Keane's contribution was crucial on many levels, in my view, not least of which was in saying: "I'm not going back." I know this is very technical but basically, to put it as simply as I can, if the prop-forward retreats, the

Big Tom: the pride of Young Munster, Tom Clifford. (© Gerry Casey)

Captain's log: Ciaran Fitzgerald takes control. (© Picsperfect)

Ireland's greatest back row? Bill McKay, Des O'Brien and Jim McCarthy. (Courtesy of the author)

Centre of the action: Gordon D'Arcy bursts through the Welsh defence. (© Picsperfect)

High flyer: Paul O'Connell, lifted by John Hayes, climbs highest. Malcolm O'Kelly (far right) awaits developments. (© Picsperfect)

Magic: Girvan Dempsey scores the first try against England in Croke Park in 2007. (© Picsperfect)

Giving something back: since his retirement, Denis Hickie has supported a number of worthy causes; here he is pictured with Sister Stanislaus Kennedy and some young fans. (© Young Social Innovators)

Simply the best: Brian O'Driscoll goes for another try. (© Picsperfect)

ABOVE: *An officer and a gentleman*: the late Lieutenant Dermot Earley meets Bertie Ahern. Dermot was one of many GAA stars who played rugby under an assumed name because of 'The Ban'. In his case, he was listed as Lieutenant Late. (© The Defence Forces)

LEFT: *Ireland's next rugby great?* Gort RFC star Adam Minogue prepares for glory. (© Teresa Scally)

Carnage: the devastation after the IRA bomb that claimed two lives and ended the career of Nigel Carr. (Courtesy of Nigel Carr)

To the rescue: Donncha O'Callaghan bringing emergency supplies to Haiti. (© Mark Stedman, Photocall Ireland)

That's how do you do it: Victor Costello gets advice on a good-will visit to India for Goal. (© Goal)

To sir with love: Donncha O'Callaghan on a UNICEF visit to Haiti. (© Mark Stedman, Photocall Ireland)

second row normally has to as well, otherwise the prop's back is arched up. Ginger knew that this would be his fate if he didn't hold his line, which meant that he went in there fighting like a tiger. It's things like that which make the difference between victory and defeat, and only someone of Moss's stature could have pulled it off.

'Ginger and Moss got on brilliantly and that made my job easier. I will always remember that, in 1982, before the Triple Crown decider against Scotland, Bill Beaumont rang Moss Keane to wish him well. "Moss, if you win, they will build a statue of you in Cork."

'"Billy, you bollix. I'm a Kerryman."

'Moss himself was confused. After the game was over, Moss approached me and said, "I'm taking the Cup to Currow next weekend. No more about it – my mind is made up."

'"But Moss, there is no trophy. The Triple Crown is a mythical trophy."

'"Is there a medal?" Moss asked.

'"No, Moss."

'"You mean to say we went to all that f**king trouble and they won't even give us a f**king medal?"

'Like so many others, Moss made Ginger feel very at home in the Ireland set-up and McLoughlin grabbed his opportunities. He was a good scrummager technically, could do well in the loose, as he showed with that famous try against England, and always gave great commitment. I was always happy to have him beside me.'

Another teammate, Donal Lenihan, has vivid memories of McLoughlin: 'Ginger was a great character. In 1983, I was chosen to tour with the Lions to New Zealand but because of injury I was unable to make the start of it. Later on, both Ginger and I were called out as replacements. Ginger hadn't trained in about two months. We had to travel to London, Los Angeles, Auckland and Christchurch. Both of us were very concerned to get there in the best shape possible and were not drinking at all. There were a lot of supporters on the plane and they were in high spirits. We hit an air pocket and a few of the fans spilled their drink all over us. We smelled like a brewery. Willie John McBride was at the airport to meet us and was not impressed.'

Tony Ward recalls his days with Ginger with a wry smile: 'Munster toured Romania in 1982. The food was absolutely dire throughout the tour. We had been warned in advance that it would be like that and we were told to bring a few bars of chocolate. Noel McGlynn was a butcher and he had the wherewithal then to bring plenty of fantastic meat, vacuum-packed, to sustain him throughout the tour and to store it and keep it fresh. He only shared his "treasure chest" with Colm Tucker and Ginger McLoughlin! The three wise men dined royally on the tour, while the rest of us watched enviously on our paltry rations.'

52

A RAY OF HOPE
RAY McLOUGHLIN

One of the greats of Irish rugby is Ray McLoughlin, who twice toured with the Lions and, had he not declared himself unavailable, would inevitably have been picked on the Lions tour in 1974. Ray's brother Feidlim also played for Ireland. Feidlim proudly said, 'We have forty-one caps between us.' What he neglected to point out was that he had only one and Ray held the remaining forty!

For Mick Molloy, Ray McLoughlin was a huge influence: 'Of course, the big hero in my first year in Garbally College was Ray McLoughlin, although, because he was a few years ahead of me in school, it wasn't until we played together for Ireland that I got to know him. He has had a huge influence in the development of Irish rugby. He was way ahead of his time as a captain. He is a great organiser and has a brilliant mind. Although he is best known in professional circles for his business activities, Ray got a first-class honours degree in chemical engineering. He applied scientific principles to his time as captain. One of the things that is most often forgotten is that Ray coached the forwards during part of Tom Kiernan's reign, but he did it in a low-profile way and kept well out of the limelight.'

Seán Lynch had a strong rivalry with his great friend: 'Ray McLoughlin was the toughest opponent I ever came up against. Nobody else ever bothered me too much, but Ray made life very difficult. He would be seen as one of the very best worldwide.'

McLoughlin is remembered by Mick Quinn for a different reason: 'I don't remember much about the build-up for my debut except that I fell asleep during Willie John McBride's team-talk! Ray McLoughlin told me that I was a cheeky bugger. Willie John was a wonderful captain because he had such a great presence. I remember when I first came onto the international scene, I addressed him as "Mr McBride".

'It was pay-for-play with a difference. I had to pay for my jersey. We beat France 6–4 for my first cap. The player who scored their try was killed by lightning some time later. The great J.P. Romeu missed the conversion. As it was my first cap, there was no way I was going to part with my jersey but I really wanted Romeu's. I went back into the dressing-room and asked Ray McLoughlin for his number-1 jersey. You have to remember that he is a very successful businessman, who headed up the James Crean Company – so he's not short of a few bob. He sold me his jersey for £10. I rushed out and swapped jerseys with Romeu. I was thrilled with myself when I returned, but suddenly the Frenchman came into our dressing-room. With his dreadful English and my awful French, communication was a problem but it didn't take me long to see that the problem was that he wanted a number-10 jersey. I used sign language and said to him: "Zero fello offo!"'

Bill McLaren gave me a typically thoughtful appraisal of perhaps Ireland's most famous prop: 'At 5 ft 11 in. and 15 st. 8 lb, he proved one of the most feared scrummagers in the world game during his 13 years (1962–75) of international rugby for Ireland, when he merited a reputation as a strongman who frequently buried or lifted opposing props with a combination of physical hardness and technical knowhow. He might be described as the thinking man's prop, for here was a bright, intelligent fellow with a science degree from University College Dublin, who made a study of the mechanics of scrummaging, then applied them to his work at the Irish coalface. On the 1971 Lions tour, he was pack leader until he got injured. When Willie John McBride took over that role, he followed in McLoughlin's tradition of playing with fire and fury. That might be why Willie John and Colin Meads had a rare old set-to in one of the Tests with punches flying but, at the end, they left the field together, and each had a huge respect for the other. That too was in the tradition and ethos of Ray McLoughlin.'

McLoughlin's status in the game was reflected when I invited Ollie Campbell to pick his world dream team from his own era. That team is:

15. Serge Blanco (France)
14. Gerald Davies (Wales) 13. Tim Horan (Australia)
12. Mike Gibson (Ireland) 11. David Campese (Australia)
10. Barry John (Wales)
9. Gareth Edwards (Wales)
1. Ray McLoughlin (Ireland) 2. Tommy Lawton (Australia)
3. Graham Price (Wales)
4. Colin Meads (New Zealand, captain) 5. John Eales (Australia)
6. Ian Kirkpatrick (New Zealand) 8. Murray Mexted (New Zealand) 7. Michael Jones (New Zealand)
Coach: Carwyn James (Wales)

53

A RENAISSANCE MAN
PAUL McNAUGHTON

Who played in Lansdowne Road, Dalymount Park and Croke Park in the one year?

For years, this has been a standard pub-quiz question. The answer is former Irish centre and current Irish team manager Paul McNaughton. In the one year, he played rugby in Lansdowne Road, played for Shelbourne in an FAI Cup final and played for Wicklow against Louth in the Leinster Senior Championship. As an international, 'Macker' was a class apart because he had the lot: good hands, strength in the tackle, exceptional in the air, elusive on the break and, most importantly, the self-belief to 'go for it' from anywhere. He – more than anyone else – put Greystones on the rugby map. Initially, though, he showed promise as a Gaelic footballer and hurler, and later at soccer, but then rugby entered his life:

'Gerry Doyle saw me playing and asked me to sign for Shelbourne, and essentially I was semi-professional for them for three years, but, as well as playing Gaelic football during the summer, I also started playing for a great Wanderers team. It wasn't always easy to keep both going simultaneously. There was one weekend when on the Saturday I played rugby in the Leinster Cup semi-final and on the Sunday I played in the FAI Cup final. The following weekend, on the Saturday, I was due to play in the Leinster Cup final and, on the Sunday, the replay of the FAI Cup final. As a result of an ankle injury, I missed out on the rugby game but, as it was the last game of the season, I took a cortisone injection and played in the soccer match only for us to lose 1–0 to Cork Hibs.

'One of the most memorable moments was playing for Shelbourne against Manchester United. They had signed Paddy Roche from us and part of the deal was that they would travel over to Dublin to play us in a friendly. My immediate opponent was Gordon McQueen and Martin Buchan was playing alongside him. Gerry Daly was in their midfield and Stuart Pearson was up front. He got their goal in a 1–1 draw.'

The realities of working life meant that McNaughton had to make hard choices, as he explains, 'After college, I decided to restrict my sporting activities and concentrate on rugby – though not fully to the exclusion of soccer. I won my first cap against Scotland in 1978.'

The high point of Paul's career in the green jersey came Down Under: 'Winning the two Tests in Australia in 1979 was an incredible achievement, especially when you consider our track record of defeats in the Southern Hemisphere since. With all the fuss about the dropping of Tony Ward, people may have missed out on how good our performances were.

'The tour provided the funniest moment in my rugby career. The night before the First Test, we had a team meeting. Our coach, Noel "Noisy" Murphy, always got very worked up when he spoke at these meetings. The problem was that he generally said the same thing each time. He always started with: "This is the most important match you will ever play for Ireland." The night before the first Test, sure enough, Murphy's first words were: "This is the most important match you will ever play." We were just after eating dinner and the room was very warm because there were 25 of us. Murphy was talking away for about five minutes and, just as he said, "Jesus Christ, ye're wearing the Irish jersey and do you realise this is the most important f**king game you will ever play?", there was a massive snore. It was, of course, Willie Duggan. Murphy said, "F**k it. I'm not doing this." Then he stormed out.

'In 1981, at the start of the season, I announced that I was emigrating to America at the end of the Six Nations. I was only 27 and at the peak of my playing career but my friends could not believe I was turning my back on my playing career. I felt lousy the following year when Ireland won the Triple Crown. It was minus 25 degrees in Chicago and I listened to the decisive match against Scotland on the BBC World Service.

'I actually played a lot of rugby in America. One of the players I came up against was the legendary South African out-half Naas Botha. One of my coaches was a then unknown South African, Kitch Christie, who steered his native country to their World Cup victory in 1995. When I returned to Ireland in 1985, I immediately started playing junior rugby with Greystones. In my first game, my brother threw me literally a hospital pass and I fractured my skull!'

54

SUPERMAC
HUGO MacNEILL

Capped thirty-seven times for Ireland, Hugo MacNeill scored eight international tries, a record then for a full-back, making him perhaps Ireland's greatest attacking full-back of all time. Having won his first full cap against France in 1981, he was one of only six players to play in all six matches of the 1982 and 1985 Triple Crown victories and he won three Test caps on the 1983 Lions' tour of New Zealand.

Having been a virtual novice in 1982, MacNeill was one of the more senior players when Ireland regained the Triple Crown in 1985.

'That year, there was a great uncertainty and apprehension before the Scotland game. We had no recognised place kicker and had such a young side. After our win, there was so much excitement and freshness that no one could sit down. I had come through the schools and universities with these guys and I really enjoyed the buzz.'

What caused Ireland's star to wane so dramatically the following season?

'We won the Triple Crown playing good rugby, but I think we got complacent the following season. If you look back at our matches in 1985, we could have lost all of those matches. We had a lot of good fortune. In 1986, we were not going to surprise people playing more of the same. We needed to advance our game but we didn't.'

Ireland's form in the post-Mick Doyle era slumped dramatically, culminating in a humiliating 35–3 defeat at Twickenham in 1988. At least the match generated one of the most celebrated stories in recent Irish rugby folklore. MacNeill went AWOL during the game. Although Ireland went in with a 3–0 lead at half-time, they were slaughtered in the second half. When the second half started, Hugo was not there and nobody knew where he was. The joke after the game was that he went in to make a phone call. By the time he came back onto the pitch, they had run in for two tries! MacNeill was involved in a similar situation in a match against France. What was the explanation for these incidents?

'It's the usual story of making a mountain out of a molehill. What happened in both cases was that I picked up head injuries in the first half and had to go off with Mick Molloy for treatment. In the French match, I returned with my head strapped so I could never understand the mystery.'

Hugo is well able to tell stories against himself: 'I was in Malahide with Ollie Campbell at a festival or something in 1982. It was not long after the Triple Crown and we had a very high profile then. At one point, I was conscious of a group of girls looking at us. I heard murmurs of: "Yes, it is." "No, it isn't."

'Shortly afterwards, I felt someone tap me on the shoulder. It was a young lady who asked me if I was Hugo MacNeill, the Irish rugby player. When I said I was, she turned around and went back to her friends. I heard her whisper: "Jaysus, I've never been so disappointed in all my life. He's nowhere near as good-looking in real life as he is on television!"

'Ollie's biggest problem is that he can't say no when people ask him to do them a favour. I rang him up one night and put on an accent and told him I was Mick Fitzgerald from Irish Marketing Ltd and was organising a beauty competition for nurses and that I wanted him to be one of the judges, knowing full well that he would hate that kind of thing. He sighed and sighed, struggling to come up with a plausible excuse. Eventually, he asked me what date the contest was. When I gave him the date, he said, "Oh, that's an awful shame. I'm really sorry but I have another function on that night. It's such a pity because I always wanted to judge a beauty contest."

'"That's no problem, Ollie," I replied. "You see, one of the prizes we are going to offer is a night out with Ollie Campbell. We'll pay for everything and it'll be first class all the way."

'"Gosh, I'm afraid I'm going to have a lot of commitments around that time. I won't have many nights free."

'"But that's the beauty of this, Ollie, we'll arrange it for any night that suits you!"

'The panic was getting ever more noticeable in his voice and I could visualise him writhing in his chair as he tried to find a way to back out of it. Eventually, he said he was backing away from that type of thing. Then I asked him if there were any of his colleagues who would be willing to do that kind of thing. He blurted out my name immediately and provided my phone number faster than you could say Tony Ward!

'Another time I was down in Cork with Moss Finn, Donal Lenihan and Michael Kiernan, and we were having lunch with five or six rugby fans. In any other place in Ireland, sports fans would have passed the time by picking their greatest-ever Irish team. Not so in Cork. They picked the worst-ever Irish team! I kept my head down as they discussed the merits of three of my predecessors for the position, expecting to have my name mentioned at any minute. After they made their choice for full-back, I remarked with relief: "I suppose I can relax now."

'Quick as a flash, someone said, "Hang on, boy, we haven't picked the subs yet!"'

55

OUR FRIENDS FROM THE NORTH
PHILIP MATTHEWS

Philip Matthews made his international debut against Australia in 1984. How did he hear about his selection?

'I was taking a tutorial of undergraduates in Queens and I knew the team was due to be announced. I felt I deserved to be selected, but it's one thing to feel that you ought to be picked and another to have the selectors think the same way. I rang the sports department at the *Ulster Newsletter* and asked was the Irish team chosen yet. They replied, "Who wants to know?" When I told them, they said congratulations, so I knew I was in.

'I have a clear memory of the crowd's roar as I ran onto Lansdowne Road for my debut. It was louder than it ever seemed afterwards. I'll never forget the hair standing on the back of my head, the leg-draining and the tongue-drying emotion. It was the speed of the game that I found hardest to adjust to.'

That day was to prove the most significant in Matthews' life, because at the post-match reception he met the daughter of former great Kevin Flynn, Lisa Flynn – the woman who would become his wife. Love stories begin in Irish rugby!

Matthews cringes at the memory: 'I was in a bit of a drunken haze at the time. I remember I was also introduced to Kevin that night and I doubt if he was very impressed. I'm pretty sure that he didn't want his daughter falling for a drunken yob! I asked Lisa to be my guest at the dinner after our next home international against England. I almost forgot about it but the rest of the lads reminded me and told me that, as a former chairman of selectors, it would not be a good idea for my international future to let his daughter down!'

There is a definite 'if only' tone to his voice as he recalls his Triple Crown triumph in 1985: 'To be honest, the magic of the whole thing largely passed me by. I regret it didn't happen later in my career, when I would have appreciated it much more. My attitude in those games was: "We beat them. Let's get off before the crowd come on." After we won the Triple Crown, I went back to Belfast. The average man on the street there was not too pushed but I know the guys down in Cork and Limerick were being feted like heroes.

'We had a nice bonus after that, with a tour to Japan. It was a fabulous place to travel. We were not really seriously challenged on the playing field. It is such a hospitable nation. Every reception we went to, we got some kind of gift. It was the closest I've ever been to being like one of the Beatles. Every time we played a match, we were mobbed by schoolgirls in the same way they mob Sumo wrestlers.

'I missed all the games the following year because of injury. We had a more mature team in 1987 and should have won the Triple Crown. The World Cup was a big disappointment. We weren't mentally prepared for the Welsh game. My clearest memory of that match was getting stamped on by Paul Moriarty. Doyler's illness should have been a rallying force but it wasn't.'

Doyle was succeeded by Matthews' great friend Jimmy Davidson but his reign ended in failure, as Matthews recalls: 'Very few people can coach players from one to fifteen but Jim could. It was a shame his period as coach didn't reap greater rewards. In the end, it wasn't working. If he had the team he wanted, playing the style he wanted, I think he would have been a success but, because he wasn't a selector, he didn't have that freedom. The compromise he was forced into did nobody any favours. There was also a personality problem of sorts. Some of the non-Ulster players never seemed to click with him and that made a difficult situation almost impossible.'

Matthews found himself Irish captain, but in some respects he sees it as a poisoned chalice: 'I looked on the captaincy as a burden. I wanted to make sure that I could be there for the rest of the lads. Perhaps my own game suffered in the process.'

As a result of his selection as Irish captain, Matthews became a hot favourite to captain the 1989 Lions tour to New Zealand but it was not to be.

'Missing out on the Lions tour was the biggest disappointment of my career. All the hype in the media for the year before was saying that not only was I a certainty for selection but I would also be captain. When Ronnie Dawson rang me to tell me I would not be travelling, it was a real bombshell.'

56

THE MAYNE ATTRACTION
BLAIR MAYNE

Second-row forward Lieutenant Colonel Robert Blair Mayne won six caps for Ireland between 1937 and 1939. With his massive frame, gained from years of lifting weights, his finest hour was the Lions' tour of South Africa in 1938, in which he played twenty tour matches, including three Tests, although, curiously, he was the only member of the party not to score on the tour. He also became Irish Universities boxing champion. He was awarded three bars on the DSO and was given the *Légion d'honneur* for his sterling service during the Second World War in North Africa.

Craving excitement, he had enlisted in the British army in 1940 and found himself deployed in the desert in North Africa under General Auchinleck, and later General Bernard Montgomery, in what was known as the Eighth Army. The opposition was formidable because the Germans were masterminded by the 'Desert Fox', Field Marshal Erwin Rommel, and his Afrika Korps wreaked havoc on the British forces before the decisive battle of El Alamein on 23 October 1942. At one point, Mayne had come very close to capturing Rommel.

The incident was subsequently the basis of a lengthy conversation with his international teammate Con Murphy: 'I asked him what he would have done if he caught Rommel. He told me without blinking an eyelid: "I would have slit his throat."

'The way he said it, I don't think he was joking. After joining the SAS, his speciality was in night raids behind enemy lines, where he destroyed 130 enemy aircraft all by himself. No less a person than Field Marshal Montgomery recommended Blair for the Victoria Cross after he saved a squadron of troops pegged down by heavy gunfire. He was some man because he lifted the wounded one by one and put them in his jeep. At the same time, he was mowing down the enemy. He was fond of a drink and it was so sad that he died so young, at just 40, after he drove his sports car into a lorry after having a few drinks too many.'

Murphy shared the reason for his admiration of Mayne with me, as he showed me an imposing picture of his great friend when I visited his home in Dublin. His face lit up like a Christmas tree as he told me, 'Because I was so small, the opposition often tried to intimidate me and sometimes tried to take me out of the game. Whenever anyone "did me damage", Blair would come and pick me up and say, "Are you OK, little man? I'll sort him out for you."

'The first chance he got, he took revenge for the assault on me and I was left alone for the rest of the game.'

Murphy got to know Mayne's heroes well: 'Blair was a big fan of Sam Walker, who was Ireland's second captain of the Lions on their 1938 tour of South Africa. History was made in the last match of the Test series, when all eight Irishmen in the panel played on the winning Lions team. Later a BBC commentator, Walker died suddenly in 1972.

'Next on his list was Bob Alexander, an exciting flanker, noted for his dribbling, who won 11 international rugby caps for Ireland between 1936 and 1939. [Alexander also played fourteen times, including all three Test matches, on the Lions tour, scoring more tries than any other forward on the tour – six. He also played cricket for Ireland, when, as a right-hand batsman and bowler, he took 29 runs in a Test match in 1932. While serving as a captain in the Royal Enniskillen Fusiliers in Burma, he was killed in action at the age of 33.]

'Blair also was a huge fan of [the winner of the 1987 Digital RWI Hall of Fame award] Mark Sugden – the master of the dummy. Sugden has become part of Irish rugby legend, particularly after he sold four dummies on the way to his winning try in 1929, the first time Ireland beat England at Twickenham.

'The biggest influence, albeit indirectly, on Sugden's career was Harry Thrift, who won 18 caps for Ireland in the opening decade of the last century. He captained Ireland once, in 1908 against England, because that day Ireland had seven players from Trinity in the side, the greatest twentieth-century representation in the international team. He was also an international-class sprinter. When Sugden was playing out-half for Trinity, Thrift came up to him and said, "Sugden, you're the worst fly-half I've ever seen. Why don't you take up snooker?"

'Sugden switched to scrum-half and the rest is history. He formed a lethal combination with the Simon Geoghegan of the 1920s, Dr Denis Cussen. A natural crowd pleaser, Cussen won fifteen caps on the wing for Ireland, scoring five tries. He also represented Ireland in the 100 metres in the 1928 Olympics in Amsterdam and was the first Irishman to break 10 seconds in the distance. Sugden also played cricket for Trinity, where he lined out alongside Samuel Beckett. Blair always said that Mark's dummies were so brilliant that you'd think you had the ball in your hands yourself. It was all in the way he used his eyes.'

57

NEVER RUN OF THE MILL
SYD MILLAR

Bill McLaren, the voice of rugby, was well able to tell stories against himself. During the 1987 World Cup, he introduced his wife, Bette, to leading rugby administrator Syd Millar. Syd took one look at Bill, one at Bette, and then said, 'Ah, Jaysus, Bette, you could have done a hell of a sight better!'

Between 1958 and 1970, Ballymena's Syd Millar won thirty-seven caps as a prop-forward for Ireland and toured with the Lions to New Zealand in 1959 and to South Africa in both 1962 and 1968, playing in nine Tests. In 1973, he began a three-year stint as coach to the Irish team, and the high point of his tenure came in 1974 when Ireland won a rare and much coveted Championship. He was succeeded by former Leinster prop Roly Meates. In 1974, Millar and his great friend Willie John McBride had their sterling services to Irish rugby acknowledged when a room was named in their honour in the Ballymena clubhouse.

Millar managed the Lions on the tour to South Africa in 1980 when Ireland had the singular distinction of supplying both the coach (Noel Murphy) and the manager.

John Robbie has fond memories of him from that trip: 'At one stage, quite near the end, we were all called into a special meeting. Syd Millar addressed us and asked if were unhappy, as he had read reports to that effect. We all said we were having a whale of time. He then asked us if we would all return to tour South Africa if selected. Ironically enough, I was the only player who indicated that I would have to think about it; everyone else said they would. In fact, Peter Morgan, the young Welsh utility player who had played in only a few games on the tour, brought the house down by saying that he'd love to come back again, as next time they might let him have a game!'

Tony Ward had reason to be grateful to Millar: 'In 1987, I had dedicated everything to winning a place in the World Cup squad and trained very hard for it. Paul Dean was the man in possession at that time and I found myself on the bench for the start of the Five

Nations. Unquestionably the biggest disappointment of my career, bigger even than Australia, if not as traumatic or as long lasting, was being dropped from the reserves bench for Ireland's match against France that season. After Ireland lost to Scotland, Ralph Keyes was selected ahead of me on the replacements. I would have thought even I could have done nothing wrong from the bench! In an article in the London *Times*, George Ace wrote, "The bench in Irish rugby is as dangerous as the trapdoor on a scaffold – you can disappear into oblivion might quickly."

'In fairness, Ralph had been showing good form for Cork Constitution and Munster but that was the ultimate low point for me. I had always managed to put my disappointments behind me up to that point, but I felt I could take no more after that and made up my mind to retire from representative rugby. However, a phone call from one of the Irish management at the behest of Syd Millar caused me to change my mind – but, boy, did I need convincing! He said that if I bit my tongue and did nothing hasty, everything would work out OK. He was correct and I was recalled to the bench for the next international. Of course, it was totally unfair on Ralph, but it highlighted the lack of logic in selection decisions.'

Asked about his outstanding memory from his Irish days, Barry McGann pauses only briefly: 'It was towards the final days of my international career. I was a sub for Mick Quinn at the time. Syd Millar was the coach then. I had the reputation of being a very laidback player but I was serious when I needed to be. Because of work, I was late for a training session, although genuinely I got there as quickly as I could. The training session at Anglesea Road was in full swing when I arrived. I went over and apologised to Syd for being late and asked him what he wanted me to do. I had a strong feeling he didn't believe I had made much of an effort to be there, but he told me to warm up. Instinctively, I rubbed my hands together and blew on them and said, "OK, coach, I'm ready."

'Moss Keane was in stitches but I'll never forget the bemused look on Syd's face. I think that incident probably cost me ten caps!'

58

MILLER'S CROSSING
ERIC MILLER

In 1997, Eric Miller seemed set to become one of the biggest names in world rugby. His career, though, had more twists than a Hitchcock thriller.

'I only began rugby when I went to Wesley College, and, after I left school, I went to play with Leicester. At the time, I wanted to be a PE teacher, so I also attended Loughborough University, which was nearby. Bob Dwyer came in as head coach with a new approach and he brought me into the first team. Dwyer had coached Australia to the World Cup in 1991.

'Within a fairly short time, I was invited to a training camp with the Irish squad in the Algarve towards the end of Murray Kidd's reign. It rained for the week! Out of the blue, I was picked for Ireland for the Italian game at the start of 1997. It happened so fast and I played for most of the Six Nations, although we didn't have the backline we have now and we didn't do as well as we have done recently.'

Then Miller found himself making headlines throughout the rugby world. 'To everyone's surprise, I was selected for the Lions that year, the first tour to South Africa after the end of apartheid in that country. The Springboks had won the 1995 World Cup and this was the first Lions tour of the professional era. I was only 21. I was the baby of the group by a few years. Scotland's Alan Tait really took me under his wing. He wore the number-11 shirt in the Tests. I got on very well with him. Things didn't work out for me as I would have liked. I got picked for the first Test but I got badly sick and they ruled me out the day after the side was announced. I was gutted. It is a day I will never forget. When you're that young, you think you'll get chances like that again, but, as you get older, you realise opportunities like that don't come around too often and you become aware of just how much you missed out on. Tim Rodber got my place and they were never going to change a winning team. I played really well between the first and second Test and got a place on the bench. I did get a run in the second Test, but in the backs, because there was no one else to go on. Jeremy Guscott had just got his famous drop goal and we were three points up with five or ten minutes to go. There was a lot of injury time and it was backs-to-the-wall stuff. I made a few tackles but never really got my hands to the ball. I damaged my quad muscle but I only discovered it when the euphoria of winning the match and the series died down. There were a few injuries before the third Test and I would have been playing had I not been injured myself. It was a run of bad luck.

'People have said that it happened too soon. My attitude was better that than not happen at all. It was a learning curve. Most people going on tour have baggage but I had none. I was there as a free spirit and that was great.

'It was a come-down afterwards and there was a lot I had to deal with in subsequent years, like the '99 World Cup when I wasn't first choice, and I had to get to grips with the injuries. I had played a lot of games on the Lions tour. I played when I was battered and bruised, and that did take its toll. I had a difficult season after that. In the second half of the season, Bob Dwyer stopped picking me for Leicester. I returned to Leinster because I felt I didn't have any balance in my life. The provincial structure was getting better here and I missed my friends and family. I always wonder, if things had been going well in Leicester would I have stayed – or should I have stayed?

'My lowest point was probably the 2003 World Cup. I was not getting a start for the big games, even though I was after playing really well. I scored two tries against Namibia and felt really strong. I was prepared not to be picked against Australia, but it was a real low time because I felt I deserved to be selected. I also missed out on the Triple Crown in 2004 with a shoulder injury, which was very disappointing, as I had been playing well before the injury.'

59

HISTORY MAKER
DICK MILLIKEN

Probably the greatest tribute to Dick Milliken's quality as a centre was that both he and his partner Ian McGeechan deprived Mike Gibson of a Test place on the 1974 Lions tour. His four Test appearances on that historic series best reflect his ability, as a protracted ankle injury ended his Irish career prematurely.

Like all the players in the squad, Milliken bought into Willie John McBride's philosophy that the Lions would 'take no prisoners' and 'get our retaliation in first'. As McBride explained to me, 'My experience on previous Lions tours had taught me that in provincial games you tend to have a bit of thuggery to soften up the tourists. Before the match against Eastern Province, I told the side that I was expecting trouble. I said to them, "Tomorrow, if anything happens, we are all in it together – and I mean all. You hit the guy that is nearest to you as hard as you can whether he has done anything wrong or not. If that doesn't stop it, you haven't hit him hard enough."

'My attitude was: hurt one of us and you hurt us all, so we'll stop it there and then. Initially, the signal I came up with was "999", the traditional alert for all emergency services, but the feeling among us was that 999 was too long, so we cut it down to 99 as an emergency measure when things looked like getting out of hand. On my signal, all 15 Lions would "take on" their nearest opponent, not only to show the South Africans that they were not going to back down, but also to reduce the risks of a sending-off as the referee was highly unlikely to dismiss an entire team. The call was used twice in the bruising third Test but was only used as a last resort.

'There is no question but that Gareth Edwards was one of the best players in the world at the time. So, if there was any thuggery, he was always likely to be targeted. At one stage during the game, he got a thump on the back of his head after he had passed the ball. Within seconds, about half the Eastern Province team were sprawling on the ground. They literally didn't know what hit them. An important marker had been put down for the rest of the tour.

'You might say we were under house arrest even before we left home. We came under tremendous pressure, spending three days in London, where the anti-apartheid movement asked us to pull out of the tour. I met the players and told them, "If you don't want to come, please leave now." There wasn't a sound. It seemed like for ever, but after a couple of moments I could wait no longer and said, "OK, then, we are all in this together."

'That was the biggest challenge of my life, trying to get coalminers from Wales and solicitors from London to mix together. Cracks could have appeared in the squad when we divided into a Test side and a midweek side, but those problems never arose because we kept on winning. I especially remember, after Alan Old broke his leg, Phil Bennett came along to say to me, "Don't worry, I'll play as often you need me."

'When we won the first two Tests, we had the Springboks reeling. I think they made ten changes in all for the third Test. That was the big one because it meant that if we won that match, we won the series.

'When I walked into the room where the team had gathered, the air was full of electricity. Usually, I would talk about the importance of the game and the reasons for wanting to win. But this time I simply asked, "Men, are we ready?"

'They looked up. They were ready.

'The first 20 minutes or so were probably the toughest of the whole tour. The pressure on us was terrible. People expected us to win, which can be fatal for any team. We made it hard on ourselves by making mistakes we'd never made before. However, we finally got it together and won 26–9.

'The feeling of greatness in that side was unbelievable. Dick Milliken deserved his place in such a team of stars. He was an outstanding player and would have gone on to even greater heights had he not had such a hard time with injuries.'

Johnny Moloney recalls one aspect of Milliken's involvement on that tour: 'There was an incredible bond on that tour from day one. No one could identify any single factor for this. There were no cliques on the team. It was the fabled "all for one and one for all". The only "particular friendship" I recall that developed was between Dick Milliken and Ian McGeechan. Dick was a hell of a player.'

60

HEALING HANDS
MICK MOLLOY

Dr Mick Molloy is almost unique among former Irish rugby internationals. He was raised in Cornamona, Co. Galway, as a native Irish speaker. The late 'Locky' Butler had been the only other international who spoke fluent Irish. Molloy was capped twenty-seven times over an eleven-year period between 1966 and 1976, most of them in partnership with Willie John McBride, and scored two international tries.

His rugby career only began when he went to Garbally College in Ballinasloe. 'At Garbally, I came under the influence of a wonderful coach and educationalist, Father Ryle. At one stage, he persuaded Harold Connolly, an Irish-American who was then the world champion hammer thrower, to come to the school to give us a demonstration. Another time he persuaded no less a player than Cliff Morgan to give us a coaching lesson. Such was his desire to learn that he was constantly seeking new ideas. He got permission from his bishop to attend the 1960 Olympics but the bishop attached a condition to the trip: Father Ryle was forbidden from watching the women swimming, in case his morals were corrupted!'

After making his mark with UCG and Connacht, Molloy was chosen to make his debut in that most intimidating of venues, Paris, in 1966. In the final trial, the Probables had won 30–3 and were selected en bloc. As was the norm, the match ended in an Irish defeat.

'There were a number of players who were a big help to me: Ray McLoughlin, Noel Murphy, Willie John McBride and Mick Doyle. Doyler was a very knowledgeable player. I got a lot of conflicting advice on what to do with my first ball but my Gaelic football experiences helped me no end. I caught the ball cleanly, marked it and kicked it well.

'We had a great team in the late 1960s. Yet we never won a Triple Crown because we lacked a top-class penalty kicker. There is absolutely no doubt in my mind that, if we had had the good fortune to have Ollie Campbell on our side at the time, we would have won at least one.'

Molloy also played rugby at county level for Surrey. He downplays the suggestion that Connacht players, especially those who continued to play for Connacht clubs at the time, found it very hard to get their place on the team: 'I knew that I would have to work very hard to hold my place. I was very careful about my diet. In fact, my problem was putting on weight! Willie John was always at least two stone heavier than me. I trained on my own and did a lot of work with weights, which gave me the strength I needed. My strength was in the loose and my mobility. I used to run five or ten miles a day, which in retrospect was useless to me.

'The highlight of my career was when we beat Australia 11–5 in 1967 in Sydney. We were the first international team to win in Australia. A disappointment for me that year was that I lost out on the opportunity to play the All Blacks when our proposed international had to be cancelled because of an outbreak of foot-and-mouth disease.

'The disadvantage for me was that I found it hard to get time off work for rugby. I had to do a lot of night duty, and, when I toured Australia in 1967 and Argentina in 1970, all my holidays went for those years on the tours. The Argentinean tour in particular was great fun. As we were Irish and largely Catholic, there was a great reception for us. What amazed me the most is that we met people who were no more than third-generation Irish and yet they were speaking in Roscommon and Galway accents. At one stage, I thought I was back in the West of Ireland!'

61

JOHNNY B. GOODE
JOHNNY MOLONEY

Johnny Moloney was a very single-minded player. In a schoolboy match, he was charging through for a try when a despairing dive by his marker robbed him of his shorts. True to form, he raced through for the try in his underpants before worrying about getting new togs! Moloney was a much underrated player, even though he won 27 caps for Ireland. He was the ultimate third wing-forward. With his athletic build, his work rate around the field and his ability to read the game, his impact was phenomenal, and his peers rate him as one of the best all-round tactical scrum-halfs they played with.

Moloney recalls winning his first cap against France in 1972: 'The joy of being selected for Ireland was heightened for me because my St Mary's clubmate Tom Grace was also picked on the team. Our careers overlapped a lot. Gracer really had a great will to win. I remember in a match for Ireland against England he was up against David Duckham, who came into the match with a great reputation. The first time he got the ball, Gracer ran into him and knocked Duckham clean over. Every time Duckham touched the ball that day, he dropped it. It was one of the best examples of a player psyching out an opponent I have ever seen. Duckham wasn't at the races that day and Gracer came out a clear winner.

'I can't remember much about the build-up to my first cap. I'm naturally a very calm person but that quality was accentuated that week. I recall that there was a wonderful dinner after the match. The French subs were in great singing voice.

'I was one of five new caps, with Tom Grace on the right wing, Wallace McMaster on the left, Con Feighery in the second row and Stewart McKinney at wing-forward. I always think of that side as a team of three fives. The five new caps, five senior stars – Tom Kiernan, Kevin Flynn, Mike Gibson, Willie John McBride and Ray McLoughlin – and five rising stars – Fergus Slattery, Ken Kennedy, Barry McGann and my two clubmates Denis Hickie and Seán Lynch. It was an ideal blend.'

With typical modesty, Moloney makes no mention of the fact that he scored the first of his four international tries on his debut. In the process, he became the first player to score a 4-point try for Ireland, helping his country to a 14–9 win at Colombes.

Moloney's rugby memories are almost all happy ones: 'The one regret, I suppose, was that we didn't win a Triple Crown. I think, were it not for the Troubles, we would have won it in 1972 when Scotland and Wales refused to travel to play us, because we won both our away matches to France and England, and the Welsh were a coming side rather than the dominant force they were later in the decade. Having said that, winning the International Championship in 1974 was great and being selected on the Lions' tour to South Africa was fantastic.'

The highlight of Moloney's career was being chosen to lead his country: 'I have much stronger memories of being made captain of Ireland than of my first cap. I was not selected for the final trial that season. John Robbie and Colin Patterson were the two scrum-halfs. I came on at half-time but did not have a great game. The convention at the time was that the team for the first international of the season was announced the evening of the trial. All the players in contention for selection gathered that evening. To be honest, in light of my performance in the trial, I was certain I would not be selected. Reluctantly, I went along just to observe the proprieties. I was stunned to discover not alone had I been selected but that I was made captain!'

One figure looms large in Moloney's comic reminiscences of his days with Ireland: 'We were playing England away. Stewart McKinney went through the pages of *Mayfair* magazine and saw the number of an escort service. He rang it up and booked a lady of the night for Mick Quinn. I had to play my part by keeping Quinny in his room and slipping out just before she was due to arrive. I only know this from hearsay, you understand, but she was wearing a raincoat with nothing on underneath but suspenders and some very skimpy underwear. Quinny had to pay her £25 just to get her out of the room. After she left, he came out into the corridor and everyone in the squad was looking out from their rooms laughing at him. It was the only time I ever saw him lost for words!'

62

HAIR-RAISING
BILL MULCAHY

One of the most curious features of Irish rugby is that everyone refers to former Irish captain Bill Mulcahy as 'Wiggs', yet hardly anybody seems to know the origin of his nickname. So was Mulcahy 'follically challenged' as a young man and had he recourse to a hairpiece?

'I deny that categorically! In fact, what happened is that as a boy I did a lot of doodling in my copy books. One of them was Wig-wam and my school friends decided that should be my nickname. Over the years, that became abbreviated to Wiggs.'

Mulcahy was born in Rathkeale, Co. Limerick, and was a doctor attached to the medical centre at Aer Lingus. He won Leinster Cup medals with Bective Rangers and a Munster Cup medal with Bohemians in 1962. A product of St Munchin's College in Limerick, there he learned the subtleties of the game, especially those carried on between broadly speaking consenting adults in the privacy of the scrum. He was capped on thirty-five occasions for Ireland between 1958 and 1965, captaining the team eight times between 1962 and 1964. His wife is a cousin of the golfer John O'Leary.

Bill is also noted for his quick wit. Once, when asked by Tony O'Reilly how he would like the ball thrown into the lineout, he replied, 'Low and crooked!'

Of all the people interviewed for this book, he was easily the most difficult to persuade because of his inherent modesty.

He made his international debut in 1958 in a historic match as part of the first-ever Irish team to defeat a touring side when Ireland beat Australia 9–6 at Lansdowne Road, thanks to a late try from Noel Henderson.

He has great memories of that time: 'It was a wonderful feeling to be on the Irish team. The previous season, I had played on the Probables side in the final trial but had been overlooked. That season, I was only on the Possibles but was selected. Your debut is always a tense affair. You've got a burning passion to do well but you run onto the field fearing that you will be a one-cap wonder rather than embarking on an illustrious international career.

'It was a tremendous experience, although I had to put off my finals. I had to sell this idea to my late mother, who was a widow, and she had more than a few misgivings about me putting my career on hold for the sake of rugby.'

Under the leadership of Ronnie Dawson, the fifth Irish player to captain a touring side, the 1959 Lions set an all-time record of 842 points and in the process ran in 165 tries. Mulcahy was one of six Irish players selected on the Lions tour. He was severely injured in a match against New South Wales after only nine games, and his loss to the side badly affected the strength of the scrum and was a significant contributory factor to the Lions' ultimate failure.

Mulcahy also recalls when he was honoured with the Irish captaincy: 'When I became captain, my big worry was that I would not be up to the job. The captain's role was very different then than it is now because we had no coach nor back-up team, so there was a lot of additional responsibilities. We had no squad sessions. Now everything is organised on a more professional basis.

'I was not an instant success at the job, to put it at its mildest. We went to Twickenham with nine new caps and got hammered 16–0. I think the sweetest moment of my career was going back to Twickers two years later and getting revenge in the best way possible by defeating them 18–5, especially because of Pat Casey's famous try under the posts. It was great that Kevin Flynn also got two tries that day. He was a wonderful player who was unlucky with injuries. It's probably true to say we hadn't a great side at the time but we had some great players. I especially remember Jerry Walsh's great commitment and I can still see him coming back from an international with two black eyes. As captain, it's important to work out your own style in terms of your own personality.'

Mulcahy laughs at the memory of one incident when he got into the spirit of things: 'After one of our trips to Paris, I was feeling very, very good at the reception, thanks to a large amount of wine. At one stage, I went out to the toilet and returned to the top table. I was chatting away in my amazingly dreadful French before I realised that I had got my directions totally wrong and instead of attending the rugby reception I was at a wedding!'

63

DOCTOR'S ORDERS
KARL MULLEN

Rugby is the only game where a man sticks his head up another man's bum and the referee allows it. Yet Irish rugby players have often had more specialist knowledge of human anatomy, as doctors played a prominent part in the golden era of Irish rugby. Apart from the peerless Jackie Kyle, there was team captain Old Belvedere's Karl Mullen. Mullen was one of Ireland's most successful captains, leading the side to their first Grand Slam in 1948, the Triple Crown in 1949 and the Championship in 1951. He also led the Lions in Australia and New Zealand in 1950.

For Jack Kyle, Mullen was an inspirational force: 'Karl was a wonderful captain. His greatest gift was to let the players play to the best of their potential. There were times, though, when he showed great tactical awareness. Before we played Wales in Swansea in 1949, he gathered us around and said, "We're going to run them into the ground."

'We had such a fit and fast back row in particular at the time that he knew we could wear them down and we did. There's a lot of talk today that "forward supremacy is the key", but at that time we were always able to win the battle of the packs, which made our job in the backs all that much easier.

'I especially remember the game against Wales at Ravenhill in front of a capacity crowd of 30,000. I'd say they could have taken four times as many had there been places for them. We were all understandably a bit apprehensive but deep down felt we could win. Karl made a point of getting the team to discuss tactics and the strengths and weaknesses of our opponents before matches. He made sure that every man had his say and it was an important part of the pre-match preparations from the point of view of contributing to the great team spirit. We also had a "council of war" at half-time and Karl kept us on the straight and narrow.'

Mullen spoke to me about the characters on that team: 'George Norton was probably the first Irishman to exhaustively practise place kicks. In his case, practice certainly made perfect. I was lucky enough to play with some great characters like Barney Mullan, who scored the first try in our Grand Slam run. He was a very colourful personality and a powerful, stocky runner. Another was John Smith, the prop from Queen's University. I remember listening to him being interviewed for the radio. He was asked on what side he played in the scrum. In his best Northern accent, he replied, "Sometimes I play on the right side, sometimes I play on the left side – but not right and left at the same time!"'

Mullen's successor as Irish captain, Des O'Brien, had a very personal memory of Karl: 'In my first two years, the players were not allowed any tickets even to buy! Before the Scotland game in Dublin in 1949, Karl Mullen was offered two tickets to buy for his parents. The team decided no tickets, no game, and there was quite a scene in the Shelbourne on the Friday night – Karl got his tickets and after that the IRFU agreed, with reluctance, to let us buy two tickets each. Big deal!'

In August 2004, Karl Mullen was catapulted back into the media spotlight when his grandson, Cian O'Connor, won a gold medal at the Athens Olympics in showjumping.

Long after his retirement as a player, Mullen was involved in one of the most famous incidents in Irish rugby. During a match he was attending, Phil O'Callaghan, one of the great folk heroes of Irish rugby, was in the thick of the action. The Old Wesley and Leinster player Bobby Macken joined Dolphin for a season, and went back to Dublin the following year. When he next played against Dolphin, Philo was standing on the wing as usual, when Macken came charging towards him, but, to O'Callaghan's surprise, he tapped the ball into touch.

Philo asked him, 'Are you afraid of me, Bobby?'

'No, but I'm afraid of running into your mouth!' he replied.

After Philo put out his shoulder, Karl Mullen was to experience his tongue at first hand when he ran on the pitch to give him medical care. Dr Mullen said, 'I'll put it back, but I warn you it will be painful.' He did and it was.

According to the story, Philo was screaming his head off with the pain. The doctor turned to him and said, 'You should be ashamed of yourself. I was with a 16-year-old girl this morning in the Rotunda as she gave birth and there was not even a word of complaint from her.'

Philo replied, 'I wonder what she bloody well would have said if you tried putting the f**kin' thing back in.'

64

FINE AND ANDY
ANDY MULLIGAN

On the day Ireland beat Scotland in 1958, Jack Kyle won his 46th cap to establish a world record of international appearances. Jack's scrum-half partner that day was Andy Mulligan, the eighth man to partner Kyle at half-back. He made his international debut against France in 1956 and won the last of his 22 caps against South Africa in 1961. He was one of ten Irish players to make the Lions' tour to New Zealand and Australia in 1959. The side was captained by Ronnie Dawson, and the eight other Irish players were Gordon Wood, Syd Millar, Bill Mulcahy, Noel Murphy, Tony O'Reilly, David Hewitt, Niall Brophy and Mick English, with Mulligan making the trip as a replacement to cover for injured players.

In recent years, Ireland have been spoiled for choice at scrum-half between Peter Stringer, Tomás O'Leary and Eoin Reddan. Mulligan had the misfortune to be around at a time when there was strong competition for the number-9 jersey.

Jim McCarthy notes that there was historical precedent for this: 'Sometimes we had two great players for the one position – most famously Tony Ward and Ollie Campbell. Johnny Hewitt was the second-best out-half in the British Isles during our glory years. He only won four caps for Ireland because he was around at the same time as Jack Kyle, but he would have walked on to any other team. The best passer of the ball I ever saw was John O'Meara but he had to contend in the latter stages of his career with a whippersnapper in Andy Mulligan. Andy was a fine player too and would have won even more caps had O'Meara not been around.'

Jack Kyle knew both Mulligan's and O'Meara's play intimately, but he was too diplomatic to give a straight answer when I asked him who was the best: 'In all my time playing for Ireland, planned tactics never came into it. I must have partnered eight or nine scrum-halfs in my time, and we'd just run out saying, "Let's do our best and see how it goes." All I would say is that both John and Andy were fine players.'

Bill Mulcahy gave me his take on Mulligan and O'Meara: 'The classic story told about Jack Kyle concerns John O'Meara's first cap, when he was to partner Jack at half-back. He was naturally a bit apprehensive about partnering the unquestioned best player in the world and was debating how he would address Jack. Should he call him Dr Kyle or Mr Kyle? John travelled up in the *Cork Examiner* van and walked meekly into the team hotel. Immediately he walked in the door, the first person to greet him was Jack who said, "Congratulations, Johnny. Delighted to see you here. Where would you like me to stand on the pitch?"

'Who else would have shown such modesty? With that confidence, it is no wonder that Johnny won so many caps for Ireland. Andy had the quality most needed in a scrum-half, which is bravery because you are in the front line. Andy was well able to deal with a big opponent coming around the corner.'

Bill McLaren testified to Mulligan's abilities on the field and off it: 'Ireland has always produced some wonderful entertainers. Tony O'Reilly and Andy Mulligan were famous for their antics. They had everybody in stitches for both Ireland and the Lions, especially with their simulation of the Queen's Christmas Day speech. They were both class players even if Mulligan never got the plaudits O'Reilly did.'

Jack Kyle greatly enjoyed some of the characters on the Irish team. He has a particular appreciation for the quick wit of Andy Mulligan, who once went up for a job from Dublin to Belfast and his prospective boss asked him, 'What religion are you, Mulligan?'

Quick as a flash, Andy responded, 'What religion did you have in mind, sir?'

Today's highly programmed game, which is dominated by patterns, is totally alien to Kyle: 'I remember my former teammate Andy Mulligan telling the story of an Irish team-talk given by my late brother-in-law Noel Henderson, when he was captain of Ireland: "Right, lads, let's decide how we're going to play this game. What do you think, Jack?"

'I responded, "A few wee punts at the line might be dandy, and maybe young Mulligan here can try a few darts of his own."

'Noel then sought Tony O'Reilly's opinion. O'Reilly replied, "The programme here says a midget's marking me. Just give me the ball and let me have a run at him."

'Then it was Cecil Pedlow's turn. Cec's answer was: "I think a subtle mix of runnin', jinkin' an' kickin' should just work out fine."

'Picking up the ball to go out, Noel summed up: "Right, lads, that's decided – Jack's puntin', Andy's dartin', Tony's runnin' and Cecil's doin' all three."'

65

NO SOFT CENTRE
BRENDAN MULLIN

Brendan Mullin was born in Israel because of his father's work with the United Nations. There, his sporting passion was soccer. It was not until second year at post-primary school that he came to live in Ireland. He was an outstanding schoolboy talent at Blackrock College, playing in a variety of positions on the wing, full-back and out-half. He also excelled at running and quickly established himself as a champion sprinter. Like Michael Kiernan, he was an athlete in the strictest sense of the word. That is one reason why they complemented each other so well and put pressure on the opposition. He won a record six Irish Schools caps in 1981 and 1982, captaining the side three times.

Mullin made his Irish debut against Australia in 1984, though he was not part of the original selection. An injury to Keith Crossan saw Michael Kiernan moving from the centre to the wing and Mullin stepped into Kiernan's place. How did he hear about his call-up to the international side?

'Mick Cuddy, who was an Irish selector then, rang my mother at home. I was in the middle of a lecture in Trinity at the time and I was shocked when my friend Mick Cooke called me out of the hall. It was a major breach of etiquette to disturb the rest of the class. It was years later before I got around to explaining the circumstances to my lecturer at the time.'

In 1985, Mullin was an ever-present in Ireland's Triple Crown side, scoring a try in the crunch match against England after he blocked down an attempted relieving kick from the English full-back.

'Morale was low after Ireland were whitewashed in the 1984 International Championships. Then "Dad's Army" was discarded and we came up with essentially a new and very young side. We played with a youthful innocence in 1985, almost arrogance. The whole season was fantastic. The Scottish match set us up well for the other games. We were losing with a minute to go but Trevor Ringland scored a try after a thrilling back movement and we won 18–15. The manner of our victory was almost as pleasing as the win itself because we played some sparkling rugby.

'The English game was a pretty torrid affair but we came out on top 13–10 with Michael Kiernan's late drop goal. That was the day Michael probably proved that he was a kicker of the highest class. We went into that campaign without a recognised place kicker, which was a big change for Ireland after the era of Ollie Campbell and Tony Ward. It was considered a big gamble but it certainly paid off. I've a soft spot for that game because I scored my first international try in that match. The following season, we were whitewashed. I think our opponents had spotted the weaknesses in our side; we had problems in the scrum and they exploited them to the full. We didn't get the bounce of the ball that season and could have won a couple of games.'

In 1989, Mullin was selected for the Lions' tour of Australia, winning one Test place, and he was the leading try scorer on the tour, with six tries. He remembers, 'Playing for the Lions was very special for me. It is the next step up after playing for your country.'

That same year, he was voted Irish Rugby Writers' Player of the Year. He also toured Japan in 1985 and Namibia in 1991, as well as playing in the World Cup in Australia and New Zealand in 1987 and South Africa in 1995.

He had to think carefully about returning to the international side: 'I was mentally tired in 1992 and work pressures were such that I felt I couldn't give rugby the commitment I needed to maintain my standard. I continued to play in a very good Blackrock side that, in a few years, went from playing in Division Two to a team that came close to winning the All-Ireland League. Meanwhile, the Irish international side seemed to be having problems in the backs. I was approached to make myself available for the Irish side. It was a difficult decision to come back on a number of levels. For a start, you are subjected to more severe scrutiny and greater criticism when you make a comeback. I worked harder to get myself into shape and I was glad I came back because I got the opportunity to captain my country. It was also a wonderful experience to compete in the World Cup in South Africa. They had the infrastructure in place, which really made it an enjoyable occasion for everyone. We had a great team spirit, though we didn't do ourselves justice in the final match.'

66

MURPHY'S LAW
CON MURPHY

When Ireland played France at Lansdowne Road on Saturday, 25 January 1947, they had 14 new caps in the side. The late Lansdowne full-back Con Murphy was the only capped player, having won three caps against England, Scotland and Wales in 1939, and was the only Irish international to survive the post-war era. He also played for Leinster before and after the Second World War, as well as in four of Ireland's unofficial internationals in 1946 and four times against the British army in 1943–5. Fittingly, Murphy's international swansong was in Ireland's record 22–0 defeat of England at Lansdowne Road. In an evaluation of Murphy's career, it is difficult to avoid the cliché 'small in stature but giant in performance'.

It was at soccer, though, that Murphy first made his mark. He played for Bohemians and was a junior soccer international. However, the most tense match he ever played in – even considering the Triple Crown decider – was in the altar boys' league. He laughed at the memory: 'Some of the lads who were supposed to be altar boys had whiskers on them!'

When I met him in his home shortly before he died, he was well into his eighties and his memory was not what it used to be. He had a particular problem with names but he seemed to find a new lease of life when he took me into the hall to see me out. I stopped to admire his impressive collection of photographs. This was the key that unlocked a tidal wave of memories of his playing days. He ran with the excitement of a boy playing his first match to provide a demonstration of the way he practised his skills with a paper ball. Lionel Messi would have been proud of the way he could still swivel. 'It's all about balance,' he said.

His passion for rugby was born while attending CUS school, particularly when he came under the tutelage of Ernie Crawford, who won 30 caps for Ireland, 15 as captain, as a full-back between 1920 and 1927, and was a noted tackler and handler. His enduring legacy to rugby today was the invention of the word 'alickadoo',

177

saying to a colleague who decided to read an oriental book rather than join in a game of poker, 'You and your bloody Ali Khadu!'

Murphy was now back on his feet, demonstrating the skill of tackling as he told me, 'Crawford taught me to tackle properly. When you look at players today, very few of them can tackle properly.'

Murphy's international debut came against England at Lansdowne Road in 1939. Ireland won 5–0 courtesy of a try from Harry McKibbin, which was converted by Sinclair Irwin. There followed a 12–3 victory over Scotland. That match featured an unusual event. Mike Sayers marked a Scottish drop-out and then dropped a goal from the mark. The Triple Crown was decided in wet weather at Ravenhill.

The match provided the nadir of Murphy's international career, and, as he relived the moment, a haunted look darkened his face: 'I can still see the ball coming down from the heavens as if it was yesterday. I missed the catch because of the slippy ball. They got a scrum and scored a try. That is the biggest regret of my rugby career because the Triple Crown literally slipped through my fingers. You don't get chances like that too often.'

Ireland lost 7–0 to Wales. One spectator in the crowd that day was Jack Kyle, who remembers, 'The war interrupted a great career for Con. He was a magnificent player. I vividly remember watching him play for Ireland and wondering if I would ever get the chance to wear the green jersey like him. At that time, of course, we had no television, so we learned about players like him on the radio. There was such excitement listening to the radio. When I worked for years in Zambia, I tuned in on the World Service to the radio. You could see the game in your imagination.'

Until he was in his eighties, Murphy ran the line for Lansdowne. He had special admiration for Philip Danaher, whom he described as an 'outstanding full-back but he should have stuck in that position because he could have been one of the very best'. Danaher is one of an elite group of Irishmen who have played in three positions on the Irish international team: full-back, wing (as substitute) and centre. He is also part of another select group: those who have played senior championship football – as he played for Limerick against Kerry in the Munster final in 1991.

Murphy was bitterly disappointed by the changing face of Irish rugby when professionalism was introduced: 'Whenever I go down to the club now, all the players are interested in talking about is money. It's not the game I love any more. I can see rugby becoming a game for only the rich clubs. My big fear is that club rugby as we know it will die.'

67

THE GEORGE BEST OF RUGBY
GEORDAN MURPHY

In the build-up to the 2003 World Cup, rugby pundits throughout the world predicted that Geordan Murphy was destined to become one of stars of the tournament and one of the giants of world rugby. Tragically, injury intervened and Murphy missed out on the world stage his rich talents deserved, having emerged as the star of the previous Six Nations. It was a catastrophic setback to Ireland's chances for glory.

Murphy cringes at one of his earliest memories from his time in Leicester: 'I had a real Homer Simpson moment standing beside this guy at the club one day. I didn't recognise him from Adam and I asked him if he got a chance to play much rugby at the club. I knew immediately from the way he looked at me that I had said something incredibly stupid. It was the Scottish international Craig Joiner. To complete my shame, when he turned around, I saw on the back of his jersey was the word Joiner!

'Mind you, since I started playing for Ireland, I find myself regularly the victim of mistaken identity. Even in the Irish squad, people mixed up my name with those of Girvan [Dempsey] and Gordon [D'Arcy]. So, now and again, I found the odd member of the Irish squad addressing me as "Girv . . . Gord . . . Geordan". The best one, though, came after Ireland famously spoiled the world champions England's homecoming party at Twickenham in 2004 when Girvan Dempsey scored that great try. As I was injured, I didn't play in the game, so I was doing some corporate work, and after the game I was in my jeans and T-shirt and a man congratulated me on scoring in the corner!

'The legendary Bob Dwyer was in charge of Leicester during my trial. In my second week of the trial, I was playing in the second team and I had six full internationals in the side with me, like Niall Malone and Dean Richards. It was just jaw-dropping. Bob said he wanted me to stay after the trial. I got a few games with the first team in my first season and played four games in a row after Christmas, but shortly after that Bob got the sack and Dean Richards replaced him.'

With typical modesty, Geordan makes no mention of the fact that

Dean Richards christened him 'the George Best of rugby' because of his exquisite skills.

'With Leicester, there are also great characters and practical jokers. We have a decent spread of them throughout the squad, but it comes as no surprise that Austin Healey was the tops in this respect. He was always willing to get a laugh and that is great to have someone like him in the squad because he kept morale up. Of course, he can rub people up the wrong way and often has done so! He does the craziest things. To give a typical example of an Austin activity, when he was away with the English squad, he was bored and decided to liven things up by having a game with the English forward Lewis Moody. They sat about ten feet away from each other with their legs apart and the idea was to throw an orange at each other's groin. The problem for Austin was that he wasn't very good but Lewis was the world champion!'

There was a general perception that, given Geordan's status in English rugby, he should have cemented his place on the Irish team much sooner. Is this a view he shares?

'I'm not sure. I think that perhaps being over here in Leicester was initially detrimental to my international career by virtue of the fact that the selectors didn't see me that often. Things really came together for me in the Six Nations in 2003. Although we lost the Grand Slam decider against England, it was a good season for me and I was so looking forward to taking it on one step further at the World Cup but it wasn't to be.

'When I woke up in the hospital in Scotland, I was devastated. Although I was morphined out, I couldn't believe it. There were a few tears shed. It was very tough to deal with. I can smile and laugh when I think about it now, but as I never made it on the plane I learned the lesson that you should never count your chickens.'

Murphy has many happy memories from his rugby career: 'One of the funniest came before playing a European Cup final with Leicester. In the warm-up before the game, I was throwing the ball around. I tried to do a clever dummy pass and ended up firing the ball into one of my teammates' groin. It made me laugh. It made him cry!'

68

NOISY
NOEL MURPHY

The Murphy family have given three generations to Irish rugby. Noel Murphy's father (also Noel) won 11 caps in the 1930s in the pack; Noel was capped for Ireland on 47 occasions in the wing-forward position and later coached the Irish and Lions teams; and his son, Kenny, was also capped for Ireland at full-back in the 1990s. This is the only time in Irish rugby history when a grandfather, son and grandson represented Ireland. Noisy's son-in-law is former Irish scrum-half and captain Michael Bradley.

'Noisy' was at the centre of one of the most dramatic episodes in Irish rugby history. In 1969, England were dispatched 17–15 in Dublin, and Ireland defeated Scotland 16–0. The Triple Crown was now on. The Cardiff Arms Park showdown is best remembered for arguably the most controversial punch in the history of international rugby when Noel Murphy was sensationally floored by Brian Price. After ten minutes, the Welsh forward broke from the ruck to do his Cassius Clay impersonation. Murphy, in his final international (after winning 41 caps and touring twice with the Lions), was left sprawling on the ground. Ireland lost 24–11.

Barry McGann remembers the game clearly: 'It was a very physical match. The press made a lot of the fact that Prince Charles was attending his first match as Prince of Wales and right in front of him Brian Price knocked out Noisy. People now will not appreciate just how sensational the incident was at the time. There was not a culture of sending players off then the way there is now, so Price continued on his merry way for the rest of the game. That was really the beginning of the great Welsh team with Gareth Edwards to the fore.'

McGann has fond memories of Murphy: 'After I left school, I went straight on to the Cork Constitution team. I'll never forget what Noisy Murphy said to me when I started off: "You just play the ball and we'll look after you."'

During Murphy's time as Irish coach, Tony Ward experienced the less tender side of his personality: 'I have had more than my share of tales of the unexpected. When, in 1979, I agreed to have my photo taken at the swimming pool in Newpark, I never dreamed that it would appear as a page-3-style photo in the *Daily Mirror* the morning of Ireland's Five Nations game, against Scotland or that RTE would show the picture in their build-up to the game, which meant that half the country saw it. It cast a big shadow over my game that day and caused great embarrassment to myself and my family – as well as earning me a real ticking off from a fuming Noel Murphy. He was fully entitled to be so annoyed.'

The high point of Murphy's coaching career came in 1980 when he was appointed to coach the Lions' tour to South Africa.

John Robbie played under Murphy on that tour: 'One of the problems, I believe, was that all the big guns on the tour – Syd Millar, Noel Murphy and captain Bill Beaumont – were all forwards and the senior players on the tour – Graham Price, Peter Wheeler, Geoff Squire and Derek Quinnell – were all forwards. I have read books on the tour where the backline was blamed, but I blame the decision-makers who framed our tactics. We had backs of the calibre of Colin Patterson, Ollie Campbell, Dai Richards, Ray Gravell, John Carleton, Clive Woodward and Andy Irvine. To say that with the amount of ball being won by the pack that this backline, or one with a few of the other players, was incapable of using it is nonsense. Instead of moving all balls early in the tour, thus developing a pattern of movement and support, the team kicked for position and drove excessively with the pack. It was good enough against the Provinces, but in the Tests it was different.'

Robbie retains a funny memory of Murphy from that time: 'Jean-Pierre Rives, the celebrated French flanker, was there as well at the end of the tour. I was in Pretoria with Noel Murphy at some function or other, and we got a lift back with some bloke in a sports car who was taking Jean-Pierre back to Johannesburg. We got hopelessly lost, and I recall that, as we sped at breakneck speed down a back road, we could see a fork ahead.

'"Go left," said Noel to the driver.

'"Please go right," said I.

'"Please go f**keeng slower!" screamed Rives, who could speak little English, from the back seat.

'The driver, a South African, was laughing so much he nearly crashed.'

69

THE LEADER OF THE PACK
DES O'BRIEN

Uniquely among former Irish rugby internationals, the late Des O'Brien's biggest sporting regret was that he never tried to qualify for the Wimbledon tennis championships. But, then again, O'Brien was not your typical rugby international. Apart from playing 20 times for Ireland, he also competed 14 times at international level for his native country at squash, as well as representing Wales at hockey, and being a reserve on the Welsh tennis team.

A renaissance man, after his retirement, O'Brien did a Master's degree in architectural history, and he spoke to me about rugby from his home, during a break from rehearsals for his performance in a Gilbert and Sullivan production.

He felt that he played his best rugby with Old Belvedere, where he starred in the first two of their consecutive Leinster Cups in the 1940s. He subsequently lined out for Wasps and London Irish, and he was leader of the pack when Ireland won the Grand Slam in 1948: 'We were the undisputed kings of wheeling the scrum. In an England game, we wheeled the scrum from our own line to their half. Another time, we wheeled our opponents' scrum seven times. Every time there was a scrum, you could see the fear in the opposition's eyes. Half of our training was spent practising dribbling. When the laws changed shortly after that, the tradition of wheeling the scrums waned dramatically and the art of dribbling died completely. I really feel half of the game died with it.

'I found the secret of leading an Irish pack was to keep them under tight control from the start, otherwise they went off like a cavalry charge, and died away in the last 15 minutes of each half. We had a very tight set scrum that only timed the shove when the ball left the scrum-half's hand. We gave a stone a man away to the 1951 Springboks and yet we could shift them back two feet at every scrum. In those days, the hooker had to fight for the ball and two feet was all he needed.

'In the five years I played for Ireland, nobody had a wife or a motor car. We either walked or cycled. This gave us a natural fitness which players don't have today. I know this might sound like boasting, but I think we were the fittest back row that ever played for Ireland. Jim McCarthy, in particular, had exceptional fitness. Our other colleague in the back row, Bill McKay, was 400 yards sprinting champion and a boxing champion. The three of us played together fourteen times for Ireland and only lost three times.'

Strangely, O'Brien's most satisfying victory did not come in either of the Triple Crown years: 'I think the match that pleased me most was when we beat Scotland 6–5 [O'Brien himself scored the try, with Noel Henderson adding a drop goal] at Murrayfield in 1951. We lost George Norton after 15 minutes so we had to play with only 14 players for 65 minutes. By the same token, the biggest disappointment of my rugby career came that same year when we only drew with Wales. That cost us the Grand Slam. It was sickening because we had the beating of them but without the injured Norton we missed easy kicks.'

On the plus side, the match spawned a friendship between O'Brien and the great Cliff Morgan, who was making his debut for Wales: 'Before the match, I sent a telegram to Cliff, which I know he still has, which read: "Congratulations, Cliff. I hope you'll be insured!" He was a bit green in his first international. During the match, he dived into the ruck and he was getting himself kicked to bits. I shouted in at him, "For Christ's sake, Cliff, get out of there fast. Do you want to get yourself killed?" After that, he never made the same mistake again.'

O'Brien marvelled at the perks players have today: 'We wore our own club socks when we played for Ireland. The clubs liked that, as did we. Wales wore letters on their backs instead of numbers at the time. Team dinners after internationals were held in Mills' restaurant in Merrion Row – just the team and half a dozen officials. Speeches were brief, as we all wanted to get to the three big dances being held from ten until three in the Gresham, the Metropole and the Shelbourne. We would be guests of all three. The night before a Dublin game, we would usually take the opposition team to the Gaiety Theatre. We had to pay for our own tickets! You were only given one jersey a season, no matter how many games you played. You could be dropped if you pinched a jersey after a game!

'I was on the first team to take a plane to a match when we went to France. Our touring party amounted to 68, of whom 40 were alickadoos!'

There was more to O'Brien than just rugby: 'When I was with London Irish, a regular spectator at our games was the great poet

Louis MacNeice. I often tried to talk to him in the bar afterwards about poetry, with no success. He always said, "I came here to watch rugby not to talk about poetry."'

O'Brien had the daunting task of succeeding Karl Mullen as Irish captain. The captaincy provided him with one of his happiest memories of playing for Ireland: 'Looking back, it was all a lot of fun! Before an international, the President of Ireland, Sean T. O'Kelly, the first Irish President to attend a rugby international, was being introduced to the teams. He was a man who was, let's say, small in stature. The match was being played in October so the grass was long. As captain I was introduced to him first. He said, "God Bless you, Des. I hope you have a good game." Then I heard a booming voice in the crowd: "Hey, Des, would you ever get the grass cut so we'd bloody well be able to see the President!"'

70

THE CLOWN PRINCE
DONNCHA O'CALLAGHAN

Although he has won two Heineken Cups with Munster, twice toured with the Lions and won a Grand Slam, Donncha O'Callaghan is the clown prince of Irish rugby. Yet he has a serious side and a big heart, as is evident in his charity work for UNICEF and his mercy mission to Haiti after the earthquake there in 2010.

O'Callaghan had to endure a disappointing start to 2011. Munster crashed out of the business end of the Heineken Cup with a defeat to Toulon, and Ireland did not start the Six Nations campaign with the fluency the team hoped for.

All came good, though, in the final game against England for O'Callaghan, as he won his 72nd cap, as Tony Ward acknowledges: 'England came to Dublin looking for the Grand Slam, but after we beat them in the cricket World Cup and our horses had done so well in Cheltenham, we couldn't let them win the rugby! Ireland produced an outstanding performance to win 24–8. It was a match which produced some notable feats. Brian O'Driscoll's try took the record [25] for most touchdowns in the Six Nations [from the flying Scotsman Ian Smith between 1924 and 1933] and Ronan O'Gara equalled Mike Gibson's all-time record of 56 appearances in the Championship. As part of my commentating duties for RTE, it was my job to select the man of the match. I picked Jonathan Sexton because he ran the game so well but I had some worthy contenders to choose from in the Irish pack, like David Wallace and Donncha O'Callaghan. Donncha was immense on that wonderful day because of the tackles he put in, his work ethic and the passion he brought for the contest. Ireland have some amazing flair players, like Brian O'Driscoll, who really catch the eye, but because of that players like Donncha sometimes do not get the credit they deserve because many people miss all the graft he brings to the team. Himself and Paul O'Connell have formed such a wonderful partnership down the years in the second row for both Munster and Ireland and their partnership has been pivotal to Munster's two Heineken Cups and the so-called "golden generation's" Grand Slam.'

Geordan Murphy is equally happy to give plaudits to O'Callaghan: 'Of course there are so many great forwards in the Irish team now who do such great work and give us such a supply of good ball. There are some great characters on the team, none more so than Donncha O'Callaghan. He is very funny and is always game for a laugh, and above all he can laugh at himself.'

Eric Miller witnessed some strange sights with the Irish team: 'As the tour of South Africa in 2004 was coming to an end, we organised John Hayes' stag party. We dressed John up in a gym-slip. The sight of a 20 st. man in a gym-slip is one that I never want to see again! Someone arranged for two strippers to come along but they weren't the stars of the show because Colin Farrell was filming there at the time and he came to join us for the party. He was a very sound guy and certainly knew how to have a good time! We gathered around in a circle with John in the middle and everyone got to ask Colin a question. Everything was going to plan until Donncha O'Callaghan – as only Donncha can – asked: "What was it like to be the star of *Titanic*?" The whole place cracked up and we nearly fell off our seats laughing.'

It was not the first time O'Callaghan had made a unique contribution. Rob Henderson required 15 stiches in his lip following a 'clash' in a Celtic League match in autumn 2004. Noticing Hendo's concern about his appearance, his ever helpful teammate O'Callaghan called him 'Bubba' – from the character in Forrest Gump.

Gordon D'Arcy rejoices in the camaraderie in the Irish squad: 'Donncha O'Callaghan is a comedian really. He drags fun out of everybody. He is the judge essentially and, if somebody is acting the maggot or arrives in with a new, flash car or has a new girlfriend, he will give them a hard time.'

The most nuanced assessment of O'Callaghan comes from Paul O'Connell: 'Donncha is a great character but also a fabulous player and really aggressive on the pitch. He has a reputation as a messer, and to be fair he deserves it! Off the pitch and away from the training ground, there's no bigger messer, and when he's around, you know there's a prank on its way. But when it comes to playing, training, diet or getting the proper rest, there is nobody more dedicated. He is a contradiction in some ways, but if you ask anyone within the squad, they will tell you that he's the most focused and dedicated of us all.'

71

TOP OF THE PROPS
PHIL O'CALLAGHAN

Like Moss Keane, Phil O'Callaghan was one of the great characters of the game. He toured three times with Irish parties, to Australia in 1967, to Argentina in 1970 and to New Zealand and Fiji in 1976. Apart from his fire on the pitch, he was also noted for his quick wit. The most oft-quoted story about him is the story of the day a referee penalised him and said, 'You're boring [the term used to describe the way a prop-forward drives in at an illegal angle into an opposing prop-forward], O'Callaghan.'

Philo's instinctive retort was: 'Well, you're not so entertaining yourself, ref.'

The referee penalised him a further ten yards.

The Dolphin player was capped twenty-one times for Ireland over a ten-year period between 1967 and 1976, although he won no caps from 1971 through to 1975. He really established his credentials when Ireland went to Australia for a six-match tour in 1967. The omens for the Test match were not favourable, as, the previous week, Ireland had lost 21–9 to New South Wales at the same Sydney venue. However, tries from Jerry Walsh and Pat McGrath, and a conversion and drop goal from Tom Kiernan, gave Ireland an 11–5 win.

O'Callaghan was one of twenty-three players selected on a depleted Irish squad (deprived of the services of Mike Gibson, Ken Kennedy, Fergus Slattery and Roger Young) to tour Argentina in 1970. The challenge facing the Irish was compounded by the fact that the tour was in August, which meant that the visitors were ring rusty after a three-month lay-off, whereas the home sides had been competing since the previous April. Moreover, Argentina were still bullish in the wake of recent victories over Scotland and Wales. Ireland lost three of their seven matches, including both Tests 8–3 and 6–3, respectively. They also lost 17–0 to an Argentine 'C' side.

To add to Ireland's problems, O'Callaghan was sent off in the first Test. He recalls, 'At one stage, we went to Boca Juniors stadium for the World Club Championship final between the Dutch and the

Argentinean champions. There is a history of crowd trouble at such venues. One of our lads was whistling on the way into the stadium. For this "crime", he was thrown into jail for 24 hours! It was a magnificent venue and a very intimidating atmosphere. It was the first time I saw fires in the stadium. The home supporters turned against their own side because they were so dissatisfied with the performance.'

O'Callaghan's disappointment about that incident pales into insignificance when compared with the pain he experienced during the darkest chapter of his career. Time may heal all but his scars are still discernible: 'The biggest disappointment of my career came in 1970 when I was dropped from the Irish team at a time when I was the number-one contender for the Lions position. I can say with my hand on my heart that I was playing my best rugby in the years I was off the Irish team.'

Despite the vagaries of the Irish selectors, rugby's prodigal son would return. In 1976, after Ireland suffered a record defeat, 26–3, at the hands of the French in Paris, O'Callaghan was restored to the front row, much to his relief: 'My happiest memory in rugby was being recalled to the Irish team for the Test match against New Zealand in 1976, having spent six years in the international wilderness. I knew back in 1970 that the next Irish tour was six years away and made a bet, of two pints, in a pub in a Cork that I would make that trip to New Zealand. I got great pleasure from claiming that bet six years on.'

O'Callaghan had the image of being a 'hard man'. Was this a fair perception?

'You have to meet fire with fire. There were times when front rows faced you like a bull facing a bullfighter. The French especially used a combination of the prop and the hooker to try and soften you up. Once you showed you could not be bullied, you were fine. I was tough and hard but fair.'

O'Callaghan is a huge admirer of the many players who soldiered with him in the Irish jersey, including Tom Kiernan, Mike Gibson, Willie John McBride, Mick Molloy, Jerry Walsh, Ken Goodall, Alan Duggan, Ken Kennedy, Noel Murphy and Barry McGann. Among their number was Barry Bresnihan, who was capped twenty-five times in the centre for Ireland between 1966 and 1971, scoring five international tries. Bresnihan went on two Lions tours, to Australia and New Zealand in 1966 and to South Africa in 1968, where he played three Test matches. On the '66 tour, he wrote himself into the history books by becoming the first replacement in representative rugby. He is the brother-in-law of Con Feighery, who was capped three times in the pack for Ireland in 1972. Con's brother Tom, a prop-forward, was also capped for Ireland.

O'Callaghan reserves special praise for one man, though: 'The best wing-forward I've ever seen was Shay Deering. He was such a whole-hearted, committed player and one of the greatest characters I've ever met on or off the field.'

One of his strongest memories is of an incident involving Barry McGann: 'The night before an Irish squad session, McGann, Shay Deering and I and a couple of others had frequented a few pubs. In fact, we were even thrown out of one of them! The squad session the next day started with some laps around the pitch. Shortly after we started off, I heard Barry shout at me: "Cal, don't leave me." I dropped back with him and we were lapped once or twice. The cruel irony of the situation was that after the session he was selected and I was dropped!'

72

PAULINE CONVERSION
PAUL O'CONNELL

One of the most striking things about spending an hour in the 2009 Lions captain Paul O'Connell's company is how often he uses the word 'lucky' about himself. His all-informing, generous and humane sensibility is also indicated by the way the litany of coaches who helped him on the way are all mentioned by name and spoken of with genuine affection and respect. His innate modesty is also evident when he is asked if he has any interest in a career in the media after rugby: 'I don't think I have the boyish good looks for a career as a TV pundit!'

Learning his craft in the second row, O'Connell believes he could not have served his apprenticeship with a more skilled instructor beside him for both Munster and Ireland: 'I think every player on the Munster team has a bit of a Mick Galwey in him. Gaillimh was very similar to Peter Clohessy, in that he was old school. He likes his pints, wasn't very fond of training, but when it came to Saturday, there was nobody who put themselves on the line more or gave more on the pitch. He was a great guy to talk to players and to get them up for a match. When you saw a man who had accomplished so much get so emotional and be so committed for every Munster game, it did inspire you to give of your best. He had a great ability to put his finger on the button for every occasion with every guy on the team in a way that got the best out of them.

'When I played for Ireland Under-21s, I was coached by Ciaran Fitzgerald and he was very "Gaillimh-like". Ciaran was very passionate and a great motivator.

'I learned a lot from Gaillimh and the Claw because they knew every trick in the game and every shortcut there was to know. Gaillimh had a very good tight game. He was clever, tactically astute and above all a great leader. When I came into the Munster squad first, Mick O'Driscoll was in the second row for Munster and he was brilliant in the lineout. I learned so much about lineout play from him. I was lucky enough to get his place on the Munster team and he was so helpful.

'"Woodie" [Keith Wood] was a great leader as well. When he pointed his finger at you and said he needed a big game from you, you wanted to give it to him because he was one of the greatest players in the world and had done it all himself.

'"Drico" [Brian O'Driscoll] has a different style of captaincy from either Gaillimh or Woodie, but when he asks you to do something, you know that anything he asks you to give he himself will give more. Some players give a hundred per cent but Drico gives a million per cent. He puts his body on the line every time and I love that about him. He's not a fancy Dan by any means.'

Paul made his debut for Ireland against Wales in the Six Nations in 2000 at Lansdowne Road. It was also Ireland's first match under Eddie O'Sullivan's tenure as Irish coach.

O'Connell made an excellent start and thoroughly deserved his debut try but left the field injured and in tears after only half an hour, although his memory is hazy: 'I think I scored the try after about 20 minutes but I got concussed in about the fifth. I don't remember anything after that. I was basically on autopilot. It was a weird thing. I was doing everything I normally would, but I just can't remember any of it.

'There were seven Munster forwards in the pack with Simon Easterby, so I felt right at home. Normally, after your first cap, everybody gets you a drink and you end up smashed. As I was concussed, that didn't happen to me. My parents were up for the game, and as my dad is such a massive rugby fan, it was a big day for him.'

Just as Paul got his taste of the big time, his career ran into problems: 'Up to winning my first cap, my career had the ideal trajectory: one upward step after another. While that day against Wales was brilliant, it triggered off a series of injuries for me which I thought would never end. Having got a concussion in the Wales match, I played for my club·two weeks later to see if I would be fit for the next international against Scotland. The problem was that I had an abscess on my tooth and, while I did play in the match, I was sick all the way home. I picked up a shoulder injury playing for Munster in the run-up to the Heineken semi-final against Castres. The morning of the match, I had to do a fitness test. That is a test I will never forget because my shoulder was standing up well and I was hitting a tackle bag which Declan Kidney was holding. The problem was that I hit it so hard at one stage I knocked out one of Declan's teeth! He was due to do an interview three-quarters of an hour later, so he had to go to the dentist to get it stuck back in. The shoulder was fine but I probably wasn't

100 per cent fit. We won the game, but in a warm-up match before the Heineken Cup final I damaged my ankle ligaments. I did manage to play against Leicester in the final, but with my shoulder and ankle problems I didn't play well.

'That summer, I made the summer tour to New Zealand, but in the First Test I damaged the same shoulder again and had to miss the Second Test. On the plane home, I ruptured a disc in my back, which I had to have an operation on. I was out for four months. I got back and played four games for Munster when I broke a bone in my thumb. I made my comeback when coming on as a sub in the Grand Slam decider against England in 2003. My proper rehabilitation only came with the tour to Australia, Tonga and Samoa. It was a tough tour. Tonga is a very poor country and we played in dreadful conditions. Samoa wasn't much better but at least we had a nice hotel.'

In August 2003, he scored two tries in the warm-up game against Wales before the World Cup. He was one of the stars of the rugby World Cup later that year, and recalls the fun off the pitch: 'Overall, the World Cup went well for me personally. It was horribly disappointing to lose to Australia. Although sometimes the media didn't believe us, we felt we had a good team. The days of moral victories mattering for us are over. We knew that, if we won that game, a lot of things could happen for us. We didn't play fabulously well against France, but a couple of defensive mistakes cost us dear. I have been on tours like that before when I was homesick, but not on that one because it was such a carnival of rugby. For two weeks, we were staying in a hotel outside Sydney by the beach, going surfing every day and swimming in the sea after training as part of our recovery. We were in Melbourne at the time of the Melbourne Cup and there was massive hysteria about it. The whole experience was the kind of stuff you dream of.'

In the absence of Brian O'Driscoll, O'Connell led Ireland in their opening 2004 Six Nations game against France in Paris: 'It was a great thrill to be selected as captain but the experience was spoiled by the fact that we lost. A few defensive errors cost us dearly.'

There was a lot of criticism of the side after that match. Was that hard to take at the time?

'We knew that we had a lot of potential in the side and that's why talk of "brave old Ireland" has no interest for us. We want to win and are not satisfied any more to play heroically but to lose. I think criticism is brilliant. It only makes you a better player, if you are mentally strong enough to take it. If someone has a go at me personally in the press, and I respect him, I think I can learn from that. If you don't respect him but he's speaking the truth, you have to take it on board. But if you know it's not the truth, you just ignore it.'

O'Connell feels that belief was crucial to Ireland's Grand Slam victory in 2009: 'Even at half-time in the game in Cardiff, when we were 6–0 down, we knew we could win.'

O'Connell's towering frame and his fierce commitment on the pitch mask his gentle nature off it, and his modesty is again in evidence when he looks back on his career to date: 'I have had a huge amount of good luck to get where I am. To take one example, when I was playing in the trial for the Irish Schools, I didn't play that well but I was lucky because the guy who was lifting me lifted me by the legs and the guy who was opposite me was getting lifted by the shorts so I had two feet on him straight away. I robbed a few lineouts off him and so I got picked. If he had got picked, it could be him doing this interview now and not me.'

There is one memory that will forever hold a special place in O'Connell's memory chest. Waking as a boy on Christmas morning was like this – the sleepy thrill before remembering its source. He loves the stories of the 'old school' before rugby went professional and the way players combined drinking and other 'extra-curricular' activities and playing. It was part of another time and place. For O'Connell, the players from that era carry the aura of another life that is half secret and half open. He got a taste of it when he spent a week with Peter Clohessy: 'I used to travel up with the Claw for internationals because we were both Young Munster and both of us lived in Annacotty. Claw was such a legend at the time that he roomed alone, but, as it was my first cap, he was asked to room with me for the week. It was a week I will never, ever forget!

'At the moment, we knock off at 11 p.m. and go to sleep. We eat a proper breakfast of muesli and scrambled eggs and drink lots of water. We also take protein shakes after training. We do our weights but go for a nap during the day to ensure that we are getting the proper rest. After having a proper dinner, we might do some video analysis but then we're in bed early.

'My week with the Claw was very different! He was old school. On the way up to Dublin, we stopped off in a petrol station. I had a tuna sandwich with no butter and a pint of milk. The Claw had a sausage sandwich with plenty of butter and lashings of brown sauce and cups of tea with shovels of sugar.

'When we were in our hotel room, he was smoking fags the whole day. We'd be getting room service up all day, every day, with various not particularly healthy dishes like mayonnaise sandwiches. I would go to sleep about 11 and he'd still be up watching the TV. I'd wake up about two to go to the toilet. Claw wouldn't be one for bringing water into the room. The TV would still be on and I would knock it off. I'd wake back up at four and the TV would be back on! I'd knock it off again. Then I would wake up again at seven. The Claw would be sitting up in the bed, smoking a fag and watching the TV.

'On our afternoon off, the Dublin lads would go home to their families but we didn't have that luxury because the journey was too far. We were staying in the Glenview Hotel and we drove up the Wicklow mountains and went to a cafe for a healthy diet of rhubarb tart, ice cream and custard!

'He did everything differently and yet before the match he was the one with the tear in his eye and he would get more up for the game than anyone else. He was the best player on the pitch against Wales by a mile. His understanding of professionalism was very different but he had a bigger heart than everyone else and that's why everybody loved him and still loves him.'

73

SUPERSTITIOUS MIND
RODNEY O'DONNELL

Rodney O'Donnell's middle name could have been 'Superstition'. He had a huge fear of anything connected with the number 13. On tour, not only did he refuse to stay in a room numbered 13, or 213, or a room on the 13th floor, but he would not even stay in a room in which the numbers added up to 13, such as 274.

He had an interesting theory about the psychology of the rugby ball. When an opponent had kicked a goal against his team, he felt much better if the ball came down in such a way that he was able to throw it back over the crossbar, his theory being that, the next time, the ball would be either unsure where to go or would lose the habit of travelling in the right direction.

When he believed in something, there could be no deviation. He always insisted on being the last man on the team bus and would patiently wait for everyone to get onto the bus regardless of the climatic conditions. He refused to walk over a line. Yet another ritual was preparing to tog out before games. He had to put on his togs in such a way that the material did not touch his skin on the way up. Should such a calamity occur, he would begin the whole process again – and, if necessary, again and again until he got it exactly right. The second part of this operation was that he would never button up his togs until he was running onto the field.

He was preoccupied with exactitudes to the point that he went around every room adjusting pictures so that they hung straight on the walls. This tendency was dramatically illustrated on Ireland's tour to Australia in 1979. In the middle of Noel Murphy's team-talk, he jumped up to the astonishment of all present to adjust the position of the telephone.

One of his most famous idiosyncrasies was his desire to get into bed each night without touching the bottom sheet. The task had to be executed with military precision. If he failed the first time he tried, he kept trying, until he got it exactly right. Only then did he allow himself to relax.

John O'Driscoll became a close friend of O'Donnell: 'Like Rodney, Willie Duggan had to be the last one on the field. The big question was what would happen when they both played together. The rest of us all ran onto the pitch. We waited and we waited but no sign of either. Eventually, Willie came running out. He was very determined to be last but Rodney was going to be last.

'I roomed with Rodney during the 1980 Lions tour, which was an unforgettable experience. He had a ritual for everything, including going to bed. He had to leave his shoes a certain way and so on. The whole saga lasted at least 20 minutes. To wind him up, once he got into bed, I would adjust the picture in the room so that it wasn't hanging straight. It was unthinkable for Rodney to even contemplate going to sleep in such an environment so he had to get up straight away and settle it. Of course, when he was up, he couldn't just jump back into bed but had to go through his entire ritual again. He did get his own back on me, though. I couldn't sleep with any light in the room so he always parted the curtains.

'A Friday the 13th fell on that tour. Ollie Campbell and John Robbie rose at 6.30 a.m. that morning and, with taping, made lines right across the lobby outside O'Donnell's room and pasted the number 13 all over the lobby and the elevator. As a result, Rodney was afraid to leave the room for the entire day!'

Tragedy struck against Griqualand West in the penultimate game of the 1980 Lions tour, which the Lions won 23–19. O'Donnell sustained a serious injury tackling the massive Danny Gerber, and although he walked off the field, when he was examined in hospital it was discovered that he had dislocated his neck between the sixth and seventh vertebrae, coming within a fraction of an inch of being paralysed for life. Prompt intervention by O'Driscoll on the pitch prevented more severe repercussions. To compound the problems, when the ambulance finally arrived the driver got lost on the way back to the hospital, depriving the Irish player of the quickest possible care.

Tony Ward was dismayed by the injury: 'It was a sad end to a potentially great career. I genuinely believe that, were it not for that injury, he would have gone on to become Ireland's greatest full-back ever.'

74

THE LIFE OF BRIAN
BRIAN O'DRISCOLL

'They call him God. Well, I reckon he's a much better player than that.' Thus spoke Stuart Barnes during the Sky Sports commentary of one of the all-time great tries.

In his first Test for the Lions in 2001, Brian O'Driscoll left the world champions, Australia, looking as slow as growing grass as he ran half the field and scythed through their defence to score one of the greatest individual tries ever seen, the very signature of genius.

Following his vintage displays for the Lions, Brian has continued his dizzying ascent to become one of the very biggest names in world rugby. Brian has been in thrall to the game of rugby for as long as he can remember. It helps that his father, Frank, as well as his cousins Barry and John, also played for Ireland.

A kind, passionate but polite, thoroughly delightful man, Frank remembers Brian's introduction to rugby with pure and undiluted happiness: 'I still recall going to see Brian playing his first match at schoolboys. I think he scored four tries on that day. After the game, people were asking who is this new kid on the block. Having been fortunate enough to play for Ireland myself, I always felt that, if Brian got the breaks, he would go on and play for Ireland. I never had any doubt about whether he had the talent, but in the past all the talented players didn't always make it for of a variety of reasons, like injury.

'One of the proudest days for me was when Brian played his first game for Ireland at schoolboy level. I remember saying to my wife, Geraldine, on the way to the match, "Do you realise that only 14 other sets of parents in Ireland are going to experience what we are going to experience today?" I was so proud of him that day. Although he has done a lot of great things on the field, I am particularly proud of him because of his discipline. He never lets his social life interfere with his rugby. It's always the other way round.'

In conversation with this writer, Eddie O'Sullivan recalled his early impressions of the brightest star in Irish rugby: 'Brian O'Driscoll burst on the scene in a pretty explosive style. I remember seeing him at school in Blackrock College when I worked there for a while. He was quite small then but suddenly got this great growth spurt and turned into a fine athlete. He has something special. He's very gifted in terms of athleticism and in terms of football skills, but he's also a very intelligent guy. He's got the key that makes him different to everyone else, in that he can perform at the highest level under the greatest pressure and still come through. That's the biggest test for any athlete, if he can perform at the highest level at the greatest pressure.'

At Blackrock College, Brian paraded all the fluent skills that would characterise his international career: great speed and an almost unique combination of attacking and defensive qualities. Those talents brought him to the attention of the international selectors.

Brian recalls the joy of his first cap mixed with disappointment of losing the match: 'My debut for Ireland came in June 1999. I had been brought on the tour of Australia, having sat on the bench for one of the Six Nations games. I played a few games on the tour before the first Test when I was selected to play in the centre with Kevin Maggs in the first Test in Brisbane. I was lucky to play for Ireland when I was so young. It was a huge honour for me and something that I had always hoped to rise to at some stage of my career, but to have come at such an early age was incredible for me and something I really cherished. I had mixed emotions because we got a bad beating, but at the same time I'd won my first cap. I probably got to enjoy my second Test more because we really pushed the Aussies all the way. I had heard people say that your first cap always goes by so quickly that you can't really take it all in and enjoy it. That was my experience too.

'At the start, things weren't going so well for Ireland. The low point was probably losing to Argentina in the World Cup back in Lens in 1999. That defeat was crushing. I think we panicked as a team towards the end and probably our 13-man lineout showed we were a bit scarce of ideas.

'I think we probably reached an equal low when we lost so heavily to England the following year. After that, a lot of changes were made and the team started to improve and we started to win again. I think, when you have bad losses as well as great victories, you become very philosophical and realise that, when you are down, the team is probably not as bad as people say you are or, when you win, you are not the world-beaters that everybody says you are.'

Happier times were around the corner and Brian dramatically announced his arrival on the world stage with a stunning performance in Paris, culminating in his three tries.

'When we went to play France, nobody expected us to even challenge the French, which probably took a lot of weight off our shoulders. I look back at the pictures and see the joy on our faces for having achieved something that Irish teams had failed to do for 28 years. We were overwhelmed at the end and it was really a fantastic feeling. For me to have scored three tries was a nice bonus!

'The third try sticks out most of all. What most people probably don't realise is that I shouldn't have been where I was when I got the ball. I was just trying to catch a breather before I got back into position but the ball squirted out in front of me and I went for the gap. That try took us to within two points of them and convinced us that we could win the game. A lot of people have remarked that Emile Ntamack didn't make a great effort to tackle me and I'm only glad he didn't come crashing into me!'

Brian is fortunate in having a temperament that gets energised rather than drained by the big occasion. The bigger the occasion, the more he likes it. In fact, as Brian explains, he is least relaxed when watching a game he is not playing in: 'I know some people will probably feel this is strange, but I was far more nervous watching the 1997 Lions tour of South Africa, when I was back home in Dublin staring at the television set, than I was on the field in Brisbane for the first Test in 2001. When you're playing, you have no time to dwell on things. Mind you, I was aware of the crowd at the Gabba. Just looking up into that sea of red as we ran out was enough to put us on our toes, but when the Wallabies appeared and the boos drowned out the cheers it was just unbelievable.'

O'Driscoll looks back on the tour with mixed feelings: 'If we had gone on to win the series, that first Test would probably have been a major highlight of my career, but because we lost the series it doesn't have the same glow in my memory. We were fairly surprised at what we achieved in the opening fifty minutes of the first Test in particular, but all the gaps were closed up for the next two Tests. When you are a part of a tour like that, every result counts in terms of morale and encouragement. The first Test gave us a big lift, but losing the other two were crushing blows.'

Brian is fortunate to have the support of such a united family behind him, particularly as he is now so much in the public eye. Brian's mother, Geraldine, is all too aware of this: 'The France game in 2000, when he scored the three tries, changed everything for Brian and indeed for us.

I first realised that when I was introduced to someone after the match and they said, "This is Geraldine O'Driscoll. She used to be Frank O'Driscoll's wife. Now she's Brian O'Driscoll's mother!"

'The France game was on a Sunday and shortly after the match we had to rush for the train to be home for work the next day. One of our daughters was in Australia at the time and she rang us on the mobile. She said, "Mum, after Brian's three tries, I'm now a minor celebrity here!"

'Probably the most interesting experience of all came in Australia during the Lions tour. After the first Test, when Brian scored the famous try, Frank and I got on the bus with a gang of Lions supporters. We sat at the back of the bus and nobody knew who we were. Then the crowd burst into song. They started singing "Waltzing O'Driscoll". Frank and I said nothing. We just nodded at each other but it was actually very emotional.'

A major landmark in Brian's career came in March 2004, when he captained Ireland to their first Triple Crown in 19 years: 'In the Scotland game, we had to wear them down a bit. These Six Nations aren't easy, and a lot of the time you mightn't pull away till the end, which was the case in this one. There was another agenda in this game. Matt Williams was coming back to Lansdowne Road. He had a point to prove because Scotland's campaign up to then had been so disastrous. Add to the mix that he literally knows the way the wind blows in the Lansdowne from his time as Leinster and Ireland A coach and his intimate knowledge of so many of the players he once coached on the Irish team. There had to be an element of proving the critics wrong.

'We weren't second-guessing what was going on in his mind. We were concentrating on playing to the best of our ability, and we felt that, if we were to do that, we could and would win the game.'

The high point of O'Driscoll's career – surpassing perhaps even the honour of captaining the Lions on the ill-fated 2005 tour – came when he led Ireland to a win over Wales in 2009 to claim the Grand Slam. Was he nervous before the game?

'Personally, I was probably more nervous going into that game than others because the stakes were so high, but I was determined not to let my teammates see that.'

Rugby has opened a lot of doors for Brian, as he explains: 'I loved the chances to play for the Barbarians because they play a seven-man game with fifteen players on the game. That's the way I'd describe it. My first experience was very exciting; even the build-up was very exciting. Playing with players you'd never have the opportunity to play with was very exciting. Just to experience it was incredible. Training with Carlos Spencer, who was a childhood hero of mine, was great. Seeing the tricks he was doing in training left me flabbergasted but I had to pretend to be taking everything he was doing in my stride!'

Which rugby player would he most like to be compared with?

'If I had to be compared with anyone, I suppose I would like to be compared with Australia's Tim Horan. He could mix his game a huge amount and was in the World Cup-winning side of 1991 at a very young age. The fact that he could mix running skills and hard tackling makes him the complete rugby player, and a lot of his skills I tried to emulate.'

Having captained the Lions, led Ireland to a Grand Slam and won the Heineken Cup twice, Brian is one of the best-known people in Ireland. He pauses for reflection when asked what advice he would give any young person today: 'The best piece of advice I've ever been given was from my old coach in UCD, Lee Smith. Lee always wrote out a couple of sentences on a piece of paper for each player before a match, telling you what he wanted you to do and what your role on the team was, but when he came around to me he said, "Just go out and play your own game." Such a small thing made a big difference and inspired me and gave me a lot of confidence to go out and play well because I thought very highly of Lee and I still do.'

75

JOHN O'DESPERATE
JOHN O'DRISCOLL

Although he played in a final trial in 1976–77, John O'Driscoll had to wait for another year before being selected for Ireland. The following season, he fractured his cheekbone in October, which caused him to miss the interprovincials, and, although his injury was not completely healed, he was selected for his second final trial. As he recalls, 'The selectors were basically experimenting with a number of different number 8s playing in different positions. I was chosen at number 8 and had a special mask made for protection. It was one of those days everything went right for me. I won my first cap against Scotland in 1978 but got knocked out during the game. When I came round, the first thing I heard was a great cheer. My replacement Stewart McKinney had scored a try. That meant no more caps for me that season.'

The Australian tour in 1979 marked the rehabilitation of O'Driscoll's international career, although, like Willie Duggan, he was not chosen on the original touring party.

O'Driscoll played in all four Tests for the Lions on the tour to South Africa in 1980. One person literally at the centre of the action was the great Welsh and Lions player Ray Gravell. It was Gravell who re-christened John O'Driscoll as John O'Desperate on the tour.

After a disappointing season in 1981, when Ireland were whitewashed, the Triple Crown unexpectedly came on the horizon for O'Driscoll when Ireland played Scotland in 1982: 'I loved the adrenalin rush I got when I played for Ireland. I always found the tension helped me to perform. That Scottish game was an exception. Although we had done brilliantly against Wales and England, the communal tension in the dressing-room that day was striking. I felt it was very unhelpful to the entire team. The one exception was Ollie Campbell, whose kicking, even by his own high standards, was fantastic that day. He settled us down.'

After Ireland won the Championship in 1983, O'Driscoll was selected to tour New Zealand with the Lions in the company of his Irish colleagues Trevor Ringland, Michael Kiernan, David Irwin, Ollie

JOHN O'DRISCOLL

Campbell, Ciaran Fitzgerald and Donal Lenihan. Although he played in two Tests, it was not the experience he hoped for: 'I was injured in the first match and didn't play for three weeks. You need to be playing on a tour like that. We were not as evenly balanced as we had been in 1980. The press were very unfair to Ciaran Fitzgerald, which didn't help. By the standards of the time, the criticism of him was way over the top. Nowadays, that kind of sustained media assault has become commonplace.'

Like so many of his colleagues, O'Driscoll has a treasure trove of memories from his playing days. One goes back to South Africa in 1980: 'The only unpardonable sin on a Lions tour is to miss training. No matter how awful you feel or how low your morale is, you simply must get out to the training field at the appointed hour. Sunday was a day for total relaxation. To pass the afternoon, Ray Gravell and I played a card game with a difference. The penalty if you lost a hand was to take a drink – a mixture of spirits and orange juice. When I lost, I noticed that Ray was adding in extra spirits to my drink. I thought I was being very clever by saying nothing and adding in a lot of extra juice. What I didn't know was that Gravell had absolutely laced the orange juice with spirits! The next morning, I had the mother of all hangovers and had to miss training.

'In June 1983, I went with Fergus Slattery to Barcelona to play an exhibition game against a French selection with the Wolfhounds. The match was to be played at midday. The evening before the game Fergus was looking for somebody to go out with him for a night on the town. In the circumstances, nobody wanted to take up his invitation, knowing the tough conditions awaiting them the next day, but eventually he recruited the replacement prop-forward. The next morning, the two lads returned from their adventures as the French team were heading out to train! Fergus was not a bit fazed. On the bus to the game, Phil Orr was taken ill and to his horror the "partying" sub had to take his place. Slats played like a man inspired, but I've never, ever seen anyone suffer on the pitch like his partner!'

Ciaran Fitzgerald has a clear memory of O'Driscoll: 'Whatever you say to players of that calibre has to be effective. Every player is different. The most important thing is to find out how to bring out the best in each player and find a strategy appropriate to his personality. In 1982, before the decisive Triple Crown match against Scotland, the *Irish Press* wrote a very critical article about John O'Driscoll, who was a superb player and central to our success that season. The day before the match, I quietly went to him in the Shelbourne Hotel and expressed my sympathy about the article. He knew nothing about it and asked to see it. He read it but said nothing. The next day he played like a man possessed.'

76

LIFE AT NUMBER 10
RONAN O'GARA

Ronan O'Gara's international debut was delayed: 'I was due to play against England in 2000 but I got injured in the run-up to the game and Eric Elwood's international career was prolonged. With hindsight, it may not have been a bad thing.

'Standing to attention as the national anthem was played before starting my first game for Ireland against Scotland at the age of 22 was very exciting.'

With his superb pair of hands and magnificent diagonal kicking, he really announced his arrival on the international stage in his second cap against Italy in Ireland's 60–13 win. Ireland led 33–0 at half-time and went into the dressing-room expecting a massive communal pat on the back from coach Warren Gatland. He took the team by surprise when he asked them: 'Are you ruthless enough to put the game out of sight? Have you the guts to put the guys away?'

O'Gara certainly had, and he gave a superb exhibition of place kicking, with a magnificent 12 kicks on target from 12 opportunities. In the process, he amassed an Irish record of 30 points, beating the old record by 6 points. O'Gara is characteristically modest when asked about the game: 'The team played well and from a personal point of view it was a satisfying performance.'

O'Gara's fame spread so rapidly that he quickly starred in an advertising campaign for an oil company. It is not an experience he is particularly keen to talk about!

One of the defining sporting images of 2001 was the sight of blood streaming from O'Gara's eye. During the Lions tour that year, Duncan McRae had repeatedly beaten him in the left eye during the match against the New South Wales Waratahs, with an 11-punch attack. O'Gara's popularity with the squad after the McRae episode was evident when everyone wanted to go and sort out 'Duncan Disorderly'.

Two and a half years later, McRae publicly pronounced his contrition for his actions and his intention to apologise to O'Gara the next time they met. By an amazing coincidence, that admission came two weeks before McRae, as the new Gloucester out-half, was due to play against Munster at Thomond Park. The previous year, the Zurich Premiership leaders Gloucester had lost 33–6 at Thomond Park in the never-to-be-forgotten 'Miracle Match'.

How does O'Gara feel about McRae now?

'I don't have any feelings about him, to be honest. There were all kinds of rumours about what freaked him out. It is not for me to comment. What was great, though, was the support I got afterwards both from within the squad and from back home, and to know that people were thinking of me and wanting things to work out well for me.'

While the focus of the media attention on O'Gara's Lions tour was on the McRae incident, Ronan himself has very different memories from the tour: 'Other people seemed to be more affected by the sight of my blood than I was. I look back on that tour with good memories and I found it to be an enriching experience. I learned a lot from that tour and have taken a number of things from that trip and incorporated them into my game. It was great to see at first hand the way players like Jonny Wilkinson train. He is so professional and goes about his game with such dedication and attention to detail. Another person I really admired was Rob Howley. He's a great player. Brian O'Driscoll had such a wonderful tournament and that famous try in the first Test will never be forgotten. I get on very well with Brian personally. As the out-half, it is important that you get on well with all the backs and forwards because you are the link between them.'

In 2003, rumours swept the country that O'Gara had been offered up to $12 million to play American football with the Miami Dolphins.

O'Gara has known the slings and arrows of outrageous rugby fortune: 'I have had a lot of great days with Munster but a few bad ones as well. The lowest points were unquestionably losing the two Heineken Cup finals. The highs include winning our two Heineken Cups and, of course, the Grand Slam with Ireland.'

Was his rivalry with David Humphreys for the Irish number-10 jersey a help or a hindrance in his march to more than 100 international caps?

'It was a bit of everything. Older journalists make a big deal out of it, and go on about it being another case of Tony Ward and Ollie Campbell, but I didn't listen to much of it. What I would say is that whoever has been the out-half for the last few years has generally done a good job. The most important thing I have learned is that a week is a very long time in sport. It can also be a long time in the way people write about you in the press. In the build-up to big games, I can't afford to let myself be distracted by paper talk. My main job is to stay cool.'

O'Gara's coolness was exemplified in the Millennium Stadium in Cardiff in 2003, when he came on as a late sub in the game. Ireland led 22–21 when Stephen Jones drop-kicked Wales ahead. Cometh the hour and cometh the man. From the restart, O'Gara got the ball 40 metres out and calmly dropped a goal to give Ireland a dramatic win. In the autumn international with Argentina in 2004, he replicated this feat with a dramatic drop goal to snatch the game for Ireland. His temperament was also shown on a sodden November afternoon at Lansdowne Road in 2002 when he held his nerve and his footing all afternoon and kicked the six penalties required to give Ireland an 18–9 victory, which led the Irish team to literally squelch around the pitch for a lap of honour. However, he immortalised himself with his drop goal against Wales, sealing the Grand Slam in 2009. Can he enjoy such games?

'I came around to thinking that I should enjoy games. Before, I would have been nervous but I went out for that game in Cardiff determined to enjoy it.'

One of the abiding memories of O'Gara's early games for Ireland was the way the great Mick Galwey put his arms around Ronan and Peter Stringer during the preliminaries to reassure them that they were going to rise to the occasion. It is not surprising to discover that Galwey features prominently in O'Gara's list of great characters: 'I suppose the two greatest characters in my time were Mick Galwey and Peter Clohessy. They were old school and are a huge loss to the game. The freshness they brought to the game and to the Irish squad was very uplifting. Probably my most abiding memory of my days in the Irish squad was when the players and management made a presentation to Peter to mark his 50th cap. Peter responded by singing the Frank Sinatra song "My Way". What an appropriate song! He did things his way or no way. That's why I liked him and admired him so much.'

77

BIG MAL
MALCOLM O'KELLY

Malcolm O'Kelly's time in the green jersey did not always go to plan. Rugby tours have a unique capacity to produce tales of the unexpected. In 2002, the Ireland rugby team visited Siberia to play a match in an area renowned for its freezing temperatures. As the players are a very pampered lot, they can normally get everything they need. On this trip, incredibly, they found there was one thing they could not get – ice-cubes!

After he roomed with Eric Miller, Malcolm O'Kelly recalled waking up and only being able to see a silhouette of a bloke not moving and not saying anything. Big Mal found the silence the scariest thing, until he discovered that Miller was relaxing by doing transcendental meditation.

O'Kelly won 92 caps for Ireland and twice toured with the Lions. Gordon D'Arcy believes he greatly benefited from O'Kelly's experience when he made himself a fixture on the Irish team: 'To take a specific example, before the France game in Paris in 2004, just as we walked out the tunnel, Malcolm turned to me and said, "Get ready for this."

'The noise from the cheering was like having someone strike you with a bat on the back of the head as you walked onto the pitch. I stood beside Mal for the anthem, and all the anthems after that, because there's something comforting about having that giant put his arm around you. Mal probably has forgotten that moment in Paris, and has his own special memory, but it is one I will always treasure.'

Rob Henderson offers an insight into O'Kelly's personality: 'Malcolm is a great character. If he was any more laidback, his head would be touching the ground.'

There was considerable controversy in the summer of 2004 when Leinster sacked their coach Gary Ella. In a subsequent article in *Ireland on Sunday*, Ella was very critical of senior players such as Brian O'Driscoll, Malcolm O'Kelly and Victor Costello for not having sufficient commitment to Leinster.

Victor Costello makes the case for the defence: 'I was over in the

States on holiday and I heard about his comments when I was on a boat in Long Island. His Leinster career ended in the summer of 2004 but there were 38 careers going backwards under his reign. Gary Ella was a bad time for Leinster.'

At the end of his career with Leinster, O'Kelly went out on a high for the province after winning the Heineken Cup.

Former Leinster manager Ken Ging was very close to big Mal: 'There are many stories in the Leinster camp about Malcolm O'Kelly's lack of organisation and his capacity for being late. The standard line in Leinster is: if you are behind Mal in the airport, you have missed your plane. A particular favourite in the squad is about the time when Mal was spotted wearing a black shoe and a brown shoe. When this was discreetly pointed out to O'Kelly, he shrugged his shoulders nonchalantly and said, "Don't worry. That's the new fashion. I've another pair at home exactly like that!"

'Big Mal was able to poke fun at his teammates also. Naturally, Brian O'Driscoll was a primary target. Such were his commercial opportunities that his colleagues joked that he can afford to live in an area that is so posh that the fire brigade is ex-directory. The ribbing particularly intensified when O'Driscoll famously dyed his hair blonde. His teammates spun the yarn that Drico had entered a Robert Redford lookalike contest. He was knocked out in the first round. He was beaten by a Nigerian. Shane Byrne had a reputation in the squad for being "careful with money". Hence the joke in the Leinster squad that he installed double-glazing windows in his home so that his children would not hear the ice-cream van. There has never been a nicer or more modest player for Leinster than Victor Costello. Yet Victor was widely quoted within the squad as boasting that Bono asked him for his autograph.

'There is a fine line between self-confidence and arrogance. Keith Gleeson stayed on the right side of that line. That did not stop Mal and the other Leinster players from recounting a tale he tells of going for a walk one night and bumping into a Stena Sealink! They also claim that at the moment he is writing a book called *Famous People Who Know Me*. The Leinster lads knew how to enjoy themselves, but when the games came around they gave of their best – none more so than big Mal. He deserved all the caps he won and it was great that he rounded off his career by winning the Heineken Cup.'

THE LIFE OF O'REILLY
TONY O'REILLY

Tony O'Reilly is very much the Roy of the Rovers of Irish rugby. Such was the speed of his progression that even before he had established himself in the green jersey of Ireland he had become a Lions legend. He has the distinction of holding the records for the most tries ever scored by a Lion and the most tries ever scored by a Barbarian. Coached at Belvedere College by the legendary Karl Mullen, he played his first match when he was six years old. His mother asked the priest what he thought of the small players on show. The Jesuit, who had no idea who she was, answered: 'The red fellow's the best.' She glowed with pride, as, of course, the red fellow was Tony. Such was his impact that, when he played in an Under-9s match, with the team leading by 30–6 at half-time, the coach told him to give the opposition a chance and pass the ball more. The young O'Reilly answered, 'Ah, Father, you're only wasting your time. If I pass it, they'll just knock it on, or drop it.'

As a schoolboy, he also excelled at soccer, playing for Home Farm, but he turned his back onthe game on foot because of an assault. During a match, he made a bone-crunching tackle on an opponent. The boy's mother rushed onto the pitch and attacked O'Reilly with her umbrella. The future Lions sensation remarked, 'Rugby is fair enough – you only have your opponent to deal with. Soccer you can keep, if it involves having to deal with your opponent and his mother.'

Belvedere also provided a nursery for O'Reilly's entrepreneurial skills. When he was seven, he was the only boy in his class to make his Holy Communion. To mark the occasion, a priest gave him an orange – an enormous luxury during the war years. Like most of his friends, O'Reilly had never seen an orange. O'Reilly subsequently claimed, 'After I ate the centre, I sold the peel for one penny per piece, thereby showing a propensity for commercial deception which has not left me since.'

TONY O'REILLY

In the 1953–54 season, O'Reilly captained Old Belvedere to the Leinster Cup final, only to see his side lose 11–3. For once, it was O'Reilly's grace in defeat rather than his powers on the field that caught the eye. Twenty-five years later, O'Reilly's sportsmanship on that occasion reaped a handsome dividend. When he was president of Heinz, the company ran into a potentially catastrophic problem over a US Federal Drugs Administration test of its tomato ketchup. While there was no threat to health, and the test was unreliable, if the FDA sustained the result, Heinz would have to recall all its ketchup in the shops, at a cost of £35 million as well as a hammer blow to its reputation. In the end, Heinz's fate lay in the hands of the president of the Del Monte Company, who had the casting vote on the adjudicating committee.

O'Reilly went to make his case personally to the man in charge. He was taken aback to be told, 'Mr O'Reilly, in my parish in San Bernardino is a parish priest called Father McCarthy. He was a scholastic when you were playing in the super-bowl many years ago in Ireland. He said you lost a game but you showed considerable style under pressure. He's a good friend of mine and he says you were a sportsman and a good fellow – I will take his word. The Del Monte Company will vote with Heinz on this.'

In 1955, O'Reilly was the star of the Lions' tour to South Africa, but in 1959 he went one better on the Lions' tour to New Zealand and Australia, amassing a staggering 22 tries. It is probably a testimony to his importance to the team that he played in more matches than any other player, 24 in all.

O'Reilly's achievements on the field do not seem to square with his own assessment of his playing style: 'I suppose you could say I was a slightly furtive player. I hung back waiting for the game to show itself to me rather than show myself to the game.'

One of the many tributes paid to A.J.F. O'Reilly down through the years was: 'Never have you satisfied so many women in the one day.' Despite O'Reilly's erstwhile reputation as something of a ladies' man, this is not what it seems. The source was Irene Johnson, rejoicing at his generous donation towards the running of the 1994 Women's Hockey World Cup.

It seems O'Reilly could also have been a film star. The late Noel Purcell recommended him to Al Corfino, the casting director of the film *Ben-Hur*, for the role that was eventually played by Charlton Heston. O'Reilly's physique made him ideal for the scenes in the galleys. Purcell arranged a meeting between the director and O'Reilly, but the rugby player never showed up. The story of O'Reilly's possible role in the film made headlines in places as far away as South Africa.

79

HERE ORR THERE
PHILIP ORR

Irish rugby has seldom produced a better prop-forward than Phil Orr. In fact, he became the world's most capped prop-forward. Of his fifty-eight caps, forty-nine were won consecutively (one short of the Scottish international Sandy Carmichael's then record for a prop-forward) from 1976 to the match against Wales in 1986. He was recalled for the last match of the 1986 Championship.

In 1976, Orr made his international debut in Paris, coming on as a late replacement for Paddy Agnew, as Ireland lost by a then record 26–3. The magnitude of the day is still with him: 'It was a very strange experience for me. I don't think people appreciate the culture shock Paris is for you, especially the first time. I remember very little about the actual game, except that it went very quickly and I was black and blue all over. I learned to react quicker after that and to look after myself better.'

Orr was one of only three Irish players, with Willie Duggan and Mike Gibson, to be selected on the Lions' tour to New Zealand in 1977. When Geoff Wheel withdrew from the tour, Moss Keane stepped in for him.

'The biggest shock for me about the Lions tour was the British press. We would get on the team bus and there would be two busloads of journalists watching everything we did. All of these guys are looking for a different angle and would dish up any dirt they could find or even a whiff of trouble. The pressure that puts you under is immense.

'I enjoyed the Irish and Leinster tours more than the Lions tours. The 1977 Lions tour lasted three and half months, which is too long. One of the things I learned is that the Irish will talk to everybody. The non-Irish Lions won't. The Lions are not very popular in Australia and New Zealand, because basically they hate the British, though they like the Irish. I particularly enjoyed Ireland's tour to Japan because it was such a different culture. I was lucky to play for a great Leinster side in the late 1970s and early 1980s. We never expected to lose and we could always shift into a higher gear whenever we were threatened in any way.'

In the final match of the 1986 season, Orr regained his place for the home game to Scotland, which Ireland lost by the narrowest of margins. The occasion was all the more memorable because he had the honour of leading the team onto the field. This event left an interesting legacy that hangs proudly today in Orr's home. Some of the Irish players penned a tribute to him and organised a singing telegram for him. He suspects Hugo MacNeill was the author. Hugo was one of Ireland's finest full-backs but on this evidence he is no Seamus Heaney! The best line of this neatly typed, lengthy ode, which Orr has had framed for posterity is: *The finest prop among the Celts*! However, it is the short handwritten message at the side which catches the eye.

The next 50 is the toughest. Sam Torrance

The celebrated golfer happened to be a guest in the Shelbourne Hotel that evening and was readily persuaded to join the festivities.

Even when he departed the Irish scene, Orr still had time for a last hurrah on the international stage: 'After the inaugural World Cup, I retired from international rugby, but later that year I was invited to play for a World XV in Japan as part of the All Blacks tour. They had Japanese players as hooker and as a scrum-half who couldn't speak a word of English between them. These are the two most important positions on the field in terms of making the calls on the pitch and giving instructions. It made absolutely no sense to have non-English speakers in those key positions in a team of essentially English speakers! We learned the Japanese for "one", "three" and "five" and limited ourselves to three calls. To confuse the opposition, I came up with the idea of using Japanese brand names so that our call would be "Honda One" in Japanese, etc. Then it was brought to my attention that one of the Japanese players worked for Honda and didn't like the company name being used in this way. So that ended my masterplan!

'We all knew the All Blacks were in a mean mood. They had defeated Japan 106–4 in the Test game. The mistake the Japanese made was scoring a try. If they hadn't had the cheek to score a try, I reckon the All Blacks would have let them off with a 50-point defeat. I can't remember much about the match expect that we were murdered in the first half at tight-head prop. All I could say by way of tactical insight at half-time was: "We're going to retreat carefully!"'

80

THE LITTLE GENERAL
COLIN PATTERSON

With his fast fingers and his ability to switch the options, Colin Patterson won eleven caps at scrum-half for Ireland between 1978 and 1980, scoring five international tries. His career was tragically ended by injury in the penultimate game of the Lions' tour of South Africa in 1980, after he'd played in three Test matches.

Patterson recalls his international debut against the All Blacks in 1978: 'One of my clearest memories of winning my first cap is of a piece written about me in a local newspaper. The journalist in question had rung my mother a few times but had been unable to contact me. Yet, when I opened the paper, I saw a big piece full of quotes from me. I tackled the journalist about this afterwards. He said, "It's the sort of thing you would have said!" Throughout my career, the amount of quotes attributed to me written by journalists who I had never even met defies belief. I didn't have that problem with the *Irish Times*. In their case, the difficulty was that I never should have been picked for Ireland in the first place. I was described as Ireland's sixth choice.'

Patterson immediately struck up an instant rapport with his half-back partner, Tony Ward, on and off the field: 'I went on *The Late Late Show* with Tony when he was the golden boy of Irish rugby. Wardy was asked if he had thought about defecting to rugby league. When Tony rejected the idea out of hand, Gay Byrne turned to me and said, "Tony is looking down on rugby league, Colin, how about you?"

'"When you are only five feet five inches, you can't afford to look down on anything," I replied.'

With his small stature Patterson was an obvious target for intimidation on the rugby pitch, but he didn't let it faze him: 'I prided myself on my ability to take punishment. The tougher it got, the better I liked it. Whenever I got crushed by somebody, I got up immediately and said to him, "Good tackle, soldier," which really annoyed them.

'At internationals, there were a number of efforts to verbally intimidate me. I never let that sort of bulls**t get to me. The best example of this was when we played Wales in 1980. Where Stuart Lane

217

wasn't going to stuff the ball up my anatomy, I can't say. I eventually turned around and said to him, "Stuart, you don't mean that."

'It was my last home game for Ireland so the BBC gave me the video of the match. When I watched it, I saw again Stuart bursting into laughter and saying, "You're a cheeky wee bol**cks."

'The more a player tried to intimidate me, the more I wound him up by waving at him in the lineout and so on. Apart from the fact that it helped me to win the psychological war, it's the only fun us small fellas get!'

In 1980, on the Lions' tour to South Africa, Patty was at the height of his powers when all was taken from him in an accidental clash. He remembers a marked lack of sympathy from some fans: 'It all began with an innocuous incident. I was screaming in agony, the pain was so intense. My situation was not helped by the fact that the referee tried to play amateur doctor with me and started poking around with my leg. I was stretchered off but they are so fanatical about their rugby out there that two fans rushed on. One took my discarded boot and the other my sock, and he asked me if I would give him my shorts.

'The Welsh players did a classic wind-up on the English player Mike Slemen, who was the leading try scorer on the tour. All of them gathered into the one room and rang him up pretending to be from the BBC World Service, with a suitable posh accent. They fed him a lot of compliments and he started blowing his own trumpet and claimed that he probably was one of the best players on the tour. Eventually, the Welsh lads could take no more and shouted, "Slemen, you're a useless b*****d."

'The Englishman was mortified that he had been caught out so badly.'

The consequent wrecked medial ligaments from his injury caused Patterson to revise his career plans. Before sustaining that injury, he had arranged to go out and play in Australia for a season. In fact, he had already bought his ticket.

Patterson was a rugby ecumenist, singing the national anthem with gusto before matches even though he was not from Nationalist stock: 'Wardy taught me the first six or seven lines of the anthem and then I discovered that I could sing it to the tune of "The Sash". I sang the first half of "The Soldier's Song" and the second half of "The Sash" just to give it a political balance!'

81

WINGING WITH THE LIONS
CECIL PEDLOW

Cecil Pedlow won 30 caps on the wing for Ireland between 1953 and 1963 and toured with the Lions to South Africa in 1955. In doing so, he followed in a great Irish tradition dating back to Larry Bulger, who was capped eight times as a winger between 1896 and 1898. He played four Test matches for the Lions in their 1896 tour of South Africa, where he became the first Irishman to score a try against South Africa and the first Irish player to score a try for the Lions. His older brother Michael was also capped for Ireland. Both also represented Ireland in athletics.

The 1955 Lions were captained and managed by Irishmen Robin Thompson and Jack Siggins, respectively. The squad featured five Irish players: Thompson, Tom Reid and Robin Roe in the forwards and Tony O'Reilly and Pedlow among the backs. O'Reilly scored no fewer than 16 tries, a record number, and emerged as top scorer.

O'Reilly celebrated his 19th birthday on the Lions' tour to South Africa in 1955. In the opening Test in Johannesburg, the Lions won 23–22, in front of the biggest crowd ever seen at a rugby game. The Springboks led 11–3 and, to compound their misfortune, the Lions lost their flanker Reg Higgins with a broken leg. At the time, no replacements were allowed, so they had to play with 14 men in front of more than 100,000 partisan South Africans. Then three tries from Cliff Morgan, Cecil Pedlow and O'Reilly gave the Lions a 23–11 lead. The Afrikaners replied with a vengeance. In the final minute, Chris Koch crashed over for a try, cutting the deficit to just one point. As Springbok goal-kicking ace van der Schyff faced a relatively easy kick to give the South Africans victory, the Irish members on the team turned to religion. The Limerick lock Tom Reid said, 'Jesus, if he kicks this, I'm turning Protestant.'

To the horror of the home fans, van der Schyff pushed his kick left of the post and the tourists won 23–22. O'Reilly's quick wit was again evident. Asked what he had been doing looking the other way as van der Schyff took the kick that would have given South Africa victory, he replied, 'I was in direct communion with the Vatican.'

It comes as no surprise that Pedlow was a massive fan of both Reid and O'Reilly as much for their comic qualities as for their exceptional skills on the pitch. Reid saw rugby as a 'little refreshment of my spirit' and was a great diplomat. On that tour to South Africa, during an official reception, O'Reilly and Reid were in a group of Lions tourists who were asked their opinion about the political situation. An awkward silence descended on the party until Reid piped up, 'Well, sir, I think nothing of it. I come from Limerick in southern Ireland and I have my own political problems.'

Reid, who suffered from bad eyesight, went to live in Canada after that tour. In 1959, he memorably linked up with O'Reilly again. After the tour in New Zealand, the Lions stopped off to play a Test in Canada. O'Reilly was standing in line before the match when he heard a loud Limerick accent booming out over the ground, 'Hello, Reilly, I know you're there. I can't see you but I can hear you all right!'

Such is O'Reilly's flair with words, it is difficult to imagine that he was once out-quipped – but miracles do happen. England beat Ireland 20–0. As he walked off the pitch, O'Reilly turned to Reid and said, '20–0! That was dreadful!'

Reid responded, 'Sure, weren't we lucky to get the nil!'

Mick English was a big admirer of Pedlow: 'What do you look for in a right winger? It doesn't matter if they are big and strong or small and compact but they need, above all, speed. They also need to be able to deceive their opponent because otherwise they can't get away, especially because generally they get very little space. That's why they need to be clever and thinking. They should have good hands and know instinctively where to turn up in both defence and attack. Cecil Pedlow ticked all those boxes and that is why he won so many caps for Ireland, why he played for the Lions and why I rate him as one of the greats of Irish rugby.'

82

POPPY
NICK POPPLEWELL

The 1990s were generally a bleak time for Irish rugby. Yet the decade produced one of the great Irish props Nick Popplewell, one of the few world-class players from Ireland of that era. His status was such that he was an automatic selection for the Lions tour in 1993. At one point, he was rucking beside Brian Moore. Poppy got a blow to the head and said to Moore, 'I can see two balls and cannot continue.'

Moore replied, 'Get back on the pitch and kick both.'

It would not be Popplewell's last encounter with Moore, who was notorious for trying to out-psych opponents before key internationals. Indeed, some of his colleagues on the English team remarked that, when he played against France in Paris, he was more focused on putting his opponent off than he was on playing his own game. There was one famous occasion when he was hoist with his own petard in Ireland's 13–12 win over England at Twickenham in 1994. The Irish players decided to start a fight with the English team early in the match, to throw the English guys off their stride. In the dressing-room beforehand, the question arose as to who should start the fight. Poppy's eyes turned to Peter Clohessy. When the match started, the Claw was looking around for a suitable person to fight with. He first considered Jason Leonard, but then thought he might be a bit of a handful to deal with, so his eyes fell on Brian Moore when there was a scrum in front of the English posts.

Moore could not be called the most handsome man in the world. One of his teammates said of him, in an alcohol-induced moment, that his front teeth are in the back of his mouth and the back teeth are in the front, and that he was born so ugly that his mother thought his face was on fire and she decided to put it out – with a shovel!

The Claw said to him, 'Listen, pal, what are you going to do for a face when Saddam wants his a**ehole back?'

Moore immediately started a bust-up and, because he struck the first blow, Ireland got a penalty and three easy points.

The 1993 Lions tour left Popplewell with many happy moments.

Naturally, it is important to have light moments on a tour whether it is with club, country or the Lions, and a popular way of breaking the monotony in a rugby tour is a 'court session', where players are judged by their peers and given an appropriate punishment for their transgressions. Inevitably, these sessions generally involve taking in more than a modicum of alcohol. People are fined for different reasons, and the more fines they get, the more alcohol they enjoy. Players are charged for incidents in training or in matches, so somebody who dropped the ball a few times in training might be charged with being a 'butterfingers'. The fine might be to drink a bottle of beer without using their hands.

On the 1993 tour, 'Judge' Paul Rendall sentenced Scott Hastings to listen to two hours of Richard Clayderman tapes on his personal stereo after he found him guilty of having his hair cut in a style that was 'an affront to what little hair Graham Dawe had left'.

At one stage on that tour, Nick Popplewell was the judge, Stuart Barnes was the defending barrister and Brian Moore was the prosecutor. Things took an unexpectedly serious turn one night before the first Test, when Moore suddenly started talking about tactics. He said, 'I've got an idea to improve our chances on this tour.'

Barnes immediately said, 'Great. When are you leaving?'

On that tour, Popplewell got to experience Barnes' unique sense of humour. In 1990, Bath beat old rivals Gloucester 6–3 in a closely fought match to reach the Pilkington Cup final. After the game, the Bath players and their significant others retreated to the Rec for a celebration. Barnes was chatting with one of the supporters and offered to buy him a drink. 'What would you like?'

The fan thought he was in heaven to have a drink bought by the Bath captain and replied, 'I'd like something tall, cold and full of gin.'

'Then come and meet my wife,' answered Barnes.

Dissatisfaction with facilities is an occupational hazard for rugby tourists. The 1993 Lions tour was no exception. The secretary of the touring party, Bob Weighill, asked for an extra pat of butter to accompany his bread roll. He took umbrage when he was told this would not be possible. 'Do you know who I am?'

'No, sir.'

The waiter listened impassively as Mr Weighill listed his auspicious catalogue of titles. Then he softly replied, 'And do you know who I am?'

'No.'

NICK POPPLEWELL

'I'm in charge of the butter.'

Tony Ward was a big fan of Poppy but prefaced his comments about him with a plea for understanding: 'Backs refer to the forwards as "donkeys" – affectionately, of course! The donkeys refer to backs as "fairies". As a fairy talking about donkeys, I will own up to not having the in-depth knowledge of front-row play that people like Ray McLoughlin have. I tend to like forwards like Poppy for their mobility. The connoisseurs of the game will say that the best forwards are technically good scrummagers. I think that the game has changed so much now that the onus is on the forwards to get around the field as Nicky did. I played with him at Greystones and it came as no surprise to me that he went on to become a world-class player with both Ireland and the Lions.'

83

THE MIGHTY QUINN
MICK QUINN

'Mine has been an eventful career.' This is Mick Quinn's summation of a life in rugby that brought him ten caps for Ireland at out-half.

Quinn was an ever-present in Ireland's Championship success in 1974, the season that provided him with his finest hour, as he recalls: 'My best game for Ireland was unquestionably against England in Twickenham in 1974. Although the final score, 26–21, was deceptively close, we hockeyed them that day – scoring four tries. It was such a wonderful feeling after the game to know that I had played to my very best and the team had performed to its best. I have an unbeaten record against England and Wales – not many Irish internationals can say that. OK, so I only played against them once!'

After the high of the Championship victory in 1974, Quinn was quickly brought down to earth: 'The one great disappointment of my career was when I was a standby for the Lions' tour to South Africa. The English fly-half Alan Old got injured near the end of the tour. I got a call at home from one of the Lions management team, Albert Ager, who told me to get ready for the trip to South Africa. An hour later, I had my bags packed and at the hall door. Then another call came from Ager, a name I will never forget, telling me that, in fact, I would not be travelling and asking me did I mind. What a question to ask? Of course, I lied and said no, but it was devastating. It turned out that, after he had called me, someone else rang Mike Gibson, who had declined the invitation to tour initially.'

Quinn, though, did get the chance to tour with Ireland, and his worst moment in rugby came on one tour with them: 'On the New Zealand tour in 1976, we were losing 15–3 to Canterbury. I was sub. From my point of view, everything was going great. When you are a sub, you don't really want things to be going well for the team, because, if it does, how else are you going to get your place back? Larry Moloney broke his arm so Tony Ensor replaced him. Wallace McMaster got injured, and, with a sinking heart, I realised I would have to play on the wing. It was my first time ever to play in that position. I was petrified and

I can tell you I wished I was wearing brown shorts!

'As I walked on, one of their players, Alex "Griz" Wyllie, came over to me and said, "You've come a long way to die, son."

'When I was in Newbridge, Father Heffernan had always drilled into me the belief that you should never let anybody intimidate you. At that stage, I made the biggest mistake of my life. I said, "Listen, pal, if my dog had a face like yours, I would shave his a**e and get him to walk backwards."

'Every chance he got after that, he clobbered me. Even when the ball was somewhere else, he kept coming at me. When I said the ball is over there, he answered, "I couldn't give a f**k where the ball is. I'm going to kill you."'

Quinn made some interesting friendships through rugby: 'At one stage, Willie John McBride and I were invited to South Africa to play for a World XV against the Springboks. I was interviewed on South African TV and asked what I thought of the main contenders for the number-10 shirt with the Springboks and if any out-half had impressed me. I mentioned that I had been taken by this new kid called Naas Botha, who I had seen play on television. The next day I was training when this fella came over to me and I recognised him as Botha. He wanted to thank me for my compliments.

'Naas was a hugely controversial figure in South Africa. They either loved him or hated him. We got on very well and I subsequently invited him to come over and get some experience in Lansdowne. I thought nothing more about it until some months later I got a phone call at home. It was Naas. He said he would like to take up my offer of hospitality. I told him that he would be welcome and asked him when would he be travelling over. Then he told me, "Well, Mr Quinn, I'm ringing you from a place called O'Connell Street in Dublin!"

'He brought his brother Darius with him, who since became a Dutch Reformed minister. He used to organise prayer meetings in my house!'

84

REID ON
PADDY REID

According to Jim McCarthy, former Irish centre Paddy Reid should have won a hundred caps for Ireland but he 'only' wore the green jersey six times. Reid is unwilling to blame anybody for his exclusion from the Irish team. His international colleague Jim McCarthy is less reticent and points out that a lot of curious selection decisions have much more to do with politics than with rugby merit – the 'you scratch my back, I'll scratch yours' syndrome. In 1948, there were two Leinster selectors, two Ulster selectors and the other selector was a Cork man. Championing the cause of a Limerick player would not have been uppermost on any of their agendas.

After a distinguished schools career with Crescent College, in 1947 Reid followed his father onto the Garryowen side, captaining them to the Munster Cup, Munster Senior League and Charity Cup in 1947, the same year he led Munster to the interprovincial championships.

'My love of rugby began when I was a five-year-old, when my father bought me my first rugby ball. He played for Garryowen and Munster, as did my father-in-law, Mick Kelly. I grew up in a home filled with rugby stories. One of my clearest memories is of my dad telling me about travelling to Belfast in 1911, when it was like going to the moon because of the poor state of communications. They visited the shipyard and read a notice on one of them which stated, "Even God can't sink this ship." It was the *Titanic*!'

He recalls with pride how his international career began in 1946, in the unofficial internationals against France and Wales: 'My first match in the green jersey was a tremendous thrill. To me, rugby is life. There could be no greater honour in my eyes than running out on Lansdowne Road for the first time.'

Reid was first capped in an official international against the touring Australians on 6 December 1947. It was not a fairytale debut, as Ireland went down 16–3. The following New Year's Day, though, saw the opening of an unexpectedly glorious chapter in the history of Irish rugby when Ireland had a shock 13–6 victory over France at Colombes.

Reid enjoyed being in the thick of the action: 'A great character in the team was Barney Mullan. The night before the game in Paris, we had a team meeting as per usual. Barney came up with the idea that, if we were under pressure during the game and got a lineout, he would call a short one and throw it out over the forwards' heads and lift the siege. True to plan, we got a lineout on our own 25. The French players were huge. They looked like mountains to us, so we needed to out-think them. Mullan threw it long and Jack Kyle grabbed it, passed it to me, I fed it to Des McKee and he returned the compliment for me to score under the posts. The glory was mine but it was Barney's tactical awareness that earned us that try.

'Travelling to Paris for us at the time was like going to the edge of the world. We were as green as grass. After our win, we were invited to a reception at the Irish embassy. Of course, champagne was the order of the day, which was a very novel experience for most of us. We were knocking it back as if it was stout! To me, the incident that best illustrated our innocence was when the Dolphin pair Jim McCarthy and Bertie O'Hanlon asked for red lemonade!'

Reid was part of Ireland's Grand Slam-winning side in 1948. Did the players receive any reward for their unique achievement?

'The only thing we got was a photo of the winning team and the team crest!'

After the campaign, Reid joined his international teammate, prop-forward Jack Daly, and 'went north' to rugby league with the Huddersfield club. What prompted this move?

'I had no job and I was getting married. It was as simple as that. It was a great experience, and I acquired great insights into life, but on a personal level it was also a major readjustment. It was a very different world. There were a lot of Australians on the team. They were all married and went home after training and matches. There wasn't the great community spirit that there had been on the Irish team.

'I played at Wembley in front of 98,000 people, but I wasn't nervous because I had taken part in big matches before. Before the game, we were introduced to the Prince of Wales. As we shook hands, I said to him, "Everyone at home is asking for you!" I returned to Ireland in 1950. I was always a homebird.'

Reid's biggest fear is that the new rugby climate might dissipate the passion for rugby in Limerick and its egalitarian structures: 'Limerick is such a stronghold of rugby because there are no class boundaries. At one stage, the Garryowen front row was a doctor, a docker and a lawyer.

'Rugby is more than recreation here. I went with a friend of mine to a match between Garryowen and Blackrock. Garryowen had a 16 st. player called Frank "The Bull" Hayes, who was what was known then as a "failed priest". We were shocked during the match when Hayes walked up behind Dave O'Leary and tapped him on the shoulder and, when he turned around, he strechered him with a punch. Much later, I asked Frank about it and told him I thought it was an awful thing for him to do. He said, "He kicked me the year before." Dave subsequently became a member of the "big five" (the Irish selectors). Some years later, he confirmed Frank's story for me.

'The club rivalry in Limerick is intense. To say there is no love lost between Young Munster and Garryowen is a massive understatement. The incident that best sums this up for me occurred in 1993 when Liam Hall and I travelled to Dublin to see Young Munster play St Mary's in the decisive match of the AIL. Munsters won. After the game, we walked past Johnny Brennan from Munsters and an elderly lady who I recognised immediately because of her strong connection with the club, though she never had any dealings with me. I turned around and said, "Congratulations, Johnny."

'Johnny told her: "That's Paddy Reid from Garryowen."

'Her reply to this information was: "I hates him!"'

85

RING(LAND) OF FIRE
TREVOR RINGLAND

Trevor Ringland will always be remembered for his fantastic tries in the green shirt and as one of the finest wingers Ireland have ever produced. He was the most impressive Irish performer on the 1983 Lions tour.

Ciaran Fitzgerald laughs at the memory of Trevor's first cap for Ireland: 'The most difficult players to handle are those making their debuts. They get distracted by the press and the hype. The worst of all, though, are relatives who want to socialise with them and fill their head with all kinds of nonsense. The best way around this is the "buddy system", to get them to room with one of the more experienced players. At the time, the young players looked up to Moss Keane as if he was God. As everybody knows, Mossie spoke in a broad Kerry brogue, which at the best of times could be difficult to understand but the new players from the North found it virtually impossible. We had a little ritual for those new players.

'I especially remember Trevor Ringland's initiation. We put him beside Moss for dinner and Trevor was in awe of him. We primed Moss to speak for two minutes in fast-forward mode! He was talking pure gibberish. Then he turned to Trevor and asked him what he thought of that. Trevor answered lamely, "I think you're right," not having a clue what Moss had said!

'Then Moss launched off again, only faster. I can still see the panic on Trevor's face. He was going green! All the lads were killing themselves, trying to keep a straight face until Trevor found out he was being wound up.'

Hugo MacNeill believes Ringland was pivotal to Ireland's Triple Crown in 1985: 'The Scots had beaten us 32–9 at Lansdowne Road the previous March and we were going into their back yard with a young team. We were whitewashed in 1984 and so many experienced players retired that year. Mick Doyle asked us, "What are we afraid of?" The answer most people would have given him was the wooden spoon. But literally from the first minute I sensed that something special was about to happen to us all. Deano moved it wide, Keith Crossan split the line, Brenny [Brendan Mullin] passed to me and the ball squirted forward as I was tackled over the line. If I had the ball in my other hand, we'd have scored a breathtaking try with our first attack. Our confidence was instantly lifted. We thought, "Wow, did we really do that?"

'The Scots got on top of us slowly and it looked like it was going to end badly, but then we produced a little piece of magic. The back row created a position on the far side; the ball went wide and through the hands of nearly every back on the team before Trevor Ringland scored in the corner. We won 18–15. That little cameo showed Trevor's importance to the team.

'I think Mick Doyle brought out the best in Trevor that year. Doyler best summed up his philosophy when he said, "I want you to run, and if that doesn't work out, I want you to run again."

'On a personal level, I had reason to be grateful to Doyler that season. I had one game that didn't go well for me. After the game, a number of journalists were calling for a change at full-back. Mick said to me in training, "Hugo, I want you in this side, OK?"

'We had a good chat and he made me feel confident again. Doyler had a great gift for man-management and I saw how well he dealt with Trevor and gave him the confidence to believe he was one of the best wingers in the world at the time – which he undoubtedly was.'

In recent years, Ringland has become a significant figure in the Ulster Unionist Party. With Hugo MacNeill, he was the brains behind the Peace International between Ireland and the Barbarians in the wake of the Canary Wharf bombing and the breakdown of the IRA ceasefire in 1996.

Colin Patterson was anxious to be something of a mentor to Ringland, drawing on his time with the Lions in 1980: 'It was a real education touring with the Welsh. That was the era when you paid for your own telephone calls home. They had three great tricks devised never to pay for a telephone. Plan A was to charm the hotel receptionist into giving them the secret code they could use to make calls without having them charged to them. Plan B was to distract the receptionist and for one of them to sneak in behind the desk and steal all their telephone bills. Plan C was, when a journalist asked for an interview, they traded it for a phone call.

'Best of all, though, was when we went into the Adidas factory. We were allowed to pick a bag of our choice and stuff it with gear. Most

TREVOR RINGLAND

of us selected the most stylish bags and filled them with gear. All the Welsh guys without exception took the biggest bags in the shop and walked out with half of the gear in the factory! In 1983, when Trevor Ringland was chosen to tour with the Lions to New Zealand, the advice I gave him was: "Be sure and stay close to the Welsh when they visit the Adidas factory!"'

86

OUT OF SOUTH AFRICA
JOHN ROBBIE

John Robbie played on a losing Lions side in 1980 and had a record of played nine, lost nine for Ireland. Before he became known for his rugby, Robbie was a child star: 'When I was very small, I was chosen to do a Christmas TV advert for Raleigh bikes. A friend of Mum's was in the advertising business, and cheeky small blond kids were always top of the shopping list. Anyway, I had to race down the stairs of a house, gaze at the presents around the tree, gasp as my eyes picked out the new bike and turn to my "parents" and utter the stunningly imaginative words: "It's a Raleigh!" The ad ended with me riding the bike around the tree. All great fun for a ten-year-old, but the trouble was that it kept reappearing each Christmas. For a gawky 14-year-old, about to crash into the nightmare of adolescence, the nightly appearance of the advert made me blush scarlet. However, for doing the ad, I received the princely sum of £21. That really was big bucks in those days, and I was most irate when Mum suggested that some of it should go to the coal bill!'

On the rugby fields, Robbie first came to prominence as captain of Trinity College. There he had some unusually motivational ploys. Before a colours match with bitter rivals UCD when Trinity were hot favourites and he felt the team were over-confident, John decided that a different type of tactic was necessary. He started with a real gut-wrenching speech. As he got to the part about how none of the team would ever forgive themselves if they lost, he made a conscious effort to start weeping. When he started to cry, the effect was electric: total concentration, and the atmosphere changed dramatically. It stayed that way, and the next day they beat UCD fairly easily.

After touring with the Lions, he made the momentous decision to take his family to strike out for the shores of the promised land in South Africa. His introduction to provincial rugby was not what he expected: 'I made my debut for Transvaal away to Griqualand

232

West. We won well, and I assumed it was drinks and bed just like at home. But I was told that all new caps had to wait outside the team room until summoned. I got called in. The room had been altered and for all the world it was like a courtroom. All the players were dressed immaculately in their number-one blazers, ties and pants, and there were three "judges" sitting at the front. Everyone was deadly serious and there wasn't a sound. I made some wisecrack as I walked in, and I was quickly told to shut up. It was all serious and I got nervous. I had to remove my shoes and stand on a chair in front of the dock. I was asked what I thought of playing for the team. Again, I made a joke but no one laughed. I was asked to sing a song, which I did; no one clapped or did anything. Suddenly, I was grabbed, turned upside down across one of the lock's shoulders with my backside up, and each member of the team with the flat of his hand gave me, in turn, a real smack across my bum. I couldn't believe it. The pain was excruciating. After they had stopped, I was angry and nearly lost my temper. Luckily, the judge told me this was just tradition, and to say nothing. Then I was turned up and hit again. I was actually crying in pain and anger. But when it stopped, the judge made a genuine speech of welcome, I was told that now I was a true Transvaal player and each player shook my hand. During this escapade, I also had to drink four or five glasses of beer. At the end it was actually quite emotional. I gather it was a fairly tame initiation, known as the *borsel* [brush], by some provincial standards, but I must say I still hated it.'

After his rugby career ended, Robbie carved out a new career in radio, working for Radio 702, and has become South Africa's answer to Joe Duffy.

On his rare trips back to Ireland, Robbie enjoys the opportunity to see the Irish team play if he can. He does not always get the reception he expects: 'I left Ireland in 1981 after we were whitewashed! In '82, Ireland won the Triple Crown and, in '83, the Championship. I timed my first trip home to Ireland in '84 to coincide with Ireland's Five Nations game against Wales. Ireland were whitewashed again that season. I had missed out on two glorious years for Ireland and came home to see them losing again, an experience I was all too familiar with from my playing days. After the Welsh game, I was still in the stand as the crowd was thinning. I heard a voice shouting, "Robbie, Robbie." I looked around until I found the owner of this voice. When I eventually

met this stranger's eye, he said, "John Robbie, I'm addressing you."
I was very flattered to be recognised and gave him the royal wave.
After all the drama, though, he took the wind out of my sails when
he said, "You're some f**king good luck charm!"'

87

THE MAGNIFICENT NUMBER 7
FERGUS SLATTERY

A product of Blackrock College, Fergus Slattery was capped more than sixty times for Ireland as an open-side wing-forward between 1970 and 1984 (a then world record for a flanker), scoring three international tries. He was part of a 19-match record back-row combination with Willie Duggan and John O'Driscoll. He captained Ireland seventeen times, including two overseas tours, to Australia in 1979 and to South Africa in 1981. It is recognised worldwide that 'Slats' on form was the best because of his presence on the field. He was always first to the break-down and first to the out-half. His angles were so good that he always managed to put the opposition under pressure, forcing either the centre or out-half to release the ball. The significance of this is that, when this happens, it is the wing-forward who is dictating the game and not vice versa. Although Slattery played his best rugby on the Lions tour of 1974 (when, with Roger Uttley and Mervyn Davies, he formed one of the finest back rows in Lions history), as he got older he read the game very well. He put his body through extraordinary punishment.

Slattery's first cap came against the Springboks in 1970 in an 8–8 draw. The terraces behind the goals at Lansdowne Road were empty and the playing surface cordoned off by barbed wire to prevent protesters from invading the pitch.

'It was a very controversial match. I was in UCD at the time and there was a forum before the game to debate whether or not Ireland should play South Africa. I spoke in favour and Kader Asmal spoke against. The weather was very bad before the match and they put straw on the pitch. It was like running into a barn. Having said that, the game lost none of its impact for me because of that. Things went pretty well for us that season. We beat Scotland 16–11 and then defeated a Wales side seeking the Triple Crown 14–0.

'Selection for the Lions' tour of New Zealand in 1971 was a natural progression. I was disappointed that I did not make the Test side but it was a terrific theatre of education. You're playing against the same guys every week and of course you're living and breathing rugby.

'For me, touring was the best part of rugby. I would have traded all my interpro appearances for one tour to France. Even though we had such great success on the Lions' tour to South Africa in 1974, it got very boring at the end. You are packing your bags every three days and everything becomes very repetitive. I decided that I would never take part in a Lions tour again.

'After that tour, I came back and played a lot of matches. I pushed myself too hard and my blood count went down. I see my career in two phases: before and after that tour. Up to then, rugby was everything for me but after that it wasn't. I had to look after my career.'

Consequently, he spent a year and a half in the international wilderness. He returned and led the Irish on the successful tour Down Under in 1979.

'Before the Australian tour, I thought we would have our work cut out to win the Tests. I think it's fair to say Australia under-performed in the first match because we caught them on the hop, but we beat them on merit in the second game.'

Surprisingly, an apparent low point of his career elicits the greatest passion from him: 'The 1981 tour to South Africa was a landmark in the development of the Irish side. We played out of our skins.'

Ireland's fine performances on the tour tempted Slattery to engage in what was to be a lucrative speculation: 'When we left South Africa, Willie Duggan asked me, "Fancy a bet on the Triple Crown?"

'The odds were a generous 14–1 and it was the first time I had ever bet on myself. Of course I was delighted to win.'

Slattery relinquished the captaincy to Ciaran Fitzgerald before the 1981–82 season. What prompted the move and how did he evaluate his successor?

'We had lost seven matches on the trot and needed a change. I was worried about Fitzie before the Australian tour in 1979 because he had a reputation for getting injured, but he held his own there and grew in stature from then on. He was made to lead and his record as captain speaks for itself. The only disappointment I had in 1982 was the Paris game. We went there as favourites but they hockeyed us.'

88

THE STRIFE OF BRIAN
BRIAN SPILLANE

After the disaster of 1984, one of the players who transformed Ireland's fortunes in 1985 was their new number 8, Brian Spillane. With Philip Matthews and Nigel Carr in the back row, he was key to Mick Doyle's philosophy of playing a running game. Having played Gaelic football, Spillane's hands were much better than the average number 8.

The Bohemians player was a young medical doctor in Limerick. Initially, he played for Munster in the second row but had been troubled by injury. When Munster selected him at number 8, he gave some great displays and was selected to make his international debut in the match against England due to take place at Lansdowne Road on 19 January, but the game was called off because of snow. As soon as the Irish squad heard the news, they all went down to O'Donoghues and some got completely drunk. That kind of thing would not happen in the professional era.

Apart from the playing demands, Spillane had to quickly learn the etiquette of being an international player. There was an unwritten code about fair play back then. Spillane saw this over two years in internationals between England and Ireland. After Ireland played England at home, they had the post-match dinner, which, for the first time, women were allowed to attend. Before the dinner, a lot of drink had been consumed and one of Spillane's Irish teammates was 'tired and emotional' and had to go to bed. When his girlfriend came down from her room, there was an English player in the lift with her. He mistakenly thought she fancied him, so he grabbed her and groped her. She was terribly embarrassed. Her boyfriend did not get to hear about it until the following day. The next year, when Ireland played the return fixture, a lineout took place and the call was made to the Irish forward in question. He was marking the English player responsible. The English guy jumped and the Irish player 'planted' him and put his opponent's nose to the other side of his face. The English player huddled up his forwards and told him the next time they got a lineout to throw the ball to him and he would plant his opponent in turn. The

English players knew about the incident the previous year and told him he deserved it. That night, the English player came to the Irish player and apologised.

Spillane ended up making his debut against Scotland in Murrayfield. The night before the team played Scotland, the Irish lads went to the cinema, as was the tradition back then. The film was *Beverly Hills Cop*, starring Eddie Murphy, whose catchphrase was: 'Get the f**k out of here.' As soon as the film was over, the lights came on and the Irish team stood up and saw that the Scottish team were sitting three rows behind them. The Irish had a popcorn fight with their Scottish counterparts, which was great fun, and the Scots started shouting at the boys in green, 'Get the f**k out of here.'

Almost as soon as the match started the next day, John Jeffrey tackled Paul Dean very late. He knew exactly what he was doing; it was too early in the game for him to be penalised. As he pinned Deano down on the ground, he whispered in his ear, 'Get the f**k out of here.'

The nice thing from Spillane's point of view was that the Irish did get the f**k out of there – but with a victory.

In the decisive Triple Crown game against England, with the score tied at 10–10, Spillane won a lineout and the resulting Irish drive led to Michael Kiernan dropping a decisive goal, setting up an explosion of noise for the remaining few minutes.

Spillane went to the inaugural World Cup in 1987. He left an enduring imprint on Donal Lenihan's memory: 'The Irish team were coached by Mick Doyle. Doyler decided he was going to get into shape on the trip because he was two stone overweight. He started to train with the backs, and when the lads saw this they stepped up a gear. At the end of the session, Doyler was in bits. Later that night, I heard that he had been taken to hospital. As captain, I went to see him that evening in hospital in a taxi. I was in the front seat and Syd Millar and Mick Molloy were in the back. At one stage in the conversation, Syd said Mick's wife, Lynne, had been on the phone and was very concerned about him and wanted to come Down Under to see him. Then he said his girlfriend, Mandy, was very worried about him and she too wanted to travel to see him. The Maori taxi driver turned to me and said with real feeling, "That stuff about holy Catholic Ireland is a load of crap!"

'When I got back from the hospital, Spillane asked, "Did he have a girl or a boy?"'

Brendan Mullin has a special memory of Spillane: 'For me, there is no better place to play rugby than Cardiff Arms Park. It just has no equal. We hadn't won there since 1967 going into the 1985 match, but we beat them 21 points to 9, with great tries from Keith Crossan and Trevor Ringland. I remember there was some discussion before the match about what we would do when the crowd started singing at us to intimidate us. Brian Spillane said, "We'll sing back at them!"

'In some of the pictures showing the arm-linked scene, you can see Brian singing at the crowd. Don't ask me what, though!'

89

THE SPRING TIDE
DICK SPRING

Dick Spring's progress in rugby was to some extent put on hold because of his years spent in London and the United States, as he explains: 'I played for two seasons with London Irish. The first season was a disaster, but when Ken Kennedy took over the captaincy the following season, we did much better. I played scrum-half in New York because I reckoned it was the only possible position a back could get the ball! Mind you, it's not easy being a left-footed scrum-half because you have to turn to get your kick in. I was offered a trial for the American side. There was no money in rugby there at the time and I would have to pay my expenses. The final trial was in Colorado and it would cost me 500 bucks to get there. I was there to make money, not to spend it on internal flights, so I declined the invitation. Shortly after, my small, younger brother, Donal, was picked to play for Ireland, so I decided I would return home and try to emulate his achievement.

'Before I came home, I had trained hard and was in good shape. I joined Lansdowne and was very annoyed to be selected on the seconds for my first match. I was on the firsts the following week. In my second year, I was made captain and we won the Leinster Cup. My chief function as captain was to get Mick Quinn to pass the ball!'

For his part, Mick Quinn speaks about his former Lansdowne colleague with genuine admiration: 'Everybody remembers Dick Spring as the player who dropped the ball which lost Ireland the game against Wales in Cardiff Arms Park in 1979. But that's a mistaken impression. He was a fantastic club player, but the Cardiff incident shattered his confidence on the international stage.'

That year evokes mixed feelings for Dick, though: 'The highlight of my career was my first cap against France. That's the game I show to my kids. I can't remember what happened in the Wales game!'

After twenty-two minutes, Ireland led 6–0 courtesy of two long-range penalties from Tony Ward. The dream of a win in Cardiff was starting to look as if it might be fulfilled. In the 25th minute, the picture changed dramatically. Davies, the Welsh fly-half, lofted a kick towards the Irish posts, but Spring was under it and there seemed to be no danger. Somehow, the ball slipped through his hands and bounced over the Irish line for Allan Martin to rush on and score a try, which Steve Fenwick converted.

While his political career flourished, Spring has never been allowed to forget that incident and has been the butt of jokes about a safe pair of hands. Throughout the enormously popular series on RTE Radio One *Scrap Saturday*, Spring was consistently referred to as 'Butterfingers'.

'It was just the luck of the draw. Nobody who ever played with me doubted my ability under a high ball. I was caught out of position and was keeping an eye out for J.P.R. Williams. There's no question but that it did affect my self-confidence from then on. The only memory people have of me is of that dropped ball. If Andy Irvine had been axed every time he dropped the ball, he would have spent a lot of time on the bench. I'm not suggesting I was as good a player as Andy, but I think that one ball should be kept in perspective.'

Two weeks later, Ireland had a welcome opportunity to redeem themselves with a home game against England. The clash with the 'auld enemy' was a bruising battle that had the Lansdowne Road crowd at fever pitch. Ireland won 12–7. Before the next game, Spring was dropped to make way for Bangor's Ronnie Elliott.

The call of politics deprived Spring of an opportunity for rehabilitation at international level: 'I was invited by the IRFU to go on the Australian tour in 1979 but I was trying to establish my new law practice and I didn't feel I could afford the time from work. There was another reason for my refusal. There were local elections on that year and I had indicated my wish to run in Tralee. I was elected but decided to play on for a year in Lansdowne out of loyalty to Paddy Boylan, who had succeeded me as captain. The next year, though, I played junior rugby with Tralee. We reached five finals but lost them all. In 1981, there was a general election and I was elected TD and was immediately made a junior minister. I played two rugby games in that capacity. In the second, I was caught in a ruck and I heard two of the opposing forwards arguing over who would be the first to kick the minister's head in. It was then I decided it was time for me to retire.'

Was Spring's rugby background an advantage to him in politics?

'There are no votes in rugby, certainly not in Kerry. John Major was quite impressed when he heard I played for Ireland. He played rugby himself when he was very young but didn't prosper at the game because at that time he was too small. I found that quite surprising because he's a tall man now. John's great passion is cricket and his moods fluctuated a lot depending on the fate of the English team. I was always wary about having sensitive negotiations about the peace process with John when England were playing. The best time to negotiate with him was when England were doing very well – mind you, that didn't happen very often!'

90

EBONY AND IVORY
DONAL SPRING

Donal Spring has an impressive sporting pedigree. His father, Dan Spring, of Kerins O'Rahillys, captained Kerry to All-Ireland football victory in 1940. His maternal uncles, the Laide brothers, of the Crotta O'Neills club, are considered among Kerry's finest hurlers. He made his debut for Ireland against Scotland in 1978, but two weeks later he missed the trip to Paris because he injured himself falling down the stairs in Trinity. He seemed destined to be the backbone of the Irish team for the next few years. However, injuries quickly intervened to curtail his caps total to seven over four seasons, which was a poor return for a player of his class. He is one of an elite group who was capped for Ireland at Schools, Under-23, 'B' and full international level.

What distinguished Spring from most number 8s was his ability to read the game, which made him a real thinking man's player. He was a great strategist and liaised very well with the defence.

His former Lansdowne colleague Mick Quinn speaks about Donal with genuine admiration: 'Donal Spring was a great servant to the club, though the competition between him and our international forward, the other Michael Gibson, was intense. If one of them sold a dummy, the other had to do the same. Gibson the younger was a class act when he was on song, and in 1979 in particular he was sensational in his four games for Ireland. Unfortunately, neither of them ever had the Ireland careers they should have because of injuries. They were both exceptionally talented, though, in different ways. Donal had more of a physical edge.'

As well as being known for his considerable rugby talents, Donal was famously among several Irish players to make a gesture against South African apartheid that would lead to an extraordinary meeting.

Towards the end of January 1981, the IRFU wrote to 44 Irish rugby players, asking if they would be available for the Irish short tour of South Africa in May–June. The letters went out amid a welter of controversy as political, clerical and media people objected to the notion of Ireland having sporting contact with South Africa. A number of Irish players declared themselves unavailable immediately. On foot of a tour of South Africa with London Irish in 1977, Donal Spring went on television to explain why he would not be travelling. Moss Keane, like Tony Ward, in a more low-key way declined to travel on 'a point of principle'. Business commitments ruled out Paul McNaughton and Mick Fitzpatrick. Ciaran Fitzgerald, then an army captain, had been informed by his superiors that he would be refused permission to travel. Perhaps the bravest decision of all was Hugo MacNeill, who was just establishing his place on the Irish team at the time. It took remarkable moral courage for an emerging star to turn down his first overseas tour with his country.

In later years, the former leader of the Labour Party in Britain, Neil Kinnock, himself a keen rugby enthusiast, would cite this gesture from the Irish players as proof that South Africa had got its integration policies wrong. Donal Spring, Hugo MacNeill, Tony Ward and Moss Keane were awarded Honorary Life Membership of Brunel University Students' Union.

In 1990, Spring was rewarded for his principled opposition to touring in South Africa when he was invited with fellow former internationals to a special meeting with Nelson Mandela, during his visit to receive the freedom of the city of Dublin. Mandela wanted to thank them personally for their courageous stand. It was an honour that touched Spring as much as, if not more than, any he had received as a player. Spring met Mandela and his then wife, Winnie, with Tony Ward and the Dunnes Stores workers who had refused to handle South African produce during the apartheid era. Mandela shook their hands and thanked each of them.

A memory to treasure.

This shows that sport is more than mere games. If Hollywood had been commissioned to write a script for the 1995 World Cup a few years later, they wouldn't have been able to come up with the fairytale ending that saw Nelson Mandela's rainbow nation upset the favourites on their World Cup debut, leaving the All Blacks to blame food poisoning. When Mandela walked out to shake hands with the players of South Africa and New Zealand in the moments before the 1995 World Cup final, it was a reminder of how powerful sport can be in symbolising friendship and reconciliation in a public forum. As he presented the trophy to Francois Pienaar, Mandela wore his Springboks jersey. Here was a man who had spent 27 years in a white man's jail, but in his first opportunity to support a white man's game he wore a white man's jersey. To witness him walk out there and shake hands with the black player Chester Williams and all the white players in the Springbok team bore eloquent testimony to sport's power to heal.

91

SHANNONSIDER
COLM TUCKER

With Rodney O'Donnell, Colin Patterson, Ollie Campbell and John O'Driscoll, Shannon's Colm Tucker was chosen on the Lions' tour to South Africa in 1980. The squad comprised the following players:

Full-backs – Rodney O'Donnell (Ireland); Bruce Hay (Scotland); Wings – Andy Irvine (Scotland); Mike Slemen (England); John Carleton (England); Centres – Ray Gravell (Wales); David Richards (Wales); Jim Renwick (Scotland); Clive Woodward (England); Utility defender – Peter Morgan (Wales); Out-halfs – Ollie Campbell (Ireland); Gareth Davies (Wales); Scrum-halfs – Terry Holmes (Wales); Colin Patterson (Ireland); Props – Fran Cotton (England); Clive Williams (Wales); Graham Price (Wales); Phil Blakeway (England); Hookers – Alan Phillips (England); Peter Wheeler (England); Locks – Bill Beaumont (England); Maurice Colclough (England); Allan Martin (Wales); Alan Tomes (Scotland); Flankers – John O'Driscoll and Colm Tucker (both Ireland); Stuart Lane and Jeff Squire (both Wales); Number 8s – Derek Quinnell (Wales); John Beattie (Scotland).

Tucker was an interesting selection because he was unable to command a regular place on the Irish team. Tony Ward, Phil Orr and John Robbie subsequently joined the squad as replacements.

The Lions tour opened Tucker's eyes to the sham amateurism that operated in rugby at the time. Almost all the Lions were sponsored with kit from their local agents of a major footwear firm, the Irish players as well as those from Britain. The Irish contingent heard that the British guys had actually received some cash as well, although it now seems a very small amount – £300 each. The Irish players convened a meeting one evening in one of the players' rooms to decide whether they would contact the firm and insist on cash. Despite two players wanting to do so, the rest felt that this would infringe their amateur status, so the motion carried was to say nothing.

Tucker saw his Irish colleagues have some bizarre experiences on the tour. Tony Ward was a sub to Ollie Campbell in the third Test in Port Elizabeth. To his horror, he discovered in the dressing-room that he had forgotten his boots. It was too late to retrieve them from the team hotel. His problem was exacerbated by the fact that nobody had a spare pair of boots to lend him. He consoled himself with the thought that he probably would not need them. The seating arrangements for the subs that day were bizarre to say the least. They were to sit on the very top row of the stadium. As the match began, Ward was making the long journey up countless flights of stairs with John Robbie when he heard somebody shouting for him. Campbell was injured in the very first moments of the match and was pumping blood. He still has a small scar on his face as a souvenir. It was panic stations all round. Robbie got a pair of boots from a ball boy for Ward to wear. At size nine, they were too big for him – but an even more serious problem was that the studs were moulded. The pitch was waterlogged that day and, even if they had been the right size, they would have been a disaster in the conditions, but they were all he had at the time.

Ward asked John Robbie what the hell he should do.

'Pray as hard as you can,' Robbie replied.

It must have worked, because Ollie somehow continued, and to this day Tucker and his colleagues don't think Noel Murphy, the coach, knows how close he was to learning that his replacement fly-half and goal-kicker in a series decider between the Lions and the Boks had arrived with no boots.

One of their teammates on the tour was the Wales legend Ray Gravell, who told me his memories of the tour and his impressions of Tucker: 'It was such a shame that Rodney O'Donnell's career ended so prematurely on that tour. Rodney was actually lucky to still have the use of his limbs after breaking his neck. If Dr John O'Driscoll hadn't been playing and shouted to the ambulance men when Rod went down not to move him, then he could have died or been paralysed. Moreover, John was only playing against the Junior Boks that day because Colm Tucker had sprained his ankle.

'Ireland also supplied two great wing-forwards on that Lions tour in Colm Tucker and John O'Driscoll. I would die for John O'Driscoll. What a player and what a man. Mind you, John and Maurice Colclough were always trying to get me pi**ed. They were always pouring rum, without my knowledge, into my soup. Colm was a much underrated player in Ireland because he did not win many caps. I guarantee you, though, there was nobody who played with him or against on that Lions tour who underestimated him. He was a fine player and always gave 110 per cent commitment. He may not have a huge profile but he was a genuine star of Irish and Lions rugby. The All Blacks found that out, too, when he brought them down to earth on that famous day when Munster beat the All Blacks in 1978.'

Tucker himself has caused some amusement for his teammates, notably when Ireland played France at the Parc des Princes in 1980. In the match programme, his surname was spelled with an 'F' instead of a 'T'.

Tony Ward experienced Tucker's particular presence up close and personal: 'I played against him often and remember him especially because he was a good ball handler and had great upper-body strength. He was a great servant of Shannon and Munster. He was unusual in that he won almost as many caps for the Lions as he did for Ireland. When I was playing for Garryowen, the crowd loved it when he had the ball tucked under his arm and he was running at me or indeed at any of the midfield backs. Although he was not the most mobile ever, because he was such a powerful player there was only going to be one winner! The attitude in Limerick when forwards came down from Dublin was one of: "Here's another pussycat." Accordingly, they got "the treatment", a real roasting from the forwards on Shannonside. Nobody could administer the treatment better than Colin!'

92

BAND OF BROTHERS
DAVID WALLACE

David Wallace is part of a unique rugby family. Two of his brothers played for both Ireland and the Lions. Richard Wallace won the first of his 29 caps on the Irish wing against Namibia in 1991 and his last against England in 1998. Like his brother Paul, he scored five tries in Test games for Ireland. Paul won the first of 45 caps in the Irish front row against Japan in 1995 and the last against Georgia in 2002.

Naturally, David was influenced by his brothers: 'Richard went out on the Lions tour as a replacement in '93. I was only 16 at the time and it was an incredible thrill for us as a family to see him playing with and against the legends of world rugby. To think of Richard playing for the Lions was inspirational for me, particularly as he was, relatively speaking, new to international rugby. I learned a lot from him about the training and the physical preparation that is required for rugby at the highest level. When Paul was selected to replace Peter Clohessy before the Lions' tour to South Africa in '97 actually began, he was looking out a partition in the airport when he saw "The Claw" coming towards him on the way home. It was awkward for him. The fact that he made it onto the Test team and was considered one of the stars of the tour was great for the family.'

That year was also a significant one for David's own emerging rugby career: 'I played in all the games on the Irish development tour to New Zealand that year but I lost my way a bit after that in the new professional environment. I was probably in a bit of a comfort zone. The following February, I won my first Ireland A cap when coming on as a replacement for Alan Quinlan against Scotland. One of my happiest memories that year was being part of the Under-21 team that won the Triple Crown. That summer, I was called to the senior squad for the summer tour to South Africa. I had been recovering from injury and I wasn't at my best and, although I played in three games, I probably didn't do myself any favours. I wasn't firing on all cylinders after that, so it took me two years to win my first cap against Argentina on Ireland's summer tour. It wasn't the fairytale debut I dreamed of and we lost, which was very disappointing. I do remember feeling a little bit nervous before the game began as we togged out, and that the crowd was very intense. I've never seen a video of the game. A week later, I won my second cap against the United States. We beat them well in the hottest temperatures I have ever played in.'

The year 2001 was to prove a big one for Wallace, as he recalls: 'I played against Italy and France in the Six Nations but the foot-and-mouth outbreak interrupted the Championship. I had been in the preliminary squad for the Lions tour, but, like other players on the Irish team, I was out of the shop window at a crucial time because of the foot-and-mouth scare. I was kind of disappointed not to make the original touring party but knew that I still might make the trip because I was on standby. I won my fifth cap in a friendly against Romania, but, as the Lions tour was progressing, I was starting to worry that I wouldn't get the call. I was going off on a summer training camp in Poland with the Irish team and was halfway there on a stop-off in Copenhagen airport when I got a phone call from Ronan O'Gara telling me that there was an injury and that I was going to be called up. I got a flight back to Heathrow and then another one on to Australia. I had 45 hours of airports and planes before I eventually got there. I then had to learn about 101 squad calls very quickly because almost immediately I had to play against New South Wales.

'It was pretty unbelievable to find myself playing for the Lions and to discover that I had made history by becoming the third member of the one family to play for the Lions – which had never been done before. I discovered pretty early on, though, that there was a negative vibe within the camp. Players like Austin Healey and Matt Dawson were unhappy not to be playing in the Test side. You can understand why they might be unhappy but then they vented their grievances with the management in their newspaper columns, which obviously did nothing to improve morale within the squad and added to the media circus.'

93

PHIL AND JERRY
JERRY WALSH

Sadly, few dreams come true, and rugby dreamers tend to see a terrific rainbow every time it rains, so when a new sensation's limitations are exposed, it can be a crushing let-down. Dreamers are forever assuring themselves that the truly great player is on the horizon but, just like the skyline, he never comes any closer. From the first of Jerry Walsh's 27 caps against Scotland in 1960, Irish rugby followers took to him with extraordinary warmth, not just because of the subtlety and invention and spirit of adventure that enabled him to terrorise opposing defenders. Above all, they loved his all-action style and relentless pursuit of every chance of taking off on an incisive run. Allied to that, his creativity on the ball, his genius for penetration and his killing finish commanded their respect. The fusion of great commitment and dazzling skills would be the stuff of cult status and instant sporting legend.

Walsh really established his credentials as a centre of note when Ireland went to Australia for a six-match tour in 1967, which saw one of the highlights of his career when Ireland became the first team from the Northern Hemisphere to beat Australia. The omens for the Test match were not favourable. The previous week, Ireland had lost 21–9 to New South Wales on the same Sydney venue. However, tries from Walsh and Pat McGrath, and a conversion and drop goal from Tom Kiernan, gave Ireland an 11–5 win.

Phil O'Callaghan has a clear memory of Walsh from that trip: 'We had a magnificent team brilliantly led by Tom Kiernan. After winning on the Saturday, we had a great celebration and we all went to Mass on the Sunday evening. Although it was the evening after the night before, one of our lads fell asleep. During the most solemn point of the Mass, he suddenly shouted out from his slumber: "Hallelujah."

'We stopped off in Hawaii. At one stage, we were standing at the side of a swimming pool. I had my back to the deep end and was pushed in by Mick Doyle. I was not able to swim and went under. The guys thought I was faking it when I didn't surface. I owe a great debt of gratitude to Terry Moore, who dived in and lifted me out of the water long enough to give me the air I needed before I went down again. The great Dr Jerry Walsh found the pole for cleaning the pool and extended it to me and I eventually hauled myself out. I asked Jerry later why he had not dived in. He said, "Why ruin the tour by having both of us drown?"'

Doyler too was a big fan of Walsh: 'Jerry Walsh was a great Irishman and a fabulous tackler. Jerry was a big fan of Gordon Brown – "Broon frae Troon" was one of the legends of rugby. He made his debut in Scotland's 6–3 defeat of the Springboks in 1969. In their next match, Scotland lost to France in Murrayfield and he was dropped for the next match against Wales. He heard the news in unusual circumstances. He was working in the bank when he was told there was someone on the phone who had to do with rugby. Gordon rushed to the phone to discover that the person on the line was his brother, Peter, who shouted down the line: "Great news – I'm back in the Scottish team!"

'"Fantastic!" Gordon shouted. "Who's out?"

'Peter replied, "You are."

'Those are the types of stories Jerry loved.

'Gordon was not always impressed by the facilities when he went on tour with Scotland. He is always remembered for his conversation with a hotel manager. "I said to the manager, 'This is supposed to be a five-star hotel and there's a bloody hole in the roof.' He turned around and said, 'That's where you can see the five stars from.'" Touring with Ireland, Jerry understood exactly what Gordon was complaining about.

'I suppose Jerry's finest hour in the green jersey came in Ireland's famous 18–5 victory over England in 1964, which was so memorable because it was Ireland's first victory in Twickenham since 1948. An hour in, Mike Gibson made a break from his own 25 and fed the ball to Jerry after a diagonal run. Jerry cleverly changed the direction of the attack from left to right and Pat Casey, the right wing that day, finished the move with a try almost under the posts. Jerry famously scored a critical try when Ireland had their first victory [11–5] Down Under against Australia in Sydney in 1967. As a proud UCC man, Jerry had the singular honour of captaining the first Irish 15 to beat the South Africans in 1965, when he led the Combined Universities to a 12–10 victory in a pulsating match in Thomond Park. Jerry then had the distinction of being the only player on both Irish teams when Ireland went on to beat the Springboks 9–6 at Lansdowne Road.'

94

DON'T PICK WARDY
TONY WARD

Throughout his career, Tony Ward would build two reputations: one for his skill on the field and the other for the controversies that restricted his appearance in the green jersey. In fact, it is somewhat surprising that he never got the nickname 'The Judge' because he spent so much time sitting on the bench. Ward took the international world by storm, and in both 1978 and 1979 he was voted European Player of the Year.

'In my prime in 1979, I had approaches from four rugby league clubs – Salford, Wakefield Trinity, New Hunslet and Blackpool – to defect to rugby league. At the time, rugby league had little appeal for me. In none of the cases did I meet the people. They were all serious offers. One came via Ronnie Teeman, one of the first football agents, who was a good friend of John Giles and wanted to sign me for New Hunslet. They rang up, but I was not interested and saved them a trip.'

Just as Ward's career was at its height, his world came apart on Ireland's tour to Australia in 1979, as he explains: 'My scoring achievements made headlines in the Australian papers. I found myself being sought out for interviews; rugby writers seemed to follow my every step. It was never my way to reject media representatives in such circumstances, as I feel they have a job to do and it's only right that one should co-operate with them. To simply run away or meet their queries with a bland, tight-lipped "no comment" was never my way. I hadn't thought that publicity about me in Europe – winning the European Player of the Year Award and so on – would have been so well known Down Under. I was rather naive in that. But they knew everything about me.

'In retrospect, I now realise – older and wiser – that if I wanted to make sure of my place on the Irish team for the first Test, I might have acted more correctly if I had gone to ground at that point and ignored the media. It would have spared me a moment that left an indelible imprint on my mind. I have pondered it again and again when reflecting on what developed into a most traumatic experience that shattered my confidence for almost two years.

'We were in the dressing-room preparing to go out for a training session for the match against New South Wales when Jack Coffey, the team manager, came over to me and said, "This is absolutely ridiculous. It's crazy what's going on – all this media stuff. I suggest that you stay away from these fellows altogether." I looked at him aghast. I didn't know what he was driving at. It was only at the end of the tour that the true relevance of his remarks that day became clear.

'I knew before I left Ireland that I was under pressure and consequently made certain that I played well in the preliminary games on that tour. I suspected certain devious undertones. I knew our coach Noel "Noisy" Murphy was no fan of mine; when he was the Munster coach, he used to call me "the soccer player" from the sideline. I still feel that it was totally unjustified and unjust. It hit me like a thunderbolt – no warning, no explanation, nobody wanted to help me. It was extremely traumatic. The immature side of me wanted to come home immediately.

'I reacted like a spoiled brat. How dare anyone drop me?! I wanted to get on a plane and get out of there. In retrospect, I'm glad I didn't, and I would like to think I learned a lot from the experience. That is what life is about – learning from experience. If we could all live with the benefit of hindsight, that would be great.'

News that he had been dropped sent shock waves through Irish rugby fans. It was like using the Shroud of Turin to clean somebody's porridge dish – a sacrilege. It had a profound effect on Ward's life as a whole. Up to '79, he had led a sheltered life, revelling in the delight of a successful career that had brought all his childhood fantasies to reality. The greatest tragedy was that he lost his inherent faith in his own ability.

However, Ward is grateful to the opportunities rugby has brought him: 'Of course, I owe my career in journalism to playing rugby. My profile also led to some unexpected offers coming my way. In 1989, Charles Haughey personally invited me in to Mount Street to run for Fianna Fáil in the upcoming general election. He explained that the party's polls confirmed that they would get a second seat in Dun Laoghaire and that if I agreed to stand in the constituency he could all but guarantee me a seat in the next Dáil. If, by some chance, that didn't happen, he would make me one of his nominees for the Senate. However, my clearest memory of him after that was of a meeting with him in RTE. It was just after the late Seán Doherty's sensational revelations about the phonetapping and just before Charlie resigned. He went into RTE to defend himself, and I happened to be on business in the sports department. I saw all these minders coming and cameras and lights filming him as he walked into the studio. I stood back and tried to make myself as invisible as possible. Then he noticed me and said, "Tony, how are you?", and chatted with me for a few minutes. I was so dumbfounded that I was unable to address him properly. The fact that he bothered to speak to me at such a traumatic time for him left a deep impression on me.'

95

WHELAN AND DEALING
PAT WHELAN

It is surprising that Pat Whelan never captained Ireland, because he had an incredible will to win. Like most hookers, he was not afraid to get physically involved, and it has been suggested that the phrase 'You live by the sword' was his motto. Whelan's preparation for big matches was somewhat unusual: he spent the afternoons before internationals in bed.

Whelan's international career saw as many lows as highs, but he still remembers the thrill of his international debut: 'The highlight of my career was definitely my first cap against England at Lansdowne Road in 1975. Running onto the pitch for the first time is a moment that will live with me until I go to my grave.'

Ireland won 12–9 in a match that also marked Willie Duggan's international debut. However, the fairy tale went sour in the next international at Murrayfield, as Ireland lost 20–13 and Whelan lost his place, much to his regret: 'I was dropped three times from the Irish team. All were intensely disappointing and the low points of my career – though it was also a huge disappointment for me to have to miss the South African tour with Ireland in 1981 because of injury. Losing cup finals with Garryowen were always crushing experiences for me. In that match against Scotland, we were up against what were certainly the best front five in the business at the time. We only lost two balls in the scrum, so I didn't anticipate I would be dropped, but I was and Ken Kennedy was recalled. Even now, I can still recall that downer, especially after winning only two caps.'

Leinster's John Cantrell then grabbed the hooker's slot, though Whelan reclaimed it on the tour to New Zealand in 1976.

In 1979, Whelan was to find himself out in the cold on the Australian tour, when he lost his place to Ciaran Fitzgerald. However, an injury to Ciaran Fitzgerald saw Whelan back in the Irish shirt for the opening match against France in 1981.

Most of his happiest memories are of off-the-field activities: 'I was fortunate in that my international days coincided with that of three of my Garryowen friends – Shay Dennison, Larry Moloney and Shay Deering. The four of us travelled up to Dublin together for squad sessions. On the way home, we had a number of stops for "light refreshments". We came home at all hours of the day and night. My wife could never understand how a training session could last 24 hours!'

Whelan was determined to learn the lessons from his experiences as a player when he took on the position of manager of the Irish team in 1995: 'I know how important it is now to treat players properly. In my playing days, it was not the norm to ring players beforehand if they were to be dropped. They never got any prior warning nor any explanation. Nowadays, as a manager, it's essential to be very communicative with players and to keep in constant touch with them.'

Whatever the future brings, Whelan will always have a vast reservoir of happy memories from his playing days to draw on, especially about the personalities he played with: 'I suppose one of – if not the – greatest characters of them all was Phil O'Callaghan, even though I once thought he cost me my place on the Irish team. Munster were playing the Wolfhounds shortly before my first cap. The Irish selectors were there, so I was all fired up to give the performance of my life, especially as my immediate opponent was the then French hooker. At one stage, we had their scrum pinned back and I was about to win a strike against the head. For a second, I could almost taste my first cap. Then, inexplicably, Philo put in his hand and pulled back the ball. Instead of getting a heel against the head, we were penalised. I can laugh at it now, but at the time I could have throttled him.

'On our tour to New Zealand in 1976, Philo came to me and said that the team needed more "bite" and that the only way we could get on to the team was to show that bite. He was absolutely correct. When we played Auckland, both of us scored extremely high on the "bite stakes" and got into the Test side.

'I scored the first try of the tour when I flopped over from five yards. I really enjoyed that experience, especially the competitive way the New Zealanders played their rugby. There was also plenty of craic off the field. I was rooming with Mossie Keane. The morning after a match, Ned Van Esbeck came into our room to call us for Mass at what seemed to us, in our "tired and emotional" state, to be an ungodly hour. All I can say is that Mossie escorted him out of our room in "typical Moss fashion". I'm not prepared to elaborate any further!'

96

TOUCH WOOD
KEITH WOOD

Among the Irish players chosen on the Lions tour in 1959 under captain Ronnie Dawson was Keith Wood's father, the late Gordon Wood. The Garryowen player was capped twenty-nine times for Ireland between 1954 and 1961 at loose-head prop, scoring one international try. After the disintegration of the Grand Slam-winning team, Ireland no longer had an outstanding pack, but, at least in the late '50s and early '60s, they had a formidable front row with Syd Millar and Ronnie Dawson.

Mick English was a close friend of Wood's, a friendship that was cemented on the Lions tour in 1959: 'Unfortunately, due to injuries to stomach muscles, I played only twice, and, with six weeks remaining and unable to play on, both Niall Brophy and I departed the scene by luxury liner for home. Niall had sat his accountancy exams in Melbourne in the first week of the tour and passed. He played against New South Wales and injured his ankle after just five minutes. No more rugby for him. Our itinerary included stops at such places as Sydney, Melbourne, Freemantle, Suez Canal, Cairo, Naples, Marseilles, Gibraltar and finally to Liverpool.

'One of the players to shine on the tour was David Hewitt, whom the New Zealanders thought was one of the best and fastest centres to play New Zealand. In some matches, David, who was a keen photographer, was very taken by the strange cloud formations one sees in New Zealand skies and, at times, when he should have been concentrating on the play, was admiring the clouds.

'One of the stars on that tour was Tony O'Reilly, who was truly magnificent on the left wing. He was top try scorer and a huge influence on those around him. It was often said that the Lions tours saw him at his peak and, when playing for Ireland, the small matter of making a living got in the way of his rugby. His time was not wasted!

'Gordon Wood had a deep admiration for O'Reilly, but, in the typical Irish way, he rejoiced in slagging him. He loved to recall how, in 1963, following Ireland's 24–5 defeat at the hands of the French, O'Reilly was dropped for the only time in his career. Although the news came as a shock, O'Reilly had arguably never consistently reproduced his Lions form in the green jersey. It seemed that, after 28 caps, his international career was over. Seven years later, in an ill-judged move, the Irish selectors persuaded him to come out of retirement to play against England at Twickenham in place of the injured Billy Brown for his 29th cap. To put it at its kindest, O'Reilly – now firmly established as a commercial giant because of his work in business – was anything but a lean, mean machine at that time. His shape prompted Willie John McBride to remark, "Well, Tony, in my view, your best attacking move tomorrow might be to shake your jowls at them."

'Ireland lost 9–3 and O'Reilly gave an undistinguished performance. In the final moments, he dived boldly into the heart of the English pack. As he regained consciousness, he heard an Irish voice shouting, "And, while you're at it, why don't ya kick his f**kin' chauffeur too!"

'The Heinz slogan is: "Beans Means Heinz". After the match, a wag was heard to say: "I never realised Heinz means has-beens!"

'Another big favourite of Gordon's was the day Sir Anthony was urged by the great Irish flank-forward Ronnie Kavanagh to harden himself with a gruelling physical regime in the mountains. O'Reilly was typically unimpressed: "Kav, it's not guerrilla warfare, it's rugby we are playing. We're not going to be asked to ford a stream at Lansdowne Road."

'On that Lions tour, Gordon showed himself to be a world-class player. I don't want to get too technical but a loose-head prop must be able to scrummage effectively at a level that is comfortable for his hooker, and Gordon could always do that for Ronnie Dawson. Technical expertise is a must because you have to be able to impart strain on opposing tight-heads, while also taking any strain they place on you. Gordon did the technical things very well, as well as playing with fire in his belly, which is the Munster way. When Keith first burst on the scene, I knew he was made from the right stuff because he was from Gordon's gene pool.'

Mick Quinn has fond memories of Gordon Wood: 'When I was eight years old, I got three coaching sessions with Keith Wood's late father, Gordon, in De La Salle Churchtown. He was an absolute gentleman and very kind. He told me, "Never go home with your knees clean." So I would always rub dirt on my knees and go home and show my father my dirty knees. Gordon patted me on the head at one stage and said, "You will play for Ireland one day." I never forgot those words.'

As those four great philosophers Abba famously suggested when they won the Eurovision in 1974, the history book on the shelf is always repeating itself, and thirty-five years later Ireland's tour to Australia would see the emergence of a new star when Gordon's son Keith earned rave reviews for his performances as a hooker. In fact, on his Ireland debut against Australia in 1994, Wood was singled out by Bob Dwyer as a potential great. As early as the first match, the potential was there. Wood went on to realise, and even exceed, those expectations with a series of dazzling performances for Ireland and the Lions (in South Africa in 1997 and Australia in 2001), which saw him selected as IRB Player of the Year in 2001. In the process, he won 58 caps and became Ireland's most-capped hooker, having surpassed the great Ken Kennedy. Wood, though, was no ordinary hooker. He kicked like a fly-half, linked like a centre, jinked like a winger and was always inspired by his father's words: 'Never be ashamed at being proud of what you are good at.'

Classically, hookers were players who won their own ball in the scrum, down whatever channel was nominated, and who could throw the ball accurately into the lineout. Woodie rewrote the manual for hookers with his play-anywhere style and willingness to kick. Indeed, there were times he seemed to play more like a full-back, apparently believing that to win without risk was to triumph without glory. Almost each time he got the ball into his hands and took off on a bullocking run, he could bring the Lansdowne Road crowd to their feet with his sharp turn of pace for such a powerful figure and his joy at running at opponents or into space. He will be forever remembered for his pivotal role in depriving England of a Grand Slam in 2001, when the Ireland v. England game was held over because of foot-and-mouth disease. He scored the crucial try with a peel move from the lineout. Yet, when a combative approach was needed, he could mix the bash with the flash.

There were some low moments, though. In 1999, he was embroiled in a ruck with the IRFU over a row about his image rights. Woodie was prepared to waive his international match fees rather than have the most distinctive face and head in rugby, apart from Jonah Lomu's, 'owned' and exploited by the IRFU sponsors. The row saw him forfeit his place on the Irish team and the captaincy.

Worse was to come, though, and 2002 was his *annus horribilis*. He played in only one of Ireland's Six Nations games and then aggravated a neck injury in the World Cup qualifier against Russia. These problems paled into insignificance compared with the personal tragedies that affected him. His brother Gordon died of a heart attack at the tender age of 41, two days before Keith was due to captain Ireland against Romania, and he missed the birth of his first child, Alexander, after being delayed on his return from the funeral. Then, two months later, his mother Pauline died on the morning of Ireland's international against Argentina.

One of the defining moments of the 2003 World Cup came when Ireland's World Cup campaign ended literally in tears when Wood poignantly cried after Ireland lost to France in the quarter-final. Within moments, he announced his retirement from rugby. His body just could not take any more, having endured 15 major operations since 1995.

In conversation with this scribe, the Irish coach Eddie O'Sullivan observed, 'I think we have lost a legend from the game of rugby and someone that will be known well after he is gone. He was written off by everybody when a disc in his neck leaked and then he wrecked his shoulder. The measure of the man is that he came back, and we said the World Cup was his goal, and nobody put more into that World Cup than Keith Wood. From a rugby point of view, I think I described him once as the identikit of the professional rugby player and that's about the highest thing you can say about him. The man pursued his profession as assiduously as he could, every minute of the day, to become the best player that he could be at any time. We've seen the retirement of a legend and I don't think he can be replaced.'

DAYLIGHT SNOBBERY
ROGER YOUNG

Belfast's Roger Young won 26 caps at scrum-half for Ireland between 1965 and 1971 and toured with the Lions to South Africa in 1968. His rugby brain and talent was immediately apparent in the Irish jersey, such as when he set up winger Pat McGrath for the crucial try against South Africa in 1965. He narrowly missed out on making history when Ireland played England in 1969: it was the first match in which Ireland made a substitution, when Terenure College's Mick Hipwell replaced the injured Noel Murphy. Later in the game, Young also had to be replaced, by Queen University's Colin Grimshaw, after sustaining an injury. However, he did have the consolation of being part of Ireland's first-ever run of five successive wins, which came in that same game – a record that was extended to six when Ireland secured a 16–0 win over Scotland at Murrayfield.

Young has a big fan in Tony Ward because of a meeting they had in 1980 during the Lions tour. Ward candidly confesses that he had no hesitation about going to South Africa once the call came: 'I wanted to be a Lion, and it was really as simple and as selfish as that, I don't deny it. I offer no justification. I didn't even think; I simply went. However, was I in for a rude awakening! The agonising tyranny of the plight of the majority struck me most forcefully on a visit to the paradisal world of a golf course in Bloemfontein on an excursion with John Robbie, Paul Dodge and Clive Woodward. We were surrounded by about 30 black youngsters in their late teens and all literally dressed in rags. They wanted to caddy for us. "Masta . . . Masta", they called me. This was the bit I could never take – people calling me master. We selected two kids, and I took them aside and I said, "This is John and Paul, and I am Tony," but, after that, they didn't call us anything at all. It really confused them. They explained that they were allowed to play golf only on a Monday morning and had to pay handsomely for the privilege. The cost was way beyond the two rand they received for the average two- or three-hour caddy. Tipping was forbidden, but we left them thinking they were millionaires. But all these little inequalities, they were simply everywhere.

'As the Lions tour progressed, events approached boiling point after the game against Transvaal in Johannesburg. We noticed that among the huge crowd of approximately one thousand people there was not one black to be seen. Then, for some strange reason, we were refused entry into the members-only bar at the Springboks' ground. To add insult to injury, in his after-dinner speech the local dignitary cracked a most inappropriate joke. Its punchline had to do with a coloured television. I can't remember the actual joke, but it was clearly a racist one and all the Lions in the room felt very uneasy.

'If I ever needed further demystification and dismantling of the idealising message we had been given about the position of blacks in South Africa, and of the dangerous Messianic arrogance of some whites, it was provided by an acutely revealing discussion with a number of wealthy women after the Orange Free State match in Bloemfontein. This was a real eye-opener for me in terms of the attitudes of whites to blacks. The women talked about the black problem and boasted about the number of servants they had. The way they were talking about them, you would think these people were the scum of the earth. They really believed this but I couldn't figure where this attitude came from. It just sickened me.

'On our final visit to Cape Town, I was one of a number of players brought to visit a children's hospital by former Irish scrum-half Dr Roger Young. It was a harrowing experience to see so many seriously disabled children, but for me what compounded their tragedy was that, even in the wards, there was segregation between whites, blacks and coloureds. It was a hospital similar to Crumlin, full of sick children – some very serious, some not so serious. Yet, within that children's hospital, there was a black children's wing and then a wing for the whites. It was unbelievable. I found it the saddest sight I had ever seen. For me, that was as much as I could take. The miserable feeling of that moment will stay with me for ever. When I left South Africa in June of that year, I did so certainly enriched for my rugby experiences, certainly content to have achieved the personal honour of Lions status, but overall I was deflated and deeply hurt by what I had seen, heard and experienced. So when, 12 months later, Ireland were to tour South Africa, I had no decision to make. My mind, no, my conscience, said no – never again.

'I had been aware of Roger's reputation as one of the greats of Irish rugby. I never saw him play, but from what I am told by those who saw him play, this reputation was richly deserved. I have never forgotten the day I spent with him in 1980. To me, he will live on in memory not just as one of the greats of rugby but as one of the greats of medicine and indeed of humanity.'

The irreplaceable Bill McLaren shared his memories of Young with me: 'I enjoyed his company because he had some nice stories. I especially liked his one about Tony O'Reilly and the time he played for the Barbarians at the Melrose Sevens tournament in the Scottish Border country, and turned out in a pair of rugby boots with no ankle guards on them. Roger told me it was the first time that the crowd had seen a player taking part in Sevens wearing dancing pumps!

'As a player, Roger could hold his own in any company, but I think we saw him at his best against the Springboks, who were a star-laden side in the 1960s with their outstanding back row of Jan Ellis, Piet Greyling and Tommy Bedford, John Gainsford in the centre, their great captain Avril Malan and, of course, the immortal second-row forward Frik du Preez. Against such exalted company, you either sank or swam, and any flaws in your game were ruthlessly exposed, but Roger not only held his own, he flourished. He deserves to be ranked as one of the greats of Irish rugby.'

98, 99 & 100

THERE'S A DARKNESS ON THE EDGE OF TOWN
NIGEL CARR, DAVID IRWIN AND PHILIP RAINEY

It was Irish rugby's darkest day.

In 1987, one of Northern Ireland's most senior judges, Lord Gibson (73), and his wife, Lady Cecily (67), were killed by a 500-lb IRA landmine at Killeen, close to the border, as they drove home to Drumbo, Co. Down, from holiday. Three prominent Irish rugby internationals, Nigel Carr, Philip 'Chipper' Rainey and David Irwin, were in a car travelling in the opposite direction to attend an Irish rugby squad training session and were caught in the blast. Nigel Carr was one of the stars of Ireland's Triple Crown triumph in 1985. He would never play rugby seriously again.

I invited the three players to re-create their journey that day with me, to help them tell their story fully.

David Irwin: 'It is the first time we've sat down as friends to talk about it and I'm very aware that the two other guys don't remember it clearly.'

Philip Rainey: 'To set the scene, we're back in Killeen, a small place between Newry and Dundalk.'

Nigel Carr: 'I was travelling with two of my great friends from university, Davy Irwin and Philip Rainey. We were going on a journey that I had taken many times, but this one changed the course of my life in many respects. It had been a mixed season, better than the year before but not as good as the one before that. Eighty-seven was a unique year from a rugby perspective, with the inaugural World Cup, and we were all terribly excited about it. So, as we drove south for a training session, there was lots of chat, banter and rugby talk. Then everything came to an abrupt end.'

David: 'The day began early because we were driving south for a session at 10.30. I remember I was driving along, chatting to the two guys, when suddenly there was a massive thud and also a giant explosion of light. The only way I could describe it was like facing a hundred flashbulbs going off at once. I was aware enough to think that a bomb had actually gone off underneath our car. My first thought was

265

that the IRA were trying to kill somebody else and they had made a mistake and we'd got mixed up in it. That sense lasted several seconds but certainly there was a huge noise and a massive flash of flight.'

Nigel: 'That's the first time I heard that description in that sort of detail. I don't remember anything. I half imagine I do remember something sometimes, but then I realise I don't. My first memory is heading back to the hospital.'

Philip: 'My memories are very short. I remember sitting behind David and him saying at one stage, "There's a fire," and that's it.'

David: 'Having experienced what I thought was a bomb in my own car, I then realised that our car had stopped in the same lane and was still pointing in the same way. I recall that my first thought was to feel my own body just to check that everything was still there. When I established that was, in fact, the case, I remember looking to my right and noting that there was a massive crater in the Belfast side of the road, and at the same time I turned around to the left and I realised that Nigel was bleeding quite badly and that the blood was coming out profusely from a neck wound. He seemed to be semi-conscious. The whole front of the car had been pushed in but particularly over on Nigel's side, and I said to him, but he probably doesn't remember it, "We've been in a bomb. You're OK. You're bleeding from your head but you're fine."

'While I was saying this to Nigel, as I looked past him through the passenger window, I could see another car, parallel to our own, pointing to Dublin, and there was a huge inferno of flames in that car, with two vague shadows of people and fire in the front seat. I assumed that it was possibly an RUC car, and then, as I panned around, I saw Philip lying sort of across the back seat – motionless. Initially, I thought he might be dead but I wasn't sure. I felt I had to get out of the car and get the guys out in case the petrol tank would explode. I wasn't totally aware of what was going on around me. As I managed to get out of the driver's door, one of the things that struck me was that two or three of the cars that had been behind us driving south actually drove around my car and passed us and drove down the road a bit, and I remember thinking at the time, "How could people drive past this?" But, in retrospect, they were that bit outside the incident and were probably in shock themselves, and the natural thing was to drive around it and get to safety.

'As I walked around the front of my car, I was aware of two or three females running up and down the road screaming hysterically.

NIGEL CARR, DAVID IRWIN AND PHILIP RAINEY

I found out afterwards that they were part of a group of nurses that were driving north, and they were actually behind Judge Gibson's car and their car had gone into the ditch. They were distraught. Again, this all happened within several seconds. A large juggernaut or lorry was driving up the road and I stopped it and told the driver to go up to the garage and ring the police and for an ambulance.

'Having done that, I went around to Nigel and tried to get the passenger door open, which was a wee bit difficult because it sort of buckled with the impact. Once I sort of got the door open again, Nigel was coming around a bit but was still very groggy. I told him I had to get him out of the car because there was a danger the car might explode. I asked him if he was in pain. He told me he was very uncomfortable in one of his thighs. I suppose, being a doctor, I would have been aware that a common type of injury in a road accident is where the dashboard is pushed in under the passenger's knees and that can cause you to fracture your femur. My initial thought was: "Oh my goodness, Nigel has to miss the World Cup because he's fractured his femur." As I tried to get him out of the passenger's side, I realised his ankles and feet were caught underneath the dashboard, and I think, between me pulling and Nigel giving some assistance, I managed to drag him out. I think one of his trainers was left struck in the car. I half-carried him and he half-walked as we went up the road and then I set him down on the grass verge. I took my belt off and tied his knees together, again assuming he had a fracture of his leg.

'I went back and spoke to Philip. He had started to come around, though he was still groggy, and I told him the car might explode and we needed to get out of there. He was able to get out himself with just a little bit of assistance from me. I took him up and sat him beside Nigel.

'At that point, the traffic had stopped about 50 yards either side and people were getting out of their cars and looking around. It seemed fairly clear to me by then what had happened, but I wasn't sure why it had happened. A plain-clothes detective came along and I asked if it had been a police car that had been blown up. He told me that it was a high court judge and his wife. It became clear that the police had been waiting to escort him the rest of the journey after the gardai had escorted him up to the south side of the border, but the car was in no-man's-land when the bomb had gone off. Then I saw that Philip had got up and was walking around, obviously concussed and not sure what was going on.

'Shortly after that, the ambulance arrived to take Philip and Nigel away. The other thing I noticed then was that one of our rugby bags was about 40 yards up the road from the car. I couldn't work out how this had happened. The explanation was that the bag flew out with the force of the explosion and then the boot had closed again.

'At that stage, the objective was to get the two guys to Daisy Hill Hospital, and I recall feeling so disappointed that Nigel was going to miss the World Cup. I gathered our valuables and bits and pieces from the car. I was told that I was going to be escorted back to Newry police station in a police car. I remember thinking, "Jeepers, we've all come through that and I'm alive, but now I have to get into a police car." I knew from living in the North that, when bombs were set off and the police came on the scene, a second bomb was sometimes set off. I was thinking, "I hope this doesn't happen to me on the way back."'

Nigel: 'We've talked before about the day, but I've never heard so much detail about it before. David was saying about my thigh injury. I don't know how he got me out because I was a lot sorer after that! I don't recall any of it. My first memory was of heading in the ambulance and hearing the medical staff whispering. I was conscious of the fact that it was only me and one other patient. I didn't know if it was either Chipper or Davy. I heard the staff talking about people being killed. My first thought was that three of us were driving in the car but there were only two of us in the ambulance. I assumed that one of my friends had been killed. Maybe I fell unconscious, because my next memory is of being in the hospital.'

Philip: 'That's the second time I've heard the story from David. It still amazes me, and Nigel and I were so lucky we had such a great guy with us. I was in his hands, and the next thing I remember was being in a theatre in hospital getting pieces of glass picked out of me.'

David: 'Once I got to Newry police station, my first job was to ring our families, who needed to know. Then the police car brought me to the hospital. I met the doctor in the corridor and my first question was about Nigel's leg. He told me that he hadn't fractured his femur, and I was so relieved and thought: "Great, he will be OK for the World Cup." But it turned out later that he had a fracture in his ankle and what is known as a "rigid abdomen", which meant internal injuries. I then found out that, although Philip had taken a bad blow to the head and was unconscious, he was basically OK.'

Nigel: 'I think I must have been given some sort of painkilling injection when I was en route. I don't recall feeling that sore. I didn't think things were that bad. I knew I had cuts and bruises, but I also had twisted joints, chipped bones, five broken ribs and internal bleeding. For the next few days, I was in acute pain. I would hold on for as long as I could and then get an injection into my backside to give me relief.'

David: 'That morning, I became more aware of what had happened. Lord Gibson had gone to the same school as me, and over the following days I learned that he and his wife were a very nice couple.'

After their 'success' with the Gibson murders, the IRA sought to repeat their coup the following year. For that reason, I brought the three players to meet the Reverend John Dinnen, the rector in Hillsborough, Co. Down. Three members of his congregation – the Hanna family from Hillsborough (Robert aged 45, his wife Maureen and their 6-year-old son James) – were killed by a bomb in Killeen, when the IRA mistook their jeep for one owned by another senior member of the judiciary, high court judge Eoin Higgins.

The deaths of the Hanna family had a profound effect on John Dinnen: 'I remember hearing the news as if it was yesterday. The first thing I had to do was to comfort the family. Although the father and mother and youngest child were killed, there were two young teenage children in the Hanna family who were not in the car that day and they needed to be consoled. I can't describe the pain and sorrow that was in their family home when I visited. They were almost numb with grief. There was incredible media interest in the story, which surprised me because I would have thought that there were so many tragedies before then in the North that people would no longer see this as an enormous national and international story. Maybe it was because there were two young children left behind that it touched such a chord, but I was under siege with people trying to look for a comment from me. My focus, though, was to prepare for the funeral.

'The church was packed and there was a massive crowd outside who could not get in. It was very hard to say anything that would bring comfort in the face of such a horrific event. I will never forget walking out of the church to the graveyard in front of those three coffins. There were flashlights going off constantly from the press photographers and there seemed to be cameras everywhere. All I could hear was the click-click of cameras. To this day, every time I preside at a funeral, the memory of that funeral comes back to me. It was just heartbreaking. Heartbreaking.'

The players then gave their reaction to John.

Philip: 'It is such a beautiful setting here, but it has such sad memories.'

Nigel: 'In many respects, it was easier that it happened to me. It would have been much harder to deal with had one of my family been caught up in the bomb. If it had happened to our close family members, it would have been much tougher to take. When children are involved, as in the case of the Hanna family, it would have been much harder, especially as we now all have children of our own.'

David: 'I think that affects me in my own role as a family doctor. I come across death frequently, but the big difference in the Hanna incident was the loss of a six-year-old child. There's an inevitability when a person gets older that they will die, but when a child of that age dies, it is much harder to comprehend. Those who are left behind are left uncertain, worrying did they suffer, and, after I heard the news, I felt an urge to write to the remaining members of the Hanna family and try to put into words what we had been through. I think the main thing I was trying to get across to them was that their family would not have suffered because things happen so fast in a car bomb. It happened to the Hannas in nearly exactly the same spot – literally 50 or 100 yards from where our accident happened. It gave me a stronger empathy with what happened.'

In the light of their experiences, I wondered what the three former internationals would say if they were to come face to face with the IRA man who had planted 'their' bomb.

David: 'I certainly would not be shaking his hand. The intelligence was that the man responsible for planting the bomb was killed somewhere else a few years later. You don't know what you would do till you're in that situation.'

Nigel: 'To be frank, I don't care to think about it. I don't know what my reaction would be.'

Philip: 'I'm ambivalent. If I met the guy, I would probably ask him why he did it and if he felt good about it. We've moved on. We're different people, better people. We're perhaps stronger people.'

It would be unforgivable if this traumatic event became all that these great players were remembered for. Tony Ward played with each of them and was more keen to play tribute to their abilities on the pitch than recall the calamity off it: 'Philip was a good full-back. He was at the right place at the wrong time because Hugo MacNeill owned the number-15 shirt for most of the time Chipper was around. I was glad he finally made it onto the Irish team in 1989.

NIGEL CARR, DAVID IRWIN AND PHILIP RAINEY

'David Irwin was perhaps the most physically competitive centre I've ever come across. Everybody dreaded playing against him. Seldom do you get a player who would get as physically involved as he did. He had a never-say-die attitude which was central to Ulster's success in the 1980s. Although he made three Test appearances for the Lions in New Zealand in 1983, in many ways, he was an underrated player in attack because he was so physically good in defence.

'In 1985, Mick Doyle saw an Irish pack that was lighter than that of the '82 team, one which could not afford to engage in hand-to-hand battle, so to speak, in set scrums, and he cut his cloth accordingly. Nigel Carr was the key figure in Doyler's set-up. Usually, he was the first to arrive to the break-down, and what many people seemed to overlook about his play was that not alone was he tremendously mobile, but he was also very strong and he was able to hold on to the ball until the other forwards were up to form the ruck or maul. It was from second-phase play that much of the damage was done to the opposition during that '85 season, and Nigel was at the heart of everything. He was as good an open-side wing-forward as ever wore the green jersey.'

CONCLUSION

For the eighty years covered in this book, great Irish rugby players from Con Murphy and Blair Mayne back in the 1930s to today's golden generation, including Paul O'Connell and Brian O'Driscoll, have been the one fixed point in a fast-changing age. The nine decades featured have not been without their troubles or their lean periods, but, even when the storm clouds have gathered, the greats of Irish rugby have not withered before their blast – and a fitter, better, stronger playing pool lay in the sunshine when the tempest had passed.

There have been times of tears, trials and tribulations. Equally, there have been days of glory and triumph. Much of this volume is bookended by Ireland's Grand Slam triumphs of 1948 and 2009.

The rugby future is not what it used to be. As we have seen in these pages, huge changes have transformed the rugby landscape, notably the switch from the amateur era to professionalism. When new challenges have presented themselves, the Irish rugby players and community have risen manfully to the task with great intelligence, imagination and innovation. This has led Munster and Leinster to become kingpins of European rugby in recent seasons. Moreover, each of the four provinces has shown an ability to produce a dazzling array of new talent, such as Jamie Heaslip, Cian Healy, Conor Murray, Jonathan Sexton, Seán Cronin, Stephen Ferris and Seán O'Brien.

The 100 players profiled in this book, for all their differences, tell us that the story of Irish rugby is an epic narrative of guts, glory and grace.

The best is yet to come.